# THE CAPTAIN AMERICA COMPLEX

# THE CAPTAIN AMERICA COMPLEX

## The Dilemma of Zealous Nationalism

ROBERT JEWETT

Foreword by
WILLIAM SLOANE COFFIN

Bear & Company
Santa Fe, New Mexico

Bear & Company Books are published by Bear & Company, Inc. Its Trademark, consisting of the words "Bear & Company" and the portrayal of the bear, is Registered in U.S. Patent and Trademark Office and in other countries Marca Registrada
Bear & Company, Inc., P.O. Drawer 2860
Santa Fe, NM 87504


ISBN 0-939680-15-7
Library of Congress Card Number 82-073362


Typesetting—Casa Sin Nombre, Santa Fe, NM
Cover Design—William Field
Printed in the United States by BookCrafters, Inc.

Publishing History

The Captain America Complex is the second edition of a title first published under the same name by Westminster Press in 1973. The present edition has been revised and updated by the author.

# TABLE OF CONTENTS

# FOREWORD

"Why do the nations so furiously rage together?" One answer to that ancient question of the psalmist was given by British historian Herbert Butterfield who wrote: "In the kind of world that I see in history, there is one sin that locks people up in all their other sins, and fastens people and nations more tightly in their predicaments, namely the sin of self-righteousness."

Although the sin is common to many, it infects different nations in different ways. The Swiss, for example, have long been inordinately proud of their neutrality, and we shouldn't overlook the money it has earned them. The French have made much of their "mission civilatrice," which frequently was supported by the Foreign Legion. For a while in the 1940s the Germans thought they were supermen, and in the 60s Nkrumah's Ghana occasionally gave the impression that it considered its solutions the answer to all African problems. As for the British—well, as one of their own has wittily explained:

"In the beginning by some mistake
Men were foreigners all created;
Til heaven conceived a nobler plan
And there was born an Englishman
Conceive the difference, if you can,
Had Adam been an Englishman."

This splendid book, *The Captain America Complex,* is about American self-righteousness, about all the things in our history and culture that keep prompting the thought in American minds that of all the nations on earth, God smiles the most on ours. Were our sense of virtue not undergirded by military power the situation would be tolerable. But when a super-power also considers itself super-virtuous—"Look out, world!"

Today the United States government seeks to concentrate all attention on the sins of others, particularly those of the Soviet Union. It appears deaf to St. Augustine's injunction, to applicable to both individuals and nations: "Do not fight evil as if it were something that arose totally outside of yourself." Moreover, our self-righteousness is pushing us once again towards the zealotry described in this book, the kind that leads to a violence which the perpetrator can view as "redemptive," provided he views his zeal as selfless. The War in Vietnam and the recent invasion of Grenada are cases in point. The clear and present danger today is not that we Americans will be overcome and overrun by communists, whether from the Soviet Union, Cuba, or from south of the border; rather it is that we may become like the exultant religious leaders in the Gospel of John who were prepared to stone to death the woman caught in adultery. Jesus, interestingly enough, disputes neither the sin nor the penalty, nor even the unfairness of stoning only the woman when obviously it takes more than one person to be caught in adultery. He simply questions the righteousness of anyone worthy of condemnation to condemn another to death: "Let him who is without sin among you cast the first stone." He takes an example of conspicuous wrong-doing and uses it not nourish self-righteousness, but rather to bring awareness of the sin common to all human beings.

We and the Soviets are not one in love, but at least we are one in sin, which is no mean bond, because it precludes the possibility of separation through judgment. Therefore their missiles should remind us of nothing so much as our own, their invasion of Afghanistan, our invasion of Vietnam. Their suppression of civil liberties at home should remind us of our complicity in the suppression of these same liberties abroad, in dictatorial countries whose governments could not maintain themselves in power without our support. Were we to repent of our self-righteousness, we Americans would abandon our present double standard: the Soviets arm, it's evil; we arm, it's for national security. Recognizing our own role in escalating the arms race, we would triple our efforts to reverse it.

In repentance lies our only hope, the hope that we can recognize today's nuclear crisis before it is validated tomorrow by disaster.

Jesus would never be "soft on communism." But I can hear him saying, "Let the nation without sin among you aim the first missile." And given Christ's far reaching mercy, I cn hear him, on some future and blessed day, addressing a repentant Soviet Union and a repentant United States with words of assurance and admonition similar to the ones he spoke to that sad and lonely figure a long time ago: "Neither do I condemn you. Go and build nuclear weapons no more."

Readers of this book, persuaded by its contents, will surely advance the coming of that blessed day.

William Sloane Coffin
February 6, 1984

# INTRODUCTION TO THE SECOND EDITION

As I put the finishing touches on this introduction, American troops have begun withdrawing after the occupation of Grenada. The public has responded with overwhelming enthusiasm to one of the most explicit expressions of The Captain America Complex in recent history. President Reagan's address on Lebanon and Grenada on October 27, 1983, evoked an immediate increase of support for the invasion from 64% to 86% of those polled by ABC News. A *USA Today* survey showed the increase jumping from 48% to 68%, which was closer to the results of other polls.[1] By whatever measure, the response was remarkable.

An examination of the rationale of Mr. Reagan's address reveals the abiding power of this complex to shape current perceptions of the world. The address linked three widely separated and distinct events in the Far East, the Middle East, and the Caribbean as part of a terrorist conspiracy centered in Moscow. He began as follows:

> My fellow Americans, some two months ago we were shocked by the brutal massacre of 269 men, women and children, in the shooting down of a Korean airliner. Now, in these past several days, violence has erupted again, in Lebanon and Grenada. . . . The events in Lebanon and Grenada, though oceans apart, are closely related. Not only has Moscow assisted and encouraged the violence in both countries, but it provides direct support through a network of surrogates and terrorists. It is no coincidence that when the thugs tried to wrest control of Grenada, there were 30 Soviet advisers and hundreds of Cuban military and paramilitary forces on the island.[2]

A more objective appraisal of these events would indicate that their causes and motivations are quite distinct. The downing of the Korean airliner was a tragic instance of bureaucratic and military bumbling, an expression of a long standing territorial paranoia in which the Soviet pilots literally had no idea of the actual identity of their target. The suicide bombing of the Marine headquarters in Beirut was a typical act of Islamic terrorism whose antecedents can be traced to centuries of religious warfare grounded in principles that are as hostile to Soviet ideology as to western imperialism. And the execution of Prime Minister Bishop of Grenada that precipitated the American invasion was the result of a power struggle between factions in the Grenadian revolutionary movement, with Cuban authorities reacting with conspicuous coolness to the violence that threatened the credibility of their position.

The link between these distantly related events is an expression of American national ideology that tends to simplify world problems as if they all stemmed from a single conspiracy centered in Moscow. Innocent victims are seen to be threatened by a demonic force whose cunning strategems encircle the world. America sees itself as the selfless, redeemer nation whose task is to protect the defenceless by its military interventions. As Mr. Reagan said of the marines killed in the headquarters building, "They've given willingly of themselves so that a nearly defenseless people in a region of great strategic importance to the free world will have a chance someday to live lives free of murder and mayhem and terrorism."[3] Under the spell of these mythic conceptions, the American public perceived the rescue of the medical students on Grenada and the successful capture of the island as a resolution of the rage and frustration it felt over the two earlier disasters. The happy ending had been achieved by violent action against the wicked just in the nick of time. One of the most striking expressions of this coherent national ideology was the videotape of the rescued students cheering the American rangers and waving their index fingers with the number one sign. America's status as the "greatest nation on earth" was confirmed by the successful completion of the rescue operation.

These sentiments are evidence of what Arthur Schlesinger, Jr. calls "a mighty comeback of the messianic approach to foreign policy" since 1980. "The convictions that presently guide American foreign policy are twofold," he writes: "that the United States is infinitely virtuous and that the Soviet Union is infinitely wicked."[4] Actually a much more subtle analysis of the messianic approach is required, as the consideration of Mr. Reagan's address on Lebanon and Grenada reveals. In addition to the tendency to stereotype, there is a need to understand the mystique of violent redemption, the theory of a grand conspiracy, the belief in the inevitable victory for the righteous and the tradition of zeal which breaks barriers of traditional law and restraint in order to rescue the innocent. Each of these aspects of the American civil religion has an extensive cultural history and each is powerfully expressed in the popular fantasies that carry the messianic ideology to the current public. What I have called the "Captain America Complex" may have derived from early American interpretation of historical events by means of

Biblical themes, but it is conveyed to the present generation by mass entertainments of the superheroic type. I believe that this study will serve to explain one of the strangest phenomena of American culture, the congruence between the popular messianism, the American superhero tale and the classic Biblical accounts of zealous warfare.

This book originally appeared at a time when national fervor seemed to be declining in American Life. When I completed the writing in the spring of 1973, the peace negotiations were already underway in Paris that might have led to an honorable end of the Vietnam War. Two years later came the retreat of the last American troops by helicopter from Saigon. Commentators and politicians intoned the message, "Never Again," while the national mood entered a period of self-doubt and more limited expectations. The 1976 election symbolized for many the beginning of national modesty. That America cannot solve the problems of the world was widely and variously stated. Yet an examination of the most popular entertainments during those years would indicate the persistence in fantasy of precisely the same ideals of zealous crusading that had been discredited in Asia. *Star Trek, Star Wars* and *Battlestar Galactica* conveyed the same conspiratorial world view and celebrated the same redemption through violence that had guided the public into the abortive Vietnamese Crusade. *Walking Tall, Superman, Superman II* and *Raiders of the Lost Ark* attracted audiences on such a scale that revealed the persistence of zealous preferences despite the adverse experience of recent history. Thus the resurgence of patriotic zeal of a militaristic type in 1980 in the wake of the Iranian hostage developments should not have been surprising to those who understood the complex.

The tragic events related to Israel's invasion of Lebanon in the summer of 1982 and the subsequent massacre of the inhabitants of Palestinian refugee camps by Christian Falangists reveal that similar complexes influence the behavior of other nations. The Syrian attacks on PLO camps near Tripoli in the fall of 1983 fit the same pattern. The tendency to stereotype the enemy and to believe in regeneration through violence is evident in many branches of Judeo-Christian and Islamic cultures. This study explores the commonly held Biblical heritage that is shared to one degree or another by Judaism, Christianity and Islam. Part of the irony of the current moment is that each of these traditions contains encouragement to identify its adversaries as the source of evil while overlooking the zealous premises that are shared by themselves, leading them into policies leading to atrocities and counter atrocities. The murderous zeal that has fractured Lebanon derives from ideological sources similar to those that led America into an abortive crusade in Southeast Asia. While usually abhorring such actions when performed by others, many Americans continue to believe that the major mistake in Vietnam was in not applying enough force, of waging war "with one hand tied behind our back." In short, we should have killed more men, women and children, if not with small arms at close range in the alleys of refugee camps, then with carpet bombs or atomic weapons at the safe distance of thirty thousand feet.

Despite these somber reflections about the persistence of the Captain America Complex, the reissuance of this book is not an act of despair, even concerning the complex itself. There is a promising side to the Captain America Complex, derived from different strands of the same Biblical tradition that provided the inspiration of zealous crusading. By explaining the fallacies in our mythic perceptions about nationalistic zeal, this book brings to the fore some contrary values of justice for the weak, equality before the law, and the preservation of the earth that are sustained by the prophetic realism of the Biblical tradition itself. The application of the critical methods of modern Biblical scholarship allows a kind of ideology-criticism that separates the healthy from the unhealthy components of a broad cultural legacy. My hope is that by recovering some of the humane and realistic components of the Biblical tradition, we may be in a position to repudiate the schizoid mindsets that threaten to destroy us, whether in the form of the Masadah Complex, the Falangist Crusader Complex, the Islamic Jihad Complex, or the Captain America Complex.

Only the first and the last chapters have been revised for this edition. With the exception of slight changes in the titles of the major divisions of the book, the material and rhetoric of 1973 is left intact. Although the references to events of the 1970s will evoke a smile of recognition, I think you will find confirmations in the news of the 1980s. And since the antidote to the Captain America Complex is derived from the same Biblical tradition that helped to form it, I appeal to your judgment to see whether the cure is worth trying. My conviction is that this complex is both our bane and our promise. It bears within itself the seeds of its own cure. The decisive need in the present moment is to rely upon the healthy side of our own American tradition, both in religion and culture, to hold our tendencies in check. While we need criticisms from friends as well as adversaries in other lands, it is the tradition to which we are attached that holds the greatest promise of changing us. Caught as we are in a schizoid state between zeal and realism, the time has come to face ourselves more squarely and to follow the path promising a way into a decent future, indeed, to any future at all.

# THE CURRENT DILEMMA

# 1

# TRACING THE NATIONAL COMPLEX

One of the puzzles about political rhetoric in America is that Biblical images for peacemaking reappear during times of crisis. It is natural for a thoroughly secularized President like Mr. Reagan to conclude an emotional speech supporting military efforts at peacemaking with "God bless you and God bless America." References to being "faithful to the cause of freedom and the pursuit of peace" are easily mixed with a definition of military casualties as "sacrifices" that must not be dishonored."[1] When one examines the rhetoric on various sides of the current debate over the Middle East, Central America, the Caribbean and the nuclear deterrent, it is clear that most Americans think of themselves as peacemakers.

To understand the peculiar shape of the current dilemma concerning peacemaking requires an exploration of the national complex. Captain America's approach to peacemaking, so to speak, derives from a pervasive tradition and its power is manifest even in the ways that many who oppose current militarization visualize the problem. The American sense of mission influences both the supporters of militant rearmament and the advocates of a nuclear freeze. Yet to a substantial degree this influence is invisible. The public is largely unaware of the origins of its convictions about peacemaking or how they are conveyed. Having originated in certain strands of Biblical thought that were popular in colonial times, these ideas came to be embodied in the American sense of mission that was expressed in language that fused secular and religious images. But even more crucial for understanding the current dilemma is the fact that these ideas were embodied in popular stories that gradually became the major channels of the national complex. To grasp the current dilemma and find ways to cope with it therefore requires an exploration of current national values, their evolution in American history, their indebtedness to the religious heritage in the Bible, and their expression in powerful stories conveyed to the public thorugh mass entertainment.

An eloquent statement of the national complex is provided by Herman Melville in his novel, *White-Jacket*. It combines religious with secular terminology to convey the sense of mission that continues to surface long after many people have lost touch with their religious roots.[2]

> And we Americans are the peculiar, chosen people—the Israel of our time; we bear the ark of the liberties of the world. . . . Long enough have we been sceptics with regard to ourselves, and doubted whether, indeed, the political Messiah had come. But he has come in *us*, if we would but give utterance to his promptings.

While the language of "chosen people" and "political Messiah" is rarely used by sophisticated Americans in the 1980s, the value and emotions associated with such ideas continue to exercise their power. A sense of . . . mission "was present from the beginning of American history, and is present, clearly, today," as Frederick Merk wrote two decades ago.[3]

In its more expansive form this sense of calling was a calling to nothing short of redeeming the entire world. Albert J. Beveridge, historian and senator, claimed precisely this at the beginning of the century. "God . . . has marked the American people to finally lead in the redemption of the world. This is the divine mission of America. . . We are the trustees of the world's progress, guardians of its righteous peace."[4]

President Wilson referred to this tradition when he assured the citizens of Cheyenne that "America had the infinite privilege of fulfilling her destiny and saving the world."[5] And despite secular tendencies, this sense of mission still prevails in Presidential speeches. Mr. Nixon has insisted that "our beliefs must be combined with a crusading zeal, not just to hold our own but to change the world. . . . and to win the battle for freedom."[6] It prevails especially in such products of popular culture as comic books. They often depict in mythic style the ideals that are widely felt but that are no longer articulated in more sophisticated circles. "Captain America is not a representative of America itself," wrote the editor of a 1970 comic book, "but of the American ideal—individual freedom, individual responsibility, moral sensitivity, integrity, and a willingness to fight for right."[7] In a letter to the editor in the same issue, a medical student refers to the problem of living up to this ideal and concludes with sentiments that many seem to share: "The fact that we retain such a high national ideal is the best of signs, and I hope that we can maintain our zeal to try to bring reality closer to the ideal."

This effort to bring reality closer to the ideal has led us straight into the confusing dilemma we face today. Shall we continue to crusade in foreign wars that are as dubious as the one in Indochina? Can reality be manipulated? Made ideal? Shall we revise or shall we eliminate our sense of mission? On the one hand there is the appeal to the tradition of a cosmic struggle "between right and wrong and good and evil," to use the words of Mr. Reagan. On the premise that the Soviet Union is the "focus of evil in the modern world," he asserts that the nation is "enjoined by Scripture and the Lord Jesus to oppose it with all our might."[8] Other voices such as the opinion editor of the *New York Times* remind us that the president also "commands awesome power that can be tragically misapplied." He leads "a fallible people, not a moral crusade."[9]

The conflicts over the proper expression of the national complex have led us repeatedly into becoming militant factions that contend for alternative versions of the "right." As Samuel Lubell noted several years ago: "These conflicts . . . have plunged us into zealous combat to remake American thinking, pressed with an intensity not known in this nation since the Civil War period. Reasoned argument and orderly debate have been shoved aside by efforts to impose beliefs through violence and other uses of power."[10]

What is there about American nationalism that lends itself to such combat? I propose to answer this by an examination of its sources and its expression in popular culture. When I trace the strands back through the American experience I discover over and over again certain Biblical ideas. These older concepts match to an amazing degree their current mythic counterparts even though separated by centuries in time and by disparities in terminology. There are, in fact, two traditions that run from the pages of the Bible down through American history, each with its distinctive approach to the mission of world redemption.

The first I would like to call *Zealous Nationalism*. It seeks to redeem the world by the destruction of the world. In the chapters that follow, I shall trace the development of this tradition from its Biblical origins to its recent expressions in American behavior and ideology. The phenomenon of zeal itself provides a fascinating access to the inner workings of our national psyche. After analyzing it in Chapter 5, I turn in subsequent chapters to the conspiracy theory of evil, to the problem of stereotyping, to the mystique of violence, and to the obsession with victory. Alongside Zealous Nationalism runs the tradition of *Prophetic Realism*. It seeks to redeem the world for coexistence by impartial justice. It also derives from the Bible, though in sections that are quite different from those popular with zealots. It can be traced through the American experience in movements and writings that sometimes criticize aspects of the dominant census. But more frequently one encounters it uneasily joined to its opposite.

My conviction is that these two strands which have long been interwoven in the American mind have always been incompatible, and that the strain has now reached the breaking point. The crusading impulse of Zealous Nationalism and the constitutional legacy of Prophetic Realism could remain in uneasy wedlock in earlier times but not in the era of atomic stalemate. My conclusion is that only the latter is capable of survival. And the specter which drives me to write is that in our present dilemma the zealous hammer which seeks to strike off the chains could destroy the world as well.

# THE SCHIZOID TRADITION

# 2

# A ROD OF IRON OR A LIGHT TO THE NATIONS

While Americans of earlier generations assumed they were the Israel of their time, we must recapture for our secular era what this meant. What sense of mission did persons such as Melville derive from the pages of Holy Writ? To assist us in our quest, this must be posed from a double perspective. First, using the tools of modern Biblical research, we will ask: How did the ancient writers themselves answer the question? What light does their experience shed on our own? Second, we will ask: How did early Americans who read the Scriptures without the benefit of modern methods understand this mission and apply it to themselves?

With these questions the agenda for our first three chapters is suggested. We begin with the traditions within ancient Israel —to be a "rod of iron" or to be a "light to the nations."

## 1

A vivid sense of mission permeates the accounts of Israel's beginnings. The father of the people, Abram, was called to leave his home and set out for an unknown land where he would become a blessing for the entire world. "Go from your country . . . and I will make of you a great nation . . . and by you all the families of the earth shall bless themselves." (Gen. 12:1-3.)[1] The belief that God would battle to achieve this mission was solidified at the time of the exodus from Egypt. Moses proclaimed that Yahweh, the God of battle, would set his people free and give them the promised land.[2] He assured those who were being pursued by Pharaoh's chariots: "Fear not, stand firm, and see the salvation of Yahweh, which we will work for you today. . . . Yahweh will fight for you, and you have only to be still" (Ex. 14:13 f.). They would be set free by violence to fulfill their mission of salvation.

This incipient form of Zealous Nationalism developed a scheme of conquest a generation after the exodus.[3] Yahweh owned the land and would wrest it from the hands of the feudal rulers of Canaan whose overlord, Pharaoh, he had already defeated. He would give it to his peasants in fulfillment of his promise to Abram. Aided by the virtual power vacuum in the rugged and largely unoccupied hill country of western Palestine, this ideology provided the impetus for the infiltration, revolution, and coalitions that established Israel in Canaan. Groups of varying racial and regional backgrounds joined the tribal confederation on the theocratic premise that Yahweh would be their king and defender. He would raise up charismatic leaders in times of emergency who would call out the volunteers for battle.[4] The response to such calls was "zeal," the passionate commitment to the national mission which matched the vehemence of the zealous God himself.

This ideology persisted in the dominant form of Israelite religion despite the emergence of the monarchy. It was particularly prominent in the Northern Kingdom, where the passionate impulse toppled one dynasty after the other. With a tenacious willingness to "fight for right," popular prophets such as Elisha stirred up revolutions. They called for total war against Yahweh's presumed enemies at home and abroad, which resulted in a disastrous series of purges and foreign campaigns. Despite the resurgence under Jeroboam II, in which military successes made possible by the nonintervention of the great empires were interpreted as Yahweh's blessings for an elect and righteous people, the Northern Kingdom was incapable of survival. It repeatedly entered into conflict with Assyria, certain that Yahweh would guarantee victory for the righteous defenders of liberty. As a result the Northern Kingdom was dismembered, the last remnant disappearing with the fall of Samaria in 721 B.C. The reliance on a pure form of Zealous Nationalism, without the tempering qualities of political realism, proved suicidal.

A few years before this collapse a new type of religious impulse emerged—Prophetic Realism. A layman from a southern village traveled to the royal sanctuary at Bethel to declare that Yahweh's justice worked impartially to thwart the excesses of believing and nonbelieving nations alike. Amos sought to shatter illusions of superior virtue and inevitable victory, warning that the Day of Yahweh would be a shock rather than a comfort (Amos 5:18 ff.). For Israel had indulged in the same sorts of war crimes for which other nations had been destroyed; her callous disdain for the life of the victim and her ruthless exploitation of the poor were destroying her from within (Amos 2:6-16). And as for the myth of superior chosenness, had not other nations also undergone exodus experiences (Amos 9:7 f.)? If the Northern Kingdom were not true to its mission of justice, what could keep it from suffering the fate of proud and brutal nations in the past?

Amos was banned from Bethel as a subversive, but Hosea took up the critique from within the Northern Kingdom itself. He attacked the mystique of violence which had been popularized by the purge of Jehu a hundred years before (Hos. 1:4-6). He thus countered the tradition of Elijah and Elisha which defined the nation as Yahweh's agency of wrath against heretics and foreigners. The matter of fighting for principle had developed, as Hosea saw it, into a blank check for assassinating one's rivals (Hos. 7:6 f.). In the space of fourteen years, this violent mystique had resulted in the murder of four kings. Atrocities came to be performed by troops and police against their fellow countrymen of different political persuasion (II Kings 15:16). The court system became corrupt and inefficient (Hos. 5:1; 7:1 f.; 10:4), because a people which believes it can rid the world of evil by killing its enemies no longer comprehends the need for the slow processes of law. Respect for authority disintegrated (Hos. 10:3) and the last boundaries of self-restraint melted away: "they break all bounds and murder follows murder" (Hos. 4:2). Religion having degenerated into a means to guarantee success and power, the chosen people had lost touch with the vitality and stability of a living faith; they had crumbled from within, and destruction was inevitable (Hos. 5:11 f.).

At first this new prophetic impulse stood on the periphery of Israel's religious consciousness, virtually drowned out by the voices of popular, nationalistic prophets in both North and South. But with the fall of the Northern Kingdom, it loomed into the foreground as the realistic appraisal of what had gone wrong with the national mission. The impulse was picked up by Isaiah, who worked among the royal elite in Judah. He saw that Yahweh refused to play favorites, that he shattered the vanity which corrupted the sense of mission. "I will put an end to the pride of the arrogant, and lay low the haughtiness of the ruthless." (Isa. 13:11.) No nation was exempt from Yahweh's moral zeal, and the course of current events confirmed the fate of those who let themselves be driven by the arrogance of power.

When Hezekiah came to power in the South after a period of subjugation to Assyria and sought to revive fervent religious nationalism, Isaiah argued for a realistic assessment of power factors. Whereas Hezekiah's sense of mission led him to assume that the revolt would produce "peace and security" in his days (Isa. 39:8), the prophet sought to expose the myth that the chosen people would always prevail. He criticized the reliance on foreign alliances and sophisticated arms systems because they clouded realism and produced a false sense of security: "Woe to those who go down to Egypt for help and rely on horses, who trust in chariots because they are many and in horsemen because they are very strong, but do not look to the Holy One of Israel or consult the Lord!" (Isa. 31:1). The devastating Assyrian invasion of 701 B.C. confirmed Isaiah's realism and shattered the basis for militant nationalism in Israel. The defeat was interpreted by many as an indication that Israel had no distinctive mission, thus opening the doors to the cynical acceptance of foreign impulses. But for Isaiah it merely confirmed the bankruptcy of popular religion and the authenticity of the deeper prophetic vision first enunciated by Amos. Isaiah saw that the calamity could provide a catharsis which might destroy Israel's illusions of superiority in virtue and power (Isa. 1:25 f.). In letting herself be purified by defeat, Israel might be able to take up her true national mission of bearing the word of God's impartial justice as the basis for world peace. The prophet envisioned that when that took place, an era of genuine tranquility might be possible. Instead of a world empire ruled from Jerusalem with a rod of iron after the submission of her enemies, there could be a voluntary confederation of nations submitting to the adjudication of their disputes by law (Isa. 2:1-4).

## 2

Israel's subsequent history reflects the dilemmas posed by these two conflicting versions of mission. By the seventh century B.C., Zealous Nationalism was on the upsurge once again. King Josiah declared independence from a declining Assyria and created an effective military system with the help of the ideology of the book of Deuteronomy. This influential work was published under his aegis to revive the zealous spirit of the ancient confederacy. It taught that Israel would always prevail in battle if it obeyed the law. It neatly incorporated the prophetic impulse into its scheme with the dogma that the Northern Kingdom had fallen because it disobeyed cultic law. Under the power of this synthesis the historical traditions were reshaped, producing the books of Joshua, Judges, I and II Samuel, and I and II Kings. The common sense of Prophetic Realism was blunted by this absorption, producing massive illusions which could lead only to disaster. When the nation was confronted within a decade by the overwhelming power of Babylon, the Deuteronomic prophets promised "peace" because Yahweh would never suffer his obedient nation to fall (cf. Jer. 8:11, 19).

The voice of realism in this situation was Jeremiah's. He opposed the popular synthesis as a dangerous and arrogant perversion of the national mission. By gestures such as shattering pottery in the Temple and walking though Jerusalem wearing the yoke of a prisoner of war, he warned about the consequences of following the course of the fanatical nationalists. He was rebuffed by the populace and imprisoned for a time as a subversive. On the eve of the Babylonian siege he was summoned by King Zedekiah, who made a final attempt to enlist him in the zealous cause. "Inquire of Yahweh for us, for Nebuchadrezzar king of Babylon is making war against us; perhaps Yahweh will deal with us according to all his wonderful deeds, and will make him withdraw from us" (Jer. 21:2). But it was too late for miracles. Jerusalem was captured and its territory dismembered. When the fanatics revolted again ten years later, with the same mistaken image of national mission and grandeur, the capital was leveled and the remnants of its population deported into Babylon. The failure to accept Prophetic Realism in the definition of the national mission had led to the annihilation of the Southern Kingdom just as it had earlier of the Northern.

During the captivity period, the two conflicting versions of mission continued to tug at the soul of the survivors. The successors of Isaiah voiced the humane, tolerant viewpoint with an interpretation of Israel as a suffering servant for the redemption of the world and of a restored temple as "a house of prayer for all peoples" (Isa. 56:7). On the other hand, Ezra and Nehemiah developed a narrow, nationalistic perspective and reestablished a cult center in Jerusalem on the basis of a legal exclusivism and a conviction that the great and terrible Yahweh was calling them into battle for the national ideals (Neh. 4:20). Their effort to reconstitute the zealous fervor came to a climax when Joel called for the scuttling of the Isaiah heritage and for a renewal of zealous warfare: "Beat your plowshares into swords, and your pruning hooks into spears; let the weak say, 'I am a warrior' " (Joel 3:10).

This call to battle was heeded in a later generation by the Maccabees, who revolted against their Hellenistic overlords in the middle of the second century B.C. They were convinced that Yahweh was leading them in battle and providing the victories against the mercenaries. They took considerable pains to follow out the Deuteronomic instruction about massacring prisoners and burning cities; at first they even took the Sabbath regulations so seriously that they suffered some serious reverses. They directed their campaign as much against their own Greek-sympathizing countrymen as against the foreign troops. Judas Maccabeus "went through the cities of Judah; he destroyed the ungodly out of the land; thus he turned away wrath from Israel" (I Macc. 3:8). The premise here is thoroughly Deuteronomic: misfortune for the chosen people is due to divine wrath provoked by traitors; if they are wiped out, wrath will be assuaged and victory then be inevitable. Judas himself clearly enunciated the zealous ideology in these terms: "It is easy for many to be hemmed in by few, for in the sight of Heaven there is no difference between saving by many or by few. It is not on the size of the army that victory in battle depends, but strength comes from Heaven" (I Macc. 3:18 f.).

This ideology worked better against the demoralized elements of Hellenistic mercenaries than it had against the Assyrians or the Babylonians. The Maccabees won their war of independence. The author of Daniel, however, was realistic enough to aver that the Maccabean warriors had contributed only "a little help" for God's cause and that elements of vainglory were present in their ideology and behavior (Dan. 11z:34). In other regards, however, he agreed with the zealous nationalists that the enemy was demonic and ought to be annihilated. The book envisioned a permanent period of world domination after Yahweh's triumph: "But the saints of the Most High shall receive the kingdom, and possess the kingdom for ever. . . . Their kingdoms shall be an everlasting kingdom, and all dominions shall serve and obey them" (Dan. 7:18, 27). Such a kingdom, of course, would be simple for the saints to administer because all its potential enemies would have been destroyed.

With the Roman invasion of Palestine, this vision of triumphant zealotry encountered the shock of reality. The struggle to define the national mission turned inward with the emergence of well-defined parties in Judaism, each offering its interpretation of the way to bring in the kingdom. The Pharisees contended that compliance with their updated version of the Deuteronomic law would bring the triumph of the saints. The Essenes and the zealot movement argued that courageous battle was required to destroy the various structures of evil: if only all Israel would rise up in arms, God's wrath would be assuaged and his angels would intervene to destroy the Roman Empire, leaving the saints to rule. The Sadducees felt that their position of power through collaboration with the Roman authorities constituted the best of all possible kingdoms, so they rejected the prophetic tradition in its entirety. All these groups, in fact, represented versions of the zealous alternative with its inflated sense of national virtue and its disdain for truly impartial justice.

Only in segments within the party of the Pharisees were there substantial elements of realism, but even these were mitigated by the spirit of Daniel which divided the world into stereotyped groups and yearned for the world domination of the saints. The synthesis of Deuteronomy and the apocalyptic triumphalism of Daniel appear to have conspired to submerge the great prophetic version of the national mission. What remained was the muddle of internecine warfare, with each faction seeing the devil in the others' camps, and with each devoutly bent on destruction. As the first century A.D. wore on, this bitter ideological strife became more and more violent. It led to intermittent but bloody guerilla warfare against the Roman legions and to the dreadful sequence of assassinations and massacres described by Josephus in *The Jewish War*. It led in the end to the rebellions against Rome in A.D. 66-70 and again in 132-135 which decimated the population of Palestine. The nation proved unable to survive with its sense of mission so fragmented by zealotry.

A clear enunciation of Prophetic Realism during this final period was set forth by Jesus of Nazareth. At the beginning of his ministry he rejected the dream of bringing the messianic kingdom through violence (Luke 4:5-8). He located evil not in the enemy but in the heart of the chosen people itself, exposing the cruelty and callous disregard for life which legalistic self-righteousness had produced (Mark 3:1-6). He reversed the idea of divine preference for the chosen people, suggesting that sinners and foreigners would be the first to be welcomed into the kingdom (Luke 4:16-30). He worked to alter the stereotypes which made zealous warfare seem necessary, picturing a hated Samaritan as humane and welcoming into his circle disciples from all sides of the ideological struggle. He warned his fellow countrymen about the dangers of subscribing to the zealot war aims, prophesying that a revolt against Rome would bring destruction to Jerusalem (Luke 19:41-44; 23:26-31). While he expressed the willingness to support the Roman Empire by paying taxes (Mark 12:13-17), he condemned its propensity to substitute brute force for its vaunted world rule of law (Matt. 26:55). At the same time, he thrust a note of realism into the minds of the disciples when one of them began to use the sword against the authorities in Gethsemane: "Put your sword back into its place; for all who take the sword will perish by the sword. Do you think that I cannot appeal to my Father, and he will at once send me more than twelve legions of angels?" (Matt. 26:52 f.). The background of the zealous ideology is visible in this citation. Zealots had expected angelic intervention in the decisive final battle with Rome, and as Josephus reports it, this expectation remained vital until the final hours of the siege in Jerusalem a generation after Jesus' death.[5] What Jesus seems to be arguing here is that an act of zealous rebellion will not guarantee the intervention of divine forces, as the nationalists assumed. And without such assistance, those who take up the sword will in all likelihood die by the sword. It is a supreme statement of Prophetic Realism.

### 3

The tragic dimension of Jesus' message concerning the national mission was not only that it was rejected and its promulgator put to death as a renegade; it was not only that it was misunderstood and distorted by those who preferred not to hear the truth about themselves—it was that the message itself came to be placed in a collection of writings which obscured its essential thrust. Jesus' message was interpreted by posterity in the light of Deuteronomy, of Daniel, and, worst of all, of Revelation. This is a matter that has frequently been overlooked by critical Biblical scholarship, concerned as it is with the analysis of the meaning of passages for their original audiences. For later generations, however, and throughout much of the course of the American experience in particular, it was the book of Revelation that placed its stamp upon the whole Bible.[6]

Revelation stands triumphantly at the end of the canon, submerging the strand of Prophetic Realism—including the message of Jesus —under a grandiose flood of zealous images and ideas. It pictures the plot of world history as a battle between God and his enemies. Over and over again it promises total victory to the saints. It urges them to keep themselves pure and undefiled while God annihilates their opponents, who are stereotyped as bestial and irredeemable. Perhaps the most insidious aspect in terms of its impact on later generations is the coalescence of the humane tradition of the Fatherhood of God and the zealous tradition of the annihilation of the enemy. For example, the idea of God's word defined in Isaiah 11:3 ff. and in the early Christian tradition as the redemptive force which would come to replace warfare as a means of adjudicating differences is transposed in Rev. 19:11 ff. into an image of annihilation. Here the fearsome rider on the white horse is called "The Word of God. And the armies of heaven, arrayed in fine linen, white and pure, followed him on white horses. From his mouth issues a sharp sword with which to smite the nations, and he will rule them with a rod of iron; he will tread the wine press of the fury of the wrath of

God the Almighty." This passage will be recognized as the inspiration for the "Battle Hymn of the Republic."[7] Julia Ward Howe, while following Revelation's use of this imagery, failed to notice that the "sword" proper and the "sword of the word" indicate two diametrically opposed methods of redemption. The one originated in the tradition of Zealous Nationalism and the other in the tradition of Prophetic Realism. Another instance of the transposition of ideas and images in Revelation is the use of "lamb" for Jesus, a term used in Isa., ch. 53, and the early Christian tradition to depict redemptive self-sacrifice. In John's Revelation the "lamb" is so ferocious an agent of war that men cry out to the towering mountains, "Fall on us and hide us from the face of him who is seated on the throne, and from the wrath of the Lamb" (Rev. 6:16). The juxtaposition of tradition and image in the phrase "wrath of the Lamb" would jar anyone not raised in the tradition of seeing the entire Bible through the lens of the book of Revelation. But with this lens, the idea of redemptive love is simply subsumed under the category of redemptive wrath and the stage is set for a long tradition of theological equivocation. Waging war out of love and destroying enemies in order to save them are the all-too-understandable results of such a perspective.

In summary, under the impact of the book of Revelation, an appealing synthesis of apocalyptic Zealous Nationalism became accessible to the uncritical mind. Its dominant feature was a dualistic premise about the participants in the battles which presumably drive history toward its predestined goal. On one side was Satan, with his allies in multiple guises, acting through a grand, conspiratorial design to destroy the saints. To the zealot every rival became an agent of this satanic host and was thus stereotyped as inhuman and irredeemable. On the other side were the saints, stereotyped as pure and entirely righteous, untouched by universal sin and maintaining a passive form of zeal while waiting for God's design of triumph to reveal itself. But with the attitudes engendered toward the enemies and the precedent of the Deuteronomic tradition, it was a short step from passive to active zeal when the saints felt themselves called to participate in the final battle of Yahweh. The mythic perspective effectively undermined any pragmatic assessment of power factors and eliminated the possibility of compromise or coexistence. Revelation encouraged a foolish optimism concerning the outcome of history. No matter how destructive the battles become, it is the saints who will prevail both in this world and in the next.

Yet enclosed within this Biblical synthesis are the completely antithetical motifs of disinterested love, individual freedom, coexistence under law, and realism about man and history. Two opposing images of God, two contradictory versions of national mission, and two different approaches to world redemption lie beside each other here in uneasy wedlock. To accept their coalescence today is to continue in the dangerous habit of "doublethink" and "double-talk." But for earlier generations of Americans, untouched by the realities which now drive this synthesis apart, the book of Revelation provided the mythic framework for the mission of the nation. The materials were there ready and waiting for the development of the Captain America Complex.

# 3

# AMERICA'S ZEAL TO REDEEM THE WORLD

Early Puritans in New England derived from the book of Revelation the dualistic world view and the belief that violence would inaugurate God's kingdom. They thought of themselves as standing in the succession of Christian warriors and martyrs which Foxe had delineated from the Bible down to sixteenth-century England. As Winthrop S. Hudson puts it, "the New England story was viewed as a continuation of John Foxe's narrative of the pitched battles between Christ and Anti-christ that had marked the course of human history from the beginning."[1] Preachers such as John Davenport, John Cotton, the Mathers, and Thomas Hooker worked on the task of building a holy commonwealth that would be invincible. Between 1629 and 1640, when their cause was in decline in England, more than twenty thousand Puritans emigrated to America with this in mind. It was the call to battle which quickened their spirits, and they were fully convinced that such warfare had to be waged in the civil realm against the forms of corruption they felt were afflicting England. John Fiske said they were animated with "the desire to lead godly lives and to drive out sin from the community."[2] Their hope was that with the successful completion of such a war, the millennial kingdom promised in the book of Revelation would surely arrive.

Michael Walzer has pointed out the decisive role of such ideas in the creation of the Puritan radicals.

> What finally made men revolutionaries, however, was . . . an increasingly secure feeling that the saints did know the purposes of God. . . . Beginning at some point before 1640, a group of writers, including Joseph Meade of Cambridge University, began the work of integrating the spiritual warfare of the preachers with the apocalyptic history of Daniel and Revelation. The religious wars on the continent and then the struggle against the English king were seen by these men as parts of the ancient warfare of Satan and the elect, which had begun with Jews and Philistines and would continue until Armageddon.[3]

These writers had shifted the thousand-year kingdom of Rev., ch. 20, from the past to the immediate future and had reinterpreted the role of the saints in martial categories. So when the revolution came in England, preachers rose in Parliament to proclaim that the final battle with Satan was at hand. As one of them declared in 1643, "when the kings of the earth have given their power to the beast, these choice-soldiers . . . will be so faithful to the King of kings, as to oppose the beast, though armed with kinglike power."[4] Stephen Marshall exhorted the troops in Parliament in 1644: "Go now and fight the battles of the Lord. . . . Do now see that the question in England is whether Christ or Anti-Christ shall be lord or king." Henry Wilkenson wrote that Parliament's "business lies professedly against the apocalyptical beast and all his complices."[5] The battle was directed, of course, not only against the Cavaliers but against moral corruption everywhere. The purge of heretics, worldlings, and the licentious was viewed as part of the same battle by which "the whore of Babylon shall be destroyed with fire and sword."[6]

When the revolution was overthrown in England in 1660, there was a sense that America had become the new bearer of Protestant destiny. Increase Mather returned to Boston the following year with this in mind, "believing it was the last stronghold of Protestantism," as Perry Miller said.[7] With such convictions, the New England colonists resisted the efforts of the Restoration regime to topple the rule of the saints. They evaded Charles II's letter of complaints in 1662, frustrated the royal commissioners in 1664 and evaded compliance with the Navigation Acts for the next ten years. Even after their charter was revoked in 1684 they resisted the efforts of Governor Andros and had the nerve to imprison him the moment they heard of the Glorious Revolution in 1688. Ernest Lee Tuveson has traced the development of millennial nationalism in *Redeemer Nation*, noting the preachers' retention of the "fanatic notion" of overturning evil by the forceful rule of the saints.[8] He noted the impact of Jonathan Edwards' ideas that with the conversion of the New World, the last corner of the globe, "divine providence is preparing the way for the future glorious times of the church, where Satan's kingdom shall be overthrown throughout the whole habitable globe."[9] As J. F. Maclear has shown, the idea that America was the millennial nation "gave to all succeeding American events a continuing cosmic importance. Thomas Prince saw the French and Indian War as 'opening the way to enlightenment the utmost regions of America' preparatory to the millennial reign."[10]

By the eve of the American Revolution this sense of being the nation to usher in the millenial age was clearly developed. Timothy Dwight's poem "America" (1771) describes the hopeless state of the world before the discovery of the new chosen land and sets forth the promise of the millennial peace which would soon be administered by the saints in America:

> Hail Land of light and joy! thy power shall grow
> Far as the seas, which round thy regions flow;
> Through earth's wide realms thy glory shall extend,
> And savage nations at thy scepter bend . . .
> Then, then an heavenly kingdom shall descend,
> And Light and Glory through the world extend.
> And every region smile in endless peace;
> Till the last trump the slumbering dead inspire,
> Shake the wide heavens, and set the world on fire.[11]

Such peace, of course, could only come through violence. In later stanzas, Dwight pictures the American warriors as joining with the heavenly host in the manner of the ancient Israelite ideology. Hugh Henry Brackenridge based his *Six Political Discourses Founded on the Scripture* (1778) on the same set of premises. He argued that King George was inspired by Satan and that Providence sided with the Americans in the great Revolution. "Heaven hath taken an active part, and waged war for us. . . . Heaven knows nothing of neutrality. . . . There is not one tory to be found amongst the order of the seraphim."[12] Perry Miller has described "how effective were generations of Protestant preaching in evoking patriotic enthusiasm" during the Revolution.[13] In particular he has traced the precedents and implications of the "day of publick humiliation, fasting, and prayer" called by the Continental Congress in 1775. All over the colonies the belief was that God would respond to such repentance, bless the impending Revolution, and usher in his era of peace for the saints. This provided a powerful motivation for carrying out a rebellion against the greatest power on earth.

What made the American Revolution constructive was in part the creative interplay with the moderate traditions of Lockean liberalism, Enlightenment egalitarianism, and common law definitions of political rights. Bernard Bailyn has shown how these traditions joined in the Revolutionary period "into a comprehensive theory of politics,"[14] This provided a definition of political liberties which were thought to be endangered by misuse of royal powers, the basis for the principle of separation of powers, the preference for resolving conflicts by lawful procedure, and the idea of federal union between existing states. These ideas reflect the impulse of Prophetic Realism, and in some instances it is possible to trace them back to the separatists and the levelers in the earlier British Revolution who carved them out of their understanding of the Biblical heritage.[15]

Without this realistic leaven the American Revolution might have been nothing more than a vicious crusade against the presumed sources of evil. The summary treatment of the unfortunate Royalists during the Revolution indicates the potential. So, while the zealous war ideology provided a powerful motivation for inaugurating and sustaining the revolutionary cause, it was the resources of Prophetic Realism which accounted for its humane result.

In the decades after the Revolution the sense of being the millennial nation expressed itself in periodic religious revivals and reform movements. They were advanced in many instances with the conviction that if the chosen people purified themselves further, they would be granted the promised dominion and peace. The evangelist Lyman Beecher wrote in 1835 that "the millennium would commence in America" because with the successful revival the conversion of the entire world was now in prospect.[16] William G. McLoughlin notes the wide-spread acceptance of these ideas which produced the "Evangelical pietism" of the nineteenth century:

> Congregationalists, Presbyterians, Baptists, Separatists and Methodists... believed that a Christian commonwealth could be achieved through the massing of the votes of the regenerate to make "a Christian party in politics." These voters would elect only converted Christians to office and these legislators in turn would enact and enforce Christian morality throughout the nation... They wanted to outlaw the Masons and the Mormons, to enact nativist laws, to enforce prohibition, to censor immorality, to prevent birth control, to maintain a Christian Sabbath, and eventually to restrict immigration and pass laws preventing the teaching of evolution.[17]

One may grant that these reform movements were in part responsible for the gradual improvements of the quality of justice during the nineteenth century. But at the same time one should notice that the intolerant spirit in which the movements advanced produced a great deal of violence and harm. The millennial hopes encouraged this harsh zealotry and led people to attach such cosmic significance to reforms that inevitable disappointments followed their achievement. The golden Jerusalem appeared neither with the revivals nor with the most ambitious of the reforms. And the greatest evil in American society—slavery—was not amenable to pietistic solutions, as the Abolitionist zealots discovered in the 1860s.

Possibly the most ominous expression of this Zealous Nationalism, however, was the sense of "manifest destiny" by which the unscrupulous wars against Mexico and the American Indians were justified. The double sense of being the virtuous nation and being called to a millennial destiny is described by several citations in Albert K. Weinberg's study. In 1845 an editorialist described the current obsession with American virtue and destiny. "It is a truth, which every man may see, if he will but look,—that all the channels of communication,—public and private, through the schoolroom, the pulpit, and the press,—are engrossed and occupied with *this one idea*, which all these forces are combined to disseminate: —that we the American people, are the most independent, intelligent, moral and happy people on the face of the earth."[18] This sense of virtue served to confirm the validity of expansion. Providence was smiling because the moral requirement for millennial mission had been met. Weinberg writes:

> Even theological literature was scarcely more abundant in references to Providence than was the literature of expansionism. For it seemed that especially in expanding our territory, as a poet wrote upon the prospect of annexing Texas, "we do but follow out our destiny, as did the ancient Israelite." The expansionist conception of destiny was essentially ethical in its assumption that "Providence had given to the American people a great and important mission...to spread the blessings of Christian liberty."[19]

It was this mission of liberty which united reform movements and manifest destiny. Herman Melville appealed to it in urging the abolition of flogging in *White-Jacket*. "Since we bear the ark of the liberties of the world, it is clear that 'the political Messiah'... has come in *us*." The consequence, as Melville put it, is that deeds which ordinarily would be classified as "national selfishness" are acceptable, since they enhance the glory and power of the messianic people: "We cannot do a good to America but we give alms to the world."[20] The task of prophetic ethics is absorbed into the redemptive mission. Even with so realistic a thinker as Melville, the provisos of realism tend to be drowned out by the messianic chorus.

This grandiose ideology had a potential for injustice which few saw at the time. If God had predestined the chosen nation to expand indefinitely, and if that expansion were for the sake of "Christian liberty," who was to demur? Yet it is a tribute to the power of Prophetic Realism that its impulse was not completely submerged. There were those who protested against the Mexican War taxes. A young congressman from Illinois by the name of Abraham Lincoln lost his seat in 1848 because he doubted Secretary of State Buchanan's claim that "Destiny beckons us to hold and civilize Mexico."[21] Hans Kohn has pointed out the countervailing witness of the McGuffey *Readers*, which "strongly denounced wars and militarism" and "had their serious doubts about the wisdom and justice of the war against Mexico."[22] They also issued warnings about the dangers of zealotry for America, particularly as posed by the radical democrats in the age of Jackson and afterward. Richard D. Mosier's study unearths such statements as the following: "Let the American dread, as the archenemy of republical institutions, the shock of exasperated parties, and the implacable revenge of demagogues."[23] These relatively conservative sentiments were combined with a doctrine of America's providential destiny to provide an example of equality and democracy to redeem the entire world. Like the sun itself, America should "shed its glorious influence backward on the states of Europe and forward on the empires of Asia." These school books were distributed by the millions, helping to shape the American sense of mission in relatively humane and responsible directions. They pictured this mission in terms of providing an example of equality and democracy to the world, though in typically grandiloquent terms. A similar approach, developed by George Bancroft, the great nineteenth-century historian. He described the American Revolution as "most radical in its character, yet achieved with such benign tranquility that even conservatism hesitated to censure. A civil war armed men of the same ancestry against each other, yet for the advancement of the principles of everlasting peace and universal brotherhood."[24] Here is a framework similar to the book of Revelation, with warfare bringing a peace which is nothing less than "everlasting." Yet it is intermixed with prophetic elements such as universal brotherhood and the preservation of life.

## 2

It was during the Civil War era that the tension between the two approaches to national mission snapped, leaving zeal against zeal to tear the nation apart. The issue behind this fateful crisis was the "peculiar and powerful interest" of slavery, to use Abraham Lincoln's words. Although the impulse of Prophetic Realism recognized from the beginning the inconsistency between slavery and the democratic ideals, it acknowledged that the Union could not survive its sudden abolition. The spread of slavery was limited by the Missouri Compromise and the Compromise of 1850, and this in effect set slavery itself on the path to ultimate extinction. But the long deadlock over the shape of northwestward expansion, hindered for decades by Southern efforts to keep an equal number of states and votes in the Senate, was broken with the Kansas-Nebraska Act and the Dred Scott decision. A plausible fear arose that slavery would expand into the western and northern states.[25] The gradual solution of the problem thus gave way to a fatal erosion of the Constitutional and legal limits, and an implicit scuttling of the democratic premise that all men were created equal. The Republican Party arose to attempt to restore the limits against the expansion of slavery, and when its candidate won the election of 1860 the slave states seceded. The reforming zeal of the North clashed against the romantic zeal of the South, producing the bloodiest war in American history.

In the North, the crusade against slavery had long been buttressed by millenial premises and had directed its attack against the gradual processes of Constitutional restraint. William Lloyd Garrison called the American Constitution a "covenant with death and an agreement with hell." In 1841 he printed a letter from an Ohio supporter which stated: "My hope for the Millennium begins where Dr. Beecher's expires, viz., AT THE OVERTHROW OF THIS NATION."[26] Although Aileen S. Kraditor has shown that the majority of abolitionists rejected Garrison's extreme anti-institutional position, the fact remains that they sought to destroy the legal protections which slavery enjoyed and the political compromises which guaranteed its existence while hindering its expansion.[27] The apocalyptic language employed by the abolitionists produced an expectation of violent upheaval. Harriet Beecher Stowe spoke of an imminent "last convulsion" which would purify the chosen people from the blight of slavery.[26] Hundreds of abolitionist preachers took up this line, until, with the opening of hostilities in 1861, Hollis Read could write *The Coming Crisis of the World: or, The Great Battle and the Golden Age,* depicting the apocalyptic strife which would usher in the millennium. It was to be the battle of the North, "carrying the standard of Christ, against the South, ranged under that of the Beast," just as in the book of Revelation.[29]

The most powerful embodiment of this zealous ideology was the "Battle Hymn of the Republic," written in 1862. Its terminology and imagery, as Tuveson shows, is derived almost exclusively from the apocalyptic portions of the Bible.[30] In the marching of the Union soldiers was "the glory of the coming of the Lord." With God himself marching on the side of the Northern armies, victory is viewed as inevitable. It would be strenuous and bloody, and many would die in the certainty that they would receive his "grace" for their faithfulness in battle. But they could fight to the last man with the certain knowledge that they were following the victorious divine trumpet:

> He has sounded forth the trumpet that shall never call retreat;
> He is sifting out the hearts of men before His judgment-seat:
> Oh, be swift, my soul, to answer Him! be jubilant, my feet!
> Our God is marching on.

Who is this martial God who leads the Northern troops into battle? Who is the "Lord" who crushes the grapes of his wrathful wine by the feet of his troops? It is none other than the loving Christ seen through the lens of the book of Revelation. The contradictory redemptive images of the peaceful suffering servant and the marching Lord of battle are joined in the final stanza. The redemptive task of the soldiers is neatly shifted from annihilating the enemy to altruistically setting men free. The unselfish mission of the suffering, dying servant is incorporated into that of the warrior. He dies, not killing others, but suffering for others. With this, the stage is set for the next hundred years of altruistic, martial zeal in America:

> In the beauty of the lilies Christ was born across the sea,
> With a glory in His bosom that transfigures you and me:
> As he died to make men holy, let us die to make men free,
> While God is marching on.

This ideology steeled the North for the long, bloody and frustrating war. In time, such war to "make men free" would not be able to halt its course until the whole world was involved. But as the following citation from Rev. George S. Phillips reveals, such prospects were in view even during the most discouraging hours of the war. "Our mission . . . should only be accomplished when the last despot should be dethroned, the last chain of oppression broken, the dignity and equality of redeemed humanity everywhere acknowledged, republican government everywhere established, and the American flag . . . should wave over every hand and encircle the world with its majestic folds. Then, and not till then, should the nation have accomplished the purpose for which it was established by the God of heaven."[31] It is the millennial hope of Rev., ch. 20, wherein the saints rule the earth after the destruction of iniquity.

The North was not alone in developing a war ideology with millennial overtones. John Hope Franklin has traced the emergence of a "militant South" in the decades prior to the war.[32] Along with a chivalrous martial tradition and a high level of regional pride, there was the conviction that "we need not fear the joust of arms—for the

God of Israel will be on the side of his children," as a New Orleans paper put it in 1855.[33] James W. Silver has shown how widespread such ideas were in the South and how decisive they were in sustaining the rebellion. "Every Confederate victory proved that God had shielded his chosen people and every defeat became the merited punishment of the same people for their sins. The war itself was a chastisement "inflicted by an Almighty arm. . . . If the people . . . were to turn with one heart and one mind to the Lord . . . He would drive the invader from our territories . . . He can turn them as he turns the rivers of water.'"[34] Benjamin M. Palmer described the South's millennial destiny before the opening of the war: "If she has the grace given her to know her hour she will save herself, the country, and the world."[35]

With mutually exclusive forms of zealous war ideology pitted against each other, and expectations of world redemption with the destruction of the other, the stage was set for a war whose ferocity and duration challenged the illusions of both sides. The expectation of a cowardly enemy was belied by those dreadful and "indecisive contests where overwhelming victory was impossible because neither side would run as they ought when beaten," to use the words of Oliver Wendell Holmes, Jr.[35] It was a tragic cycle of destruction, with every prospect of increasing in brutality and injustice no matter which crusading army won the battle. Nothing short of the enemy's bloody annihilation would promise to appease the voracious appetite of such a zeal.

The impulse of Prophetic Realism during this tragic conflict expressed itself most prominently in the work of Abraham Lincoln, and especially in his second inaugural address. The speech alludes to the expectations of both sides, noting not only the irony that "both read the same Bible, and pray to the same God" for opposite ends, but also that neither was completely justified in its assessment of the holiness of its cause. If the South should not "dare to ask a just God's assistance in wringing their bread from the sweat of other men's faces," the North must recall the admonition to "judge not that we be not judged." The sense of moral superiority which sustains zealous warfare is thrust aside in view of the fact that "the Almighty has His own purposes."[37] The judgment falls on "both North and South," and in some mysterious and tragic fashion the continued suffering of both may have its meaning in the impartial judgment of God. Lincoln continued:

> If we shall suppose that American Slavery is one of those offences which, in the providence of God, must needs come, but which,

> having continued through His appointed time, He now wills to remove, and that He gives to both North and South, this terrible war, as the woe due to those by whom the offence came, shall we discern therein any departure from those divine attributes which the believers in a Living God always ascribe to Him? Fondly do we hope—fervently do we pray—that this mighty scourge of war may speedily pass away. Yet, if God wills that it continue, until all the wealth piled by the bond-man's two hundred and fifty years of unrequited toil shall be sunk, and until every drop of blood drawn with the lash, shall be paid by another drawn with the sword, as was said three thousand years ago, so still it must be said "the judgments of the Lord, are true and righteous altogether."

This is the heart of the argument, for it shatters the simple identification of either cause with God's justice. As Lincoln wrote in the note to Thurlow Weed shortly afterward, such a message would not be "immediately popular. Men are not flattered by being shown that there has been a difference of purpose between the Almighty and them."[38] Yet until they would grow humble enough to acknowledge that "difference in purpose," they would be neither humane nor realistic.

It is the matter of humaneness which receives emphasis at the end of the Second Inaugural. It is juxtaposed with the issue of moral resolve in a manner which powerfully counters zealous ideologies. The zealot is so caught up in his moral crusade that persons cease to matter. He becomes implacable, cruel, and deadly. Mercy in such an ideology is a sign of weakness, a betrayal of the holy cause, a step toward compromise with evil. But for the same reason that charity is antithetical to zealotry it is consistent with faithful resolve to carry out a task when no absolutes are available. Lincoln speaks of a "firmness in the right" in proportion as "God gives us to see the right," that is, in mysterious and fragmentary fashion. Since every man's version of the "right" is subject to the provisos of Prophetic Realism, one must never hold to it with fanaticism, destroying life in the process. Yet Lincoln's kind of "firmness" involved a very high level of steadiness in face of the high cost required during the war to keep the democratic experiment from breaking up. The complex thought is expressed in a single sentence at the close of the address:

> With malice toward none; with charity for all; with firmness in the right, as God gives us to see the right, let us strive on to finish the work we are in; to bind up the nation's wounds; to care for him who shall have borne the battle, and for his widow, and his orphan—to do all which may achieve and cherish a just, and a lasting peace, among ourselves, and with all nations.

Charity and realism are the consequences of Lincoln's stance. Since he was spared fanaticism by his understanding of impartial divine justice, he was set free not only to respond in charity to the needs of fellowmen but also to deal realistically with the tangle of historical responsibility. The realism is visible in the grasp of what truly makes for "a just, and a lasting peace," not annihilation of the wicked but care for the victim. And who is to deny that Lincoln's plans for reconstructing the South, based on these principles of charity, would have accomplished a great deal more to "bind up the nation's wounds" than all the purges of the Radicals?

In a single short address Abraham Lincoln exposed the living source of both charity and realism within the framework of God's mysterious purposes for his "almost chosen people." By breaking with zealous appropriations of that purpose, he opened the nation to its natural resources of mercy and common sense. And he did so without scuttling the sense of national purpose, without leaving the nation adrift on a trackless, amoral sea.

## 3

When President Andrew Johnson sought to implement a Lincolnesque reconstruction program, it was wrecked by the combination of Southern intransigence, Northern radicalism, and a lack of political tact. One is tempted simply to place the major share of blame on the Radicals, but the dilemma they faced so illuminates our current crisis that it deserves a more judicious analysis. It is not enough to assert, as a current history text does, that Thaddeus Stevens and Charles Sumner were simply destructive zealots: "In the remorseless manner in which the Radicals drove through their program, we see evidences of a revolutionary spirit that would stop at nothing to attain its ends."[39] For what were the ends so zealously sought? The irony was that they were the ideals of humane, prophetic realism: the enforcement of equal rights for former slaves and the dismantling of a social structure perceived to be undemocratic. In the chaos of the South after 1865, it appeared that neither was being accomplished. Major General Carl Schurz reported after his extensive investigations that former rebels were rapidly returning to power in the new state and local governments. Blacks were being subjugated to the most barbaric pressures to force them back into their "places." Schurz reported that a "veritable reign of terror prevailed in many parts of the South."[40]

This situation posed to the country a dilemma so deep and pervasive that it is with us yet. To protect the rights of blacks required an unprecedented incursion of federal power into the affairs of local governments. As the British historian W. R. Brock states, "The concept of negro equality demanded interference with the processes of local government on a scale never before contemplated in America or in any other nation."[41] Yet to acquiesce in the continued violation of basic human rights was to deny the thrust of the American mission. The Radicals took the libertarian horn of this dilemma and carried it out until 1877 with remorseless zeal, enacting a series of unconstitutional measures in Congress and coming close to impeaching a President who thwarted their design.

Several factors closely related to Zealous Nationalism helped to defeat Radical Reconstruction. The chosen nation ideology had always emphasized the Anglo-Saxon peoples as the bearers of the millennial destiny. When combined with the stereotyping which Zealous Nationalism encourages, it produced a widespread feeling in both North and South that the blacks were inferior and unsuited for full participation in the democratic process. At the same time the North felt it had emerged from the war as God's purified nation whose destiny had been confirmed by victory. Prominent preachers suggested that the bloodshed had burned out the "base alloy" of slavery and other sins so that the chose nation could fulfill its millennial task. Horace Bushnell grieved that America's sins had brought her "to the point where only blood . . . can resanctify what we[North and South] have so loosely held and so badly desecrated." But now a new sense of unity had been produced, so that "the sense of nationality becomes even a kind of religion."[42] Marvin R. Vincent preached as early as 1864 that "God has been striking, and trying to make us strike at elements unfavorable to the growth of a pure democracy . . . , preparing in this broad land a fit stage for the last act of the mighty drama, the consummation of human civilization. . . . Who shall say that she shall not only secure lasting peace to herself, but be, under God, the instrument of a millennial reign to all the nations?"[43] Lasting peace was now assumed because evil had been cleansed through war. The "saints" could easily rule the cleansed world without having to deal with the work of Satan. As Robert Penn Warren suggested, the victorious North felt "redeemed by history, automatically redeemed," but at the same time, the reforming impulse "burned itself out in the slavery controversy," not to reappear for another generation.[44] A seemingly contradictory set of attitudes resulted: complacency about the existence of evil among the saints and a petulant impatience at any resistance to their rule. The same philosophy produced both the zeal of the Radical Republicans and the complacency about the corruption of the nation as a whole.

In the decades after 1877 the millennial language was gradually infused with secular terms, and the nation became, as Maclear puts it, "preoccupied with progress of every kind—biological, technological, and cultural, as well as spiritual and moral."[45] The evolutionary terminology was grafted onto the Redeemer Nation concept. Social Darwinism justified material progress and expansion. Success was readily identified as evidence of virtue. Horatio Alger became the new form of saint to be given rule over the world.

It was not long before these ideas were combined to produce a new and imperialistic ideology. One of the most influential exponents of imperial nationalism, according to recent studies,[46] was Josiah Strong, who served as secretary of the American Home Missionary Society. In 1885 he placed the evangelizing of the American West in the context of America's destiny to place the stamp of Christ on the entire world. Since the Anglo-Saxon peoples represent the great ideas of civil liberty and "pure spiritual Christianity," God is preparing them with their prosperity and their power to be "the die with which to stamp the peoples of the earth." With the western expansion now at an end, America is ready to enter "the final competition of races... [as] the representative, let us hope, of the largest liberty, the purest Christianity, the highest civilization—having developed peculiarly aggressive traits calculated to impress its institutions upon mankind... Can anyone doubt that the result of this competition of races will be the 'survival of the fittest'?"[47] Their calling, in other words, is to "Anglo-Saxonize mankind" for the sake of Christ, and when this is done by missionary and imperial expansion, the "coming of Christ's kingdom in the world" will have been hastened. But if this task was pictured in martial terminology, with America as "God's right arm in his battle with the world's ignorance and oppression and sin,"[48] its role was to be the servant rather than the master of the world. This fragment of Prophetic Realism is absorbed into Zealous Nationalism in Strong's book, *Expansion Under New World Conditions:* "This race has been honored not for its own sake but for the sake of the world. It has been made... powerful not to make subject, but to serve;... free not simply to exult in freedom, but to make free; exalted not to look down, but to lift up."[49] The note of unselfish mission is combined with a powerful sense of cultural and racial superiority which would inevitably lead to imperialistic warfare against the presumed enemies of progress. What other alternative would there be when lesser nations resisted the "stamp" of Anglo-Saxon civilization?

These ideas led directly to the Spanish-American War. It was clearly an unnecessary conflict, the Spanish having acquiesced to American demands before the mysterious sinking of the *Maine*. The enormous groundswell of crusading spirit swept the country headlong into war. Henry Watterson editorialized in 1898: "It is a war into which this nation will go with a fervor, with a power, with a unanimity that would make it invincible if it were repelling not only the encroachments of Spain but the assaults of every monarch in Europe.... It is not a war of conquest. It is not a war of envy or enmity. It is not a war of pillage or gain.... We find in it the law supreme... the law of man, the law of God. We find it in our own inspiration, our own destiny... [which] says that liberty and law shall no longer be trampled upon... by despotism and autocracy upon our threshold. That is the right of our might; that is the sign in which we conquer."[50] It was, in short, a war to make men free, the natural consequence of the ideology expressed by the "Battle Hymn of the Republic." Its aims were altruistic and thus victory was inevitable, even if all the nations of the world were opposed. Henry van Dyke's sermon on Thanksgiving Day 1898 put this thought very succinctly: "Not for gain, not for territory, but for freedom and human brotherhood! That avowal alone made the war possible and successful.'"[51]

This tidy little war with Spain helped to consolidate the synthesis between prophetic ideals and Zealous Nationalism. As Walter Millis notes, it helped to generate "the notions of the national destiny and the national responsibility in the global context" which were to guide American behavior in the new century.[52] That it was so easily and cheaply won served to deepen illusions of America's virtue and destiny. The thesis that America won because her aims were virtuous was easily transposed to imply that since America had won, that proved her virtue. The saints could gain ascendancy without even getting their hands dirty—proof that they were saints indeed! There were, after all, only 460 Americans killed in battle. But the shock of reality was present, even in this triumphant scene. The Filipinos refused to submit to American benevolence: They resisted the imperialistic design, so that brutal coercion had to be used, even as the supposedly degenerate Spaniards had used it in Cuba. The election of 1900 saw America divided between the imperialists and the anti-imperialists, the latter representing with some precision the position of Prophetic Realism. But voices like that of Albert J. Beveridge were to prevail. In his speech before the Union League Club in 1899, Beveridge concluded:

> Retreat from the Philippines...would be the betrayal of a trust as sacred as humanity....And so, thank God, the Republic never retreats...American manhood today contains the master administrators of the world, and they go forth for the healing of the nations. They go forth in the cause of civilization. They go forth for the betterment of man. They go forth, and the word on their lips is Christ and his peace, not conquest and its pillage. They go forth to prepare the peoples, through decades and maybe centuries of patient effort, for the great gift of American institutions. They go forth not for imperialism, but for the Greater Republic.[53]

To retreat—to accept defeat—would be to deny the millennial destiny to redeem the world. In a very real sense, the form such world redemption was to take is revealed in the reference to "the great gift of American institutions." Since these are to be Christ's means of bringing peace in Beveridge's view, to advance them by force is not imperialism, but the "betterment of man." The "healing of the nations," which Beveridge cites from the description of the heavenly Jerusalem in Rev. 22:2, would come when American democracy had swept over the world.

But could the "Greater Republic" be imposed by a zealous crusade? Were the attitudes and policies implicit in such an effort not antithetical to the very democracy one desired to advance? This was the dilemma which Beveridge's oft-cited speech before the Senate in 1900 tried to answer. It is precisely the same dilemma we face in the latter phases of the Indochina war. Though the Philippine campaign resisted the mythic solution, Beveridge insisted that "lasting peace can be secured only by overwhelming forces in ceaseless action until universal and absolutely final defeat is inflicted on the enemy." If some people charge "that our conduct of the war has been cruel," one must keep in mind that "we are dealing with Orientals....They mistake kindness for weakness, forbearance for fear." The "chief factor" in the delay of total victory has been "American opposition to the war." And as for the charge that the crusade was antithetical to the Declaration of Independence, Beveridge insisted that it "applies only to people capable of self-government," not to these "Malay children of barbarism." The crusade was grounded in something "deeper even than any question of constitutional power," so let not such matters stand in the way. For God "has marked the American people as His chosen nation to finally lead in the regeneration of the world."[54]

In retrospect one can see that Beveridge's zealous ideology had to set aside the very democratic values it sought to advance. Here was the dilemma that would one day tear the myths asunder. The coalescence of zeal and realism might stand the pressure of the Spanish navy and the Philippine guerillas, but could it survive a massive shock? As we shall see, it would begin one day to break apart precisely at the fissures Beveridge tried so eloquently to fill.

## 4

With American participation in World War I, the price of such zealotry was paid, though in relatively small installments. The nation had entered the war after much hesitation, because of Germany's violation of neutrality on the high seas. But the justification President Wilson developed had little to do with self-defense. It came straight out of the tradition of Zealous Nationalism. It was combined in such a remarkable fashion with motifs of Prophetic Realism that a modern synthesis was achieved. Part of the cost of the war was the revelation of the internal contradictions in this synthesis and their serious consequences.

Prior to our entrance into the war Wilson led America in the role of the righteous neutral, waiting for others to exhaust themselves before stepping in to enforce a lasting peace. The sense of saintly aloofness was visible in his refusal to declare war even after the sinking of the *Lusitania:* "There is such a thing as a nation being so right that it does not need to convince others by force that it is right."[55] There was room here for realistic statements of the need for world government. "It will be absolutely necessary that a force be created as a guarantee of the permanency of the settlement so much greater than the force of any nation now engaged . . . that no nation . . . could face or withstand it." Wilson also saw that the hope for total victory was antithetical to true peace. "It must be a peace without victory. . . . Victory would mean peace forced upon the loser. . . . Only a peace between equals can last. Only a peace the very principle of which is equality and a common participation in a common benefit."[56]

Would such principles of coexistence prevail when the saints themselves came into the battle? His war message to Congress in

April 1917 reveals they could not. Wilson was apparently conscious of the possible contradiction, since he took such pains to deny it. "My own thought has not been driven from its habitual and normal course by the unhappy events of the last two months. . . . I have exactly the same things in mind now that I had in mind when I addressed the Senate on the 22nd of January last."[57] He went on to reiterate "the principles of peace and justice in the life of the world" which had been his constant aim. But then he slipped into a zealous line of argument which contradicted his principles of coexistence and peace without victory. Since the German imperial government was driven by the lust for "selfish and autocratic power" and harbored "cunningly contrived plans of deception or aggression," it was impossible to coexist with it. "We are accepting this challenge of hostile purpose because we know that in such a government, following such methods, we can never have a friend; and that in the presence of its organized power, always lying in wait to accomplish we know not what purpose, there can be no assured security for the democratic governments of the world." The recourse was to the traditional crusade for millennial goals:

> The world must be made safe for democracy. Its peace must be planted upon the tested foundations of political liberty. We have no selfish ends to serve. We desire no conquest, no dominion, . . . We are but one of the champions of the right of mankind. We shall be satisfied when those rights have been made as secure as the faith and the freedom of nations can make them.[58]

As in the "Battle Hymn of the Republic," Americans would die unselfishly to set men free. The elements of Prophetic Realism had been absorbed once again into the ideology of Zealous Nationalism, and it was the spirit of the book of Revelation which animated the whole.

A powerful surge of enthusiasm approaching hysteria swept over the country. Theodore Roosevelt told the Harvard Club, "If ever there was a holy war, it is this war."[59] Jess Yoder's study of preaching during World War I shows the wide dispersion of this crusade ideology.[60] Randolph H. McKim proclaimed from his Washington pulpit: "It is God who has summoned us to this war. It is his war we are fighting. . . . This conflict is indeed a crusade. The greatest in history—the holiest. It is in the profoundest and truest sense a Holy War. . . . Yes, it is Christ, the King of Righteousness, who calls us to grapple in deadly strife with this unholy and blasphemous power."[61] An Episcopal minister wrote in the *Atlantic Monthly: "The complete representative of the American Church in France is the United*

*States Army overseas.* Yes, an *army*, with its cannon and rifles and machine-guns and its instruments of destruction. The Church militant, sent, morally equipped, strengthened and encouraged, approved and blessed, by the Church at home."[62]

In sermons such as these the apocalyptic battle of the saints against the beast is in view. Henry van Dyke, acting as a Navy chaplain, wrote an additional stanza for the "Battle Hymn" which was widely used in training camps:

> We have heard the cry of anguish, from the victims of the Hun,
> And we know our country's peril if the war-lord's will is done.
> We will fight for worldwide freedom till the victory is won,
> For God is marching on.[63]

This redemptive war of the saints for the freedom of the world was precisely what President Wilson had advanced. And while it proved effective in stirring a country to enthusiastic mobilization, it bore within it the seeds of bitterness to come. Despite the grandiose promises, the democratic countries proved less virtuous than had been supposed, and the obsession with security led to postwar arrangements which fell short of making the world safe for democracy. President Wilson sought to halt these tendencies, but the mixture of realism and zealous pretensions in his own thought and in the country as a whole made it impossible.

A curious feature of the American character has come to the fore after each great war: a sudden disinterest in the aftermath followed by a long period of disillusionment. Many causes for this pattern have been suggested, but I would submit that the zealous ideology itself has a great deal to do with it. The unquestioned premise was that a victorious crusade would truly make the world safe. It was an idea derived from the book of Revelation that after the destruction of the Beast the world would automatically come under the control of the saints. When this did not happen, a long and counterproductive withdrawal resulted. The irony of the situation was that President Wilson's thought contained a wider amalgam of the two contradictory impulses than was the case with the population as a whole. His advocacy of the League of Nations stood in the tradition of Prophetic Realism. But while this was integrated with zealous premises in Wilson's mind, it was peripheral for the country as a whole. The public was more consistent than Wilson, in one sense, by reacting on the zealous premises alone and thus being terribly disillusioned when millennial peace did not follow the victory. Having been stirred by Wilson's rhetoric to a "war to end all wars,"

Americans were unable to incorporate any thought of complex institutions to adjudicate future conflicts. To admit that such institutions were necessary was to doubt the validity of the crusade. It also meant coexisting with nations that seemed as degenerate as those the crusade had purged. The rhetoric about unselfishness had encouraged such illusions of moral superiority that accommodation to such evils was repulsive to them. Refusal to participate in the League of Nations was thus perfectly consistent. Isolationism was the logical consequence of the zealous crusade.

The tragic results of this reversion of the isolation of the "saints" are still being felt in the world, according to Hans Kohn. Since the United States refused to provide the League with the prestige and the force it required, there was no effective way to sustain the small democracies in Eastern Europe when Germany's military power revived. As Wilson had warned in his speeches favoring American entrance into the League, such factors would produce another great war within twenty-five years.[64] The refusal to cooperate in sustaining a balanced international economy made the fall of these democracies, including Germany, inevitable. The devastation of World War II and the subsequent spread of Communism were made possible by the fateful decisions of 1919 and 1920. Yet the illusions shaped by the great crusade made the public incapable of comprehending its own complicity in this tragedy. As the inevitable disillusionment deepened, it brought a growing lack of faith in the democratic ideals with which zeal had been joined. It produced the moral cynicism and the hunger for alien ideologies which would serve to erode democracy itself.

## 5

World War II provided the circumstances under which the realistic and zealous elements in American nationalism would come increasingly into tension with each other. The country was seriously divided during the opening phases of the conflict in Europe and Asia, with isolationist and pacifist sentiments setting the tone. The realists felt that intervention against Hitler was called for in the late '30s. By November 1941 they had convinced only 20 percent of the population of the rightness of their cause.[65] Despite the horrors of Fascism, America seemed to lack what Harry Schermann called for in 1941: a war philosophy "so basic that no wedging doubts can shake it."[66] President Roosevelt came to favor intervention much earlier than the country as a whole, entering into cooperation with England on lend-lease and armed merchant ships, and placing embargoes on Japanese trade. A divided public and a hostile Congress would not support all of those measures so they were carried out covertly by the Administration. By the time of the Atlantic Charter, August of 1941, conflicting tendencies were clearly visible within Roosevelt's position. The Charter set forth the traditional ideas of Wilsonian political realism, such as renunciation of territorial aggression, national self-determination, and "the establishment of a wider and permanent system of general security."[67] But these were joined with a zealous resolve concerning "the final destruction of the Nazi tyranny." These sentiments were repeated and strengthened in the October 1941 message to the nation in which a stereotyped version of Nazi war aims was set forth: "In place of the churches of our civilization, there is to be set up an international Nazi church. In place of the Bible, the words of *Mein Kampf* will be imposed and enforced as Holy Writ. And in place of the cross of Christ will be put two symbols —the swastika and the naked sword. A god of blood and iron will take the place of the God of love and mercy."[68] The issue before the nation was therefore one of cataclysmic significance, and it appeared as if irrevocable commitments had already been made to a crusade. A familiar mind-set revealed itself in these early statements of Roosevelt: beside his humane and courageous pragmatism emerged a harsh and crusading zeal. Compared with that of Woodrow Wilson, the amalgam was much less satisfactory. When Roosevelt resorted to zealous stereotypes, he approached a level of crudity never possible for Wilson.

After Pearl Harbor, these tendencies were consolidated into a crusade to rid the world of totalitarianism and to make it safe for the saints. Roosevelt said, in his December 8, 1941, statement to Congress, "No matter how long it may take us to overcome this premeditated invasion, the American people, in their righteous might, will win through to absolute victory. . . . We will not only defend ourselves to the uttermost but will make very certain that this form of treachery shall never endanger us again."[69] The radio address the next day called in a similar manner for an unlimited crusade: "I repeat that the United States can accept no result save victory, final and complete. Not only must the shame of Japanese treachery be wiped out but the sources of international brutality, wherever they exist, must be absolutely and finally broken."[70] An uncompromising zeal manifests itself in such statements, and the tradition of warfare against the demonic Beast to usher in the era of peace shows through the secularized terminology. It was perfectly consistent that

Roosevelt should have proposed the "unconditional surrender" formula at Casablanca and accepted the "Morgenthau Plan" for reducing Germany after the war to an agricultural province. These facets of total warfare were of immense help to enemy propagandists and may well have lengthened the war by eliminating any hope for negotiations with the potential resistance elements in Germany and Japan.[71] But they were welcomed by an American public nurtured in the crusading tradition.

The popular rendition of the anti-Fascist crusade contained a somewhat larger portion of religious terminology. The first American casualty of the war was buried in St. Paul's Cathedral in London while the other volunteers in his squadron sang the "Battle Hymn of the Republic."[72] One thinks of the popular war song, "Praise the Lord and pass the ammunition... and we'll all stay free!" Henry Wallace went the farthest along this line to speak in apocalyptic terms of the "fight between a free world and a slave world.... Through the leaders of the Nazi revolution Satan now is trying to lead the common man of the whole world back into slavery and darkness.... We shall cleanse the plague spot of Europe, which is Hitler's Germany, and with it the hell-hole of Asia—Japan. No compromise with Satan is possible."[73] Preachers echoing this line tended to emphasize moral requirements for victory. Peter Marshall suggested that victory for the chosen nation would not be given by God without recovery of her holiness: "We are fighting for total victory, but we shall never achieve total victory unless we fight for total Christianity.... A nation obedient to the laws of God would lead the world."[74] This moral emphasis reflects the traditional premise that only a righteous nation will triumph. It is reflected in the remarkable religious revival that took place in the early years of the war within the armed services themselves. Stanley High described the "War Boom in Religion" and cited a veteran chaplain who said: "Compared to the last war, the religion in this army looks like a revival.... There is more religion per square mile in an army camp than in any civilian area of the country." This revival was motivated by the zealous explanation of the reverses in the early years of the war. As High observed, there was a "widespread feeling that the present state of the world is largely a result of the standards we've been trying to live by."[75] Alter those standards and victory would follow. In the popular mind the zealous premises remained.

Sermons in some Protestant churches, however, did not offer the facile hope of victory through revival. Jess Yoder's study of such preaching concluded that the "prevailing theological emphasis which stressed the sinful nature of man was dramatized by the rise of fascism and the approaching war. Thus in contrast to World War I, World War II was not considered holy; it was not ushering in the kingdom of righteousness, but a tragic manifestation of sin."[76] Influential ministers like Halford E. Luccock warned against leading the public to be "so bespattered by the blood of the dragon Hatred that its mind could not be turned toward a magnanimous Christian peace."[77] Reinhold Niebuhr developed realistic proposals about European reconstruction which were later taken up in the Marshall Plan; he was among the first to recognize the dangers of Russian domination of a prostrated Europe. Wendell Willkie popularized the idea of "One World" united in peace under international agreements. The students at Harvard were urged by James Bryant Conant to avoid "dogmatism and a holier than thou attitude" and to be responsible for the postwar world without the illusion that American institutions could easily be extended to the world.[78]

It is worth noting, however, that these realistic impulses did not come from persons who at the same time advocated zealous crusading. The impulses which seemed in tension within a man like Roosevelt came to be advocated by separate groups and persons. It was no longer widely possible to hold both at the same time. Roosevelt himself became more and more dominated by the crusade as the war progressed, losing much of his realism in relation to his Russian allies and the situation which would result after their troops arrived in Berlin and Manchuria. He apparently believed that Russia's agreement to cooperate in founding the United Nations would guarantee the peace of the postwar world. He was elated by the "tremendous success" of the "Declaration of Four Nations on General Security" in 1943, which established the basis for the future world organization. Secretary of State Cordell Hull struck this note in his report to Congress on this agreement: "As the provisions of the Four-Nation Declaration are carried into effect, there will no longer be need for spheres of influence, for alliances, for balance of power, or any other of the special arrangements through which, in the unhappy past, the nations strove to safeguard their security or to promote their interests."[79] The subsequent willingness to bow to Soviet demands for a veto in the United Nations and for hegemony in Eastern Europe and parts of Asia were consistent with such premises. After all, was not Russia on the side of the saints, and was the crusade not being fought "so that we do not have to live in a totalitarian world"? If, as Roosevelt said, the "sources of international brutality, whereever they exist" were "absolutely and finally broken" by the war, why should one listen to dyspeptic realists? As William Henry Chamberlin said, "such realism was at a hopeless discount in a crusading atmosphere."[80]

The legacy of World War II was this disjunction between the crusading and the realistic impulses. But more than that, it presented the crusading impulse itself with severe credibility problems. No one could forget that it was really the attack on Pearl Harbor which forced America into the war, that self-defense rather than crusading idealism played a major role. And the disappointing aftermath of the war confirmed the warnings of the realists. It showed the shallowness of hoping that with the defeat of Fascism the totalitarian threat to the modern world would be eliminated.

This realization, however, was slow to dawn on mainstream America, where the assumptions of Zealous Nationalism continued to dominate. After all, America had achieved its goal of "unconditional surrender." Its record of never having lost a war was impressive, especially when this victory was the third since 1898 to be achieved with minimal suffering on the part of the saints, compared with the casualties suffered by their enemies. The jocular faith that "God looks after children, drunks, and Americans" seemed confirmed.[81] Its optimism seemed assured; the difficult could be done immediately and the impossible would take only a little longer. Americans wanted to return to their traditional isolation, the job of cleansing the world having been accomplished. But with the rapid return of troops in 1945, threats arose which confirmed the predictions of the realists and stimulated a new phase in Zealous Nationalism.

# 4
# THE FRUSTRATION OF ZEALOUS NATIONALISM

Ever since the close of World War II, Zealous Nationalism in America has confronted an unprecedented dilemma. For the first time, a mortal threat followed immediately upon the successful completion of a crusadel; the very existence of the nation was jeopardized; and the solution of another great crusade did not seem to be feasible. The gigantic size of the adversaries and the threat of atomic extinction marked limitations that all but the foolhardy had to admit. Yet for most of this period the assumptions that had informed American thought and behavior for more than three centuries continued to be accepted. The incongruity between ideology and necessity was so great that a chronic state of frustration set in. The country gradually learned to live with it, but in a schizoid state, torn between zeal and realism.

## 1

The story of the frustrated crusade begins with Winston Churchill's epochal "Iron Curtain speech" on March 5, 1946, at Fulton, Missouri. As summarized by one observer, Churchill warned, in effect, that "to check the expansion of the Communist bloc, the English-speaking peoples—a sort of latter-day 'master race'—must sooner or later form a union. They should immediately contract a military alliance and coordinate their military establishments. They must lead 'Christian' civilization in an anti-Communist crusade."[1] It was the American people, the bearers of the zealous tradition, rather than Churchill's fellow countrymen, who responded to his call.

First they had to experience a series of frustrating reverses which overcame the illusion that World War II had eliminated the threat to freedom. Disagreements over the occupation of Germany, Austria, and Japan arose very quickly. Russian pressure on Iran, Greece, and Turkey mounted. The Chinese Communist armies began their campaign to wrest control from the Nationalists. Although there were voices such as General George Patton, calling for an immediate military crusade, it was a group of realists who set the tone for the initial American response. Among them were George Marshall and George Kennan in the State Department, columnists such as Walter Lippman and Dorothy Thompson, and theorists such as Hans Morgenthau and Reinhold Niebuhr. They had anticipated the power struggle and were prepared to suggest policies immediately. They were supported by a Senate leader, Arthur Vandenburg, who underwent a remarkable conversion from isolationism to international realism after witnessing the rocket bombing of London. His speech to the Senate in 1945 provides a glimpse of the shift that occurred. "I have always been frankly one of those who has believed in our own self-reliance. . . . But I do not believe that any nation hereafter can immunize itself by its own exclusive action. . . . I want maximum American cooperation. . . . I want a new dignity and a new authority for international law. I think American self-interest requires it."[2] Modern weapons dispelled the illusion of the security of the chosen nation after the unconditional surrender of its enemies. It was time to take cooperation and international law seriously. Under Vandenburg's leadership there was bipartisan support for realistic measures such as the refugee and rehabilitation acts, the support for Greece and Turkey, the lenient arrangements for the British loan, and most importantly, the Marshall Plan.

A key figure in this productive but short-lived period was George F. Kennan. He developed the strategy of "containment" and guided the policy planning committee of the State Department in developing the Marshall Plan, which had a positive effect on European recovery. Kennan's view of the situation was that the United States would have to coexist with Russia for an unstable span of time. The best that one could hope for was to limit the scope of conflict between them and wait for more favorable circumstances. His long experience in Russia led him to understand the peculiar combination of insecurity and cynicism which shaped its foreign policy. By calmly containing her belligerent tendencies, the United States could hope to see a milder form of behavior after Stalin's death. Kennan advanced such ideas while explicitly rejecting the idealistic, crusading, pretentious aspects of American foreign policy. He criticized the "American dream" of being "innocent of every conscious evil intent," and the sort of "adolescent self-esteem" which it encouraged. He exposed the illusions that had guided American policy through the twentieth century, producing the feeling that the world wars and the disorder were "monsters that had arisen from nowhere, as by some black magic. We deluded ourselves with the belief that if they could be in some way exorcised, like evil spirits, through the process of military defeat, then nothing would remain of them and our world would be restored to us as though they had never existed. "[3] In response to Russian threats in 1946, Kennan spoke against the "hysterical sort of anticommunism" that was replacing the earlier stereotype of the well-intentioned, cooperative Russians that the Roosevelt administration had propagated. He pointed out repeatedly that Russian foreign policy advanced not through military conquest but through political pressures, subversion, and propaganda. The fears that they wanted to sweep across Western Europe and provoke an atomic war were "largely a creation of the Western imagination."[4] In the face of calls for great anti-Communist crusades, he quietly insisted: "These people are not ogres; they are just badly misguided and twisted human beings, deeply involved in the predicaments that invariably attend the exercise of great power."[5] Kennan's choice of the term "invariably" indicates his appraisal of the perennial dilemma of power and the extent of his break with the zealous stereotypes. But the stereotypes persisted, leading to the military distortion of the containment policy, locking the United States into the military alliance system, and blocking potential negotiation. Kennan resigned from the State Department in 1950 because he was unable to counter these tendencies. As he saw it, the difficulty lay not so much in the complex dilemmas of foreign policy as in the "deep inner crisis" which the postwar threat provoked within America itself.[6]

This crisis must be understood in the light of the ideology that continued to shape the thinking of less sophisticated Americans. Unlike the handful of realists who stood close to centers of power for several years after the war, most Americans experienced a double frustration. They were baffled at the inexplicable emergence of the Communist threat so soon after the successful crusade, and they were perplexed by the lack of a clear-cut crusading response on the part of their Government. Tradition and experience led them to yearn for a quick and total solution when a seemingly demonic force threatened the mission of the chosen nation to redeem the world for freedom. These feelings came to the fore in the wake of the Russian toppling of Czechoslovakia and the Berlin blockade in 1948. A Chicago reporter described the "cold fear" which was "gripping people hereabouts." He put his finger on the "reluctant conviction that . . . relentless forces are prowling the earth and that somehow they are bound to mean trouble for us. . . . All winter, confidence in peace has been oozing away. With the Czech coup, it practically vanished."[7] A faint image of the elusive, demonic adversary is evoked in this description of the mood in the winter of 1947-1948. The crusade against totalitarianism had somehow failed, and the forces of darkness were "prowling" about once again. The times evoked a feeling of impending showdown, of standing on the eve of the apocalyptic battle.

The crisis deepened in 1949 with the fall of Nationalist China, the explosion of the first Soviet atomic bomb, and the sensational Alger Hiss case. As Eric F. Goldman wrote, "1949 was a year of shocks, shocks with enormous catalytic force." They "loosed within American life a vast impatience, a turbulent bitterness, a rancor akin to revolt" which were unparalleled in American history.[8] The desire for an easy crusade against the forces of darkness was countered by the fear of vast atomic destruction. Yet it seemed inconceivable that the chosen nation should have to endure a stalemate. The Alger Hiss case seemed to provide an explanation. As Congressman Richard Milhous Nixon said after investigating the Hiss case and spearheading its prosecution, "the nation acquired a better understanding, vital to its security, of the strategy and tactics of the Communist conspiracy at home and abroad." He felt that it revealed the "crisis with which we shall be confronted as long as aggressive international Communism is on the loose in the world."[9]

From the perspective of Zealous Nationalism, the cause of America's frustration seemed perfectly clear. The threat to her mission must come from a demonic conspiracy, centering in Moscow, with its tentacles reaching out to intellectuals such as Alger Hiss and to fellow travelers and liberals who unknowingly supported the party line. The thing to do was to purify the camp of such traitors, and Nixon's zealous prosecution of the Hiss case was matched by a flood of incidents all over the country. Loyalty oaths were demanded. Extensive security files were gathered on private citizens. Political beliefs came under the inquisition of un-American activities committees. Libraries and schools and churches were purged of seemingly dangerous books, thoughts, and persons. The farther this cleansing zeal went, the more it conflicted with the cherished traditions of freedom of thought and expression. Enraged disputes broke out between crusaders and libertarians. The campaign to cleanse the nation so that it could accomplish its thwarted task of setting the world free threatened to destroy the very freedoms it sought to preserve.

The dilemma was compounded by the frustrating limits of the international situation. Russia was too large to defeat or to occupy, and its development of atomic weapons quickly led to a stalemate. To maintain a crusade in the international arena required a new level of frustrating double-talk. It had to be a crusade that was not a crusade, an unlimited campaign against evil, but with limits lest a greater evil result. Harry S. Truman was the first President to be caught in this dilemma. He picked up the containment impulse from his advisors and translated it into a new form of limited, American crusade. In the message to Congress during the Greek and Turkish crisis in March 1947 he stated:

> We shall not realize our objectives . . . unless we are willing to help free peoples to maintain their free institutions and their national integrity against aggressive movements that seek to impose upon them totalitarian regimes. This is no more than a frank recognition that totalitarian regimes imposed in free peoples, by direct or indirect aggression, undermine the foundations of international peace and hence the security of the United States. . . . I believe that it must be the policy of the United States to support free peoples who are resisting attempted subjugation by armed minorities or by outside pressures. . .
>
> We cannot allow changes in the status quo . . . by such methods as coercion or by such subterfuges as political infiltration.[10]

Two worlds appear in this speech, the "free" world and the "totalitarian" world, but the definition is clearly ideological rather than empirical. Turkey and Greece are classified as "free" because they are not under Communist domination, not because their citizens enjoy rights of free speech or assembly. It is a Wilsonian program of millennial nationalism, with the source of disorder assigned to the nondemocratic peoples and the mission defined as redeeming the world through the spread of democracies. The commitment is remarkably open-ended: "free peoples" anywhere on the globe qualify for aid whether they are strategically important or not and whether a change in their ruling class actually threatens world peace or not.

The Truman Doctrine marked a decisive step away from the realistic premises of containment as understood by George Kennan. It transposed the course of containment into a protracted crusade. By the time of his inaugural address of 1949, President Truman had hardened this into an elaborate two-world theory and a commitment to "strengthen freedom-loving nations against the dangers of aggression"[11] by means of defense pacts and economic development. His "Point Four" plan to assist the "free peoples of the world" was an unconditional commitment for the indefinite future. Its goal was nothing less than a secularized form of the millennial age of peace: "Steadfast in our faith in the Almighty, we will advance toward a world where man's freedom is secure. To that end we will devote our strength, our resources, and our firmness of resolve. With God's help, the future of mankind will be assured in a world of justice, harmony, and peace."[12] This rhetoric appealed to the religious and national sensibilities of a people and led them into an effort that would occupy them for the next twenty years or more. If "one result of containment was the encouragement of a holy crusade against communism," as Arthur A. Ekirch has suggested,[13] it was President Truman who synthesized the two. Despite the resignation of Kennan and the protests of other realists, there was little comprehension of how antithetical it would be to the humane traditions of freedom it sought to enhance. As the Pentagon Papers now reveal, the crusade led immediately to the involvement in Indochina. By the end of 1949 President Truman had approved the policy goal to "block further Communist expansion in Asia." Even so realistic a diplomat as Dean Acheson had succumbed by February 1950 to the mythical picture of aggressive Communism and supported military aid to the French with an early version of the domino argument: "The choice confronting the U.S. is to support the legal governments in Indochina or to face the extension of Communism over the remainder of the continental area of Southeast Asia and possibly westward."[14]

The Korean War exposed the fallacy in this synthesis of containment and crusade. At first there was widespread support for the clear-cut solution of battle. President Truman referred to the "complete, almost unspoken acceptance on the part of everyone that whatever had to be done to meet this aggression had to be done."[15] Criticism emerged only after it became apparent that a total war would not be waged. The Russians and the Chinese would not be bombed; the bulk of American troops would be held in reserve to protect Europe while MacArthur's men fought their desperate battles. A crusade Americans could understand and support, but a "police action"? The idea seemed ridiculous, not only because limited war was so antithetical to zealous ideology but also because Truman himself had been so successful in popularizing the stereotype of demonic Communist aggression. Americans had not been reared to deal with such demonic aggressors by limited means. The proper way to handle the Beast was to destroy him in the apocalyptic battle! So there was a wave of enthusiastic support in the fall of 1950 when MacArthur's troops were authorized to cross the thirty-eighth parallel to create a "unified, independent and democratic Korea." But when the Chinese intervened and President Truman prudently refused to widen the war into China itself, the cauldron boiled over. Americans were enraged and appalled as the United Nations forces were driven back down the peninsula without retaliation against China itself. General MacArthur agitated for a change in policy and was dismissed, intensifying the crisis. The scope of American outrage is indicated by the Gallup poll report that 69 percent favored MacArthur and 29 percent the President.[16]

The issue that MacArthur raised was logical and penetrating, given the assumptions of Zealous Nationalism. If one is engaged in a crusade against Communism, why not carry it to its logical conclusion? He wrote Representative Joseph Martin, the Republican minority leader, that it "seems strangely difficult for some to realize that here in Asia is where the Communist conspirators have elected to make their play for global conquest, and that we have joined the issue thus raised on the battlefield; that here we fight Europe's wars with arms while the diplomats there still fight it with words; that if we lose the war to communism in Asia the fall of Europe is inevitable; win it and Europe most probably would avoid war and yet preserve freedom. . . .There is no substitute for victory."[17] The ideology here was the same as Truman's except that it was more consistent. It had the same picture of monolithic world Communism, bent on world conquest by force of arms. It betrayed the same apocalyptic mood, the belief that if Communism wins anywhere, it will inherit the entire globe, while if one stops it somewhere, he thwarts the Beast's power everywhere. Neither MacArthur's nor Truman's vision provided access to the real situation in Korea or Europe, in Moscow or Peking. But it was a vision shared by the country as a whole, and from that vantage, MacArthur's position seemed unassailable. In a crusade there is no substitute for victory. The book of Revelation would attest to that.

The one insurmountable problem with MacArthur's crusade was the risk of a full-scale war with a country too vast to occupy and too independent to accept infringement of its vital interests. And as close as Korea was to Siberia, it ran a serious risk of provoking Russian intervention as well, particularly if success against the Chinese could be attained. Truman was sensible enough to give up his crusading hopes in the face of such prospects. When the crunch came, his synthesis of zeal and realism disintegrated, and he opted for a stalemate in Korea.

But for many Americans, to give up the crusade was to give up the most crucial aspect of the moral heritage. Enormous crowds turned out to meet MacArthur in San Francisco and Washington. After his powerful address to Congress, he was greeted by seven million people in New York City in a "reception that exceeded Lindbergh Day or Eisenhower Day or the excitement of V.J."[18] The outburst of sentiment was so intense and sustained that Senator James Duff of Pennsylvania said, "The country is on a great emotional binge."[19] The Texas Legislature applauded MacArthur's statement that "Never before have we geared national policy to timidity and fear. The guide, instead, has invariably been one of high moral principle and the courage to decide great issues on the spiritual level of what is right and what is wrong. . . . We now practice a new and yet more dangerous form of appeasement . . . on the battlefield."[20] People believed MacArthur's intimations that "insidious forces from within" America were leading to the Korean stalemate and to America's eventual enslavement to Communism.[21] Here was the familiar faith, untainted by considerations of prudence or power politics, a faith shaped by the Civil War and the Spanish-American War, and enunciated by a leader victorious in the great world wars. If the crusades worked then, why not now? If the righteous nation was granted total victory over the agents of wickedness through every engagement of the mythic past, what frustrated it now? Could it really be that a dark conspiracy had undermined the land of the free? The only other possibility in the popular mind was to give up the faith itself, and this would imply that those who died in Korea had died in vain. They would not deserve the zealot's honor if their war were less than a divine crusade. In MacArthur's words, to "die in some halfhearted and indecisive effort" was to die without righteous cause. It would not be a matter of dying to make men free.

The issue between Truman and MacArthur was so sharply drawn that it revealed the dilemma of Zealous Nationalism with definitive clarity. The strands of zeal and realism, joined in various ways since the Puritan era, parted for a moment to show their mutually exclusive character. In the face of the pressures of the atomic age, their synthesis was no longer feasible. If one chose to retain the zealous heritage alone, the results would be suicidal. Only the tradition of

Constitutional restraint and the common sense of a former haberdasher from Missouri kept the majority of Americans from embarking on precisely such a course in 1950. But since their optimism and heritage kept them from admitting such prospects, the principal result was a frustration so deep and pervasive, so bitter and revulsive, that its effect may yet be felt in American life.

## 2

The Eisenhower Administration was swept into office by a landslide vote after a campaign that capitalized on the national frustration. The issues of Communism, corruption, and Korea were linked in such a way as to appeal to the widespread feeling that subversion and degeneracy had caused the Korean stalemate. The spirit of the campaign is captured by this excerpt from the Republican platform, written by John Foster Dulles, which relates to the liberation of peoples under "Communist enslavement":

> We shall again make liberty into a beacon light of hope that will penetrate the dark places. It will mark the end of the negative, futile and immoral policy of "containment" which abandons countless human beings to a despotism and godless terrorism, which in turn enables the rulers to forge the captives into a weapon of our destruction.... The policies we espouse will revive the contagious, liberating influences which are inherent in freedom. They will inevitably set up strains and stresses within the captive world which will make the rulers impotent to continue in their monstrous ways and mark the beginning of the end.[22]

This platform linked the zealous crusade to the light-to-the-nations theme, a motif from the tradition of Prophetic Realism. The world was to be converted by the example of liberty, bringing the "godless" tyranny of Communism to its apocalyptic "end." A potent new ideological synthesis is manifest here, one whose legacy is still very much a part of American civil religion. It provides an answer as to how the world could be converted now that the conditions render unfeasible the traditional forms of martial crusading.

To decipher this answer we must start with the conviction that Wilson's great crusade, which Dulles had served as legal counsel during the Versailles negotiations, failed simply because it had not really been tried.[23] As Dulles said later: "What was wrong was the spirit which dominated the principal victors. They abandoned initiative and sense of mission. That role was left to be taken over by evil spirits who brought the peace to a quick and ignominious end."[24] He proposed to reactivate that program by the infusion of evangelical, millennial Christianity, the variety current in the liberal Presbyterian circles in which he was reared. The conviction matured in the two international conferences that Dulles attended in 1937. The contrast between the League of Nations consultation in Paris and the World Council of Churches conference at Oxford made an impact on him which was described by his son Avery: "He found that people of different nationalities were able to reach agreements transcending their short-term national self-interest and prejudices and see things in a much larger perspective. I think the contrast of these two conferences . . . convinced him that Christianity was of tremendous importance for the solution of world problems of peace and international justice."[25] How would "Christianity" provide the solution? By producing saints devoid of "short-term national self-interest"! This has been the theme of countless Protestant sermons in the past hundred years: if people would only be converted to idealism, then war and poverty and labor strife and injustice and every other social problem would be eliminated. Dulles put the thought this way in November 1944: "If we all concerned ourselves with idealism, of which there is no limit, there would be no competition for possessions. We would wish to share our spiritual values with all."[26] When everyone becomes Christian, the selfishness which causes world conflict will be eliminated. The illusions of Revelation are clearly presupposed here, that when the saints alone survive the apocalyptic strife, the millennial era of peace will automatically begin. The saints are intrinsically peaceful and atheists are inherently destructive; so to convert the latter by American example would achieve Wilson's goal of world peace.

In a speech delivered on January 16, 1945, Dulles spelled out how this millennial ideology could guide the "collaboration" with the Russians who obviously did not share the evangelical faith. "We do not want tolerance which reflects a conscious abandonment or lowering of ideals. . . . We cannot agree to solutions which fall short of our ideals if thereby we become morally bound to sustain and perpetuate them. . . . It is the possibility of change which is the bridge between idealism and the practical incidents of collaboration."[27] Here is a definition of tolerance which eliminates any permanent coexistence with an adversary. A cold war of indefinite duration is the logical consequence. In this speech the future Secretary of State suggested "four principles of conduct" to guide the nation through this protracted crusade. First "our government should adopt and publicly proclaim its long-range goals. These should stem from our Christian tradition and be such as to inspire and unify us." Here is the theme of proclaiming the high ideals that would convert the heathen and usher in the millennium. When he became Secretary of State, Dulles declared that "a first phase of our quest for peace must be to restore our moral influence. . . . The United States must make it clear, clear beyond any doubt, that it has no thought of using economic or military might to impose on others its particular way of life. Unless we do make that clear we shall not be able to assume moral leadership in the world."[28] In short, the chosen nation must lack that fatal self-interest which is the bane of power politics, so that its good example would be a light to the world.

There is a complex irony here. The claim of having such perfect disinterestedness is so blatantly self-righteous that it could never have the power to convert anyone. Moreover, the idea shields one from the realization that the conversion one seeks for others is, in fact, precisely an imposition of the saints' "particular way of life." Finally, the pious renunciation of any selfish use of "economic or military might" leaves one open to an uncritical use of such force under the impulse of the crusade.

The second principle mentioned in 1945 was "fearlessly and skillfully [to] battle" for our ideals. As Dulles later explained: "What we need to do is to recapture to some extent the kind of crusading spirit of the early days when we were darn sure that what we had was a lot better than what anybody else had. We knew that the rest of the world wanted it, and needed it, and that we were going to carry it around the world."[29] But what if there were nations that refused this beneficent gospel? The crusading premise is that evil must be either converted or destroyed. Even if such destruction were not a present possibility, in the case of an adversary as large as Russia, the will to battle must remain. For as the third principle implies, the frustration of the saints can never be accepted as anything more than temporary. "No particular set-back need be accepted as definitive." If one is confronted with a situation like that of Eastern Europe after World War II, one may be forced to put up with it for a while, but should never acquiesce in the matter. To "compromise" would be to give up the faith, to give in to the Antichrist. And the fourth principle in the statement of Christian politics is to judge the worth of an administration by its long-term faithfulness to the mission of world redemption. In other words, a zealous nation should not be measured by the destructiveness of its current policies but rather by the purity of its motives and goals.

The major shifts in Dulles' foreign policy were all implicit in this ideological statement. "Liberation" was the millennial goal, sanctified by the "Battle Hymn of the Republic" and put into modern idiom by Woodrow Wilson. It was to be achieved by international evangelism, in which the righteous nation would win the world for Christ and for peace by its high example. When the world was liberated, it would necessarily accept the tenets of Christianity as Dulles understood them and would thereby presumably cease to be an arena of conflict. The corollary was a rigid stereotyping of the "Free World" as invincible, courageous, and just, and of the unconverted "Communist World" as doomed to extinction, yet ruthless, cunning and unjust. Within this ideology, coexistence with the unconverted was excluded; compromise was defined as doing violence to high ideals; neutralism was fence-sitting between Christ and Satan; and accommodations were never accepted on more than a temporary basis. In practice, "liberation" implied a constant crusade by every feasible means to eliminate the adversary, either by conversion, or if he brought it upon himself, by violence. So deterrence, which took the form of massive retaliation after Dulles' speech in 1954, was the temporary expedient to be used against those who refused such conversion or who insisted upon Satanic conversions in return. Any readjustment of frontiers or stabilization of spheres of influence had to be adamantly opposed on the grounds that force was being used to deprive men of their right to hear the gospel. Such acts were defined as "aggressive" and must be deterred with overwhelming force regardless of the merits of the case.

The thing that baffled Dulles and his followers was how such an idealism could be viewed as self-righteous, provocative, and threatening to world peace. He was particularly piqued when church leaders criticized his version of the crusade. "The Church people," he wrote in 1958 to his brother-in-law, the Reverend Deane Edwards, "have been clamoring for a long time for the application of moral principles to public affairs and to foreign relations. Now when we try to do that, and explain what we are doing, . . . we are accused of hypocrisy."[30] This was baffling because the hypocrisy was invisible when one accepted the ideology itself. The theological double-talk of the book of Revelation was so pervasive that the crusade to bring in the millennium through the conversion of the world seemed entirely benign. It kept Dulles from seeing that his ideals of freedom and equality under law were antithetical to his zealous crusade, which stereotyped the enemy and sought either to convert or to destroy him. It would take a staggering series of reverses and crises, the alienation of allies, the hostility of the entire neutral world, and which stereotyped the enemy and sought either to convert or to destroy him. It would take a staggering series of reverses and crises, the alienation of allies, the hostility of the entire neutral world, and the shattering of every attempt to negotiate, before the nation could begin to recognize the internal contradictions that Dulles was never able to see.

The story of this frustration may be divided roughly into three phases. Until President Eisenhower's heart attack in September 1955 the crusading and realistic impulses within the Administration seemed to hold each other in check. Despite the threat to "unleash" Chiang Kai-shek, the President decided to settle for a stalemate in Korea. His survey of the deep Chinese fortifications convinced him that a rollback was not feasible. It was an embarrassing blow to the liberation policy. Another came when Eisenhower prudently decided not to intervene in the Indochina war. The President had supported recommendations for military aid for France, and echoed the domino theory in his press conferences. When the clinch came, he was too realistic to commit American troops to an endless land war in Asia.

Dulles, however, made frantic but abortive visits to the Western allies to get support for a coalition to replace France in the war. He was left with the humiliating task of participation in the Geneva Conference when he was "absolutely immovable," as the Alsops put it, in opposing "a settlement which would or could lead to Communist victory in Indo-China."[31] As Gerson's study noted, Dulles had felt that any "promise to sustain communist domination of Vietnam, Laos, and Cambodia would be out of the question."[32] Still, under the pressure of the debacle at Dienbienphu, Dulles' seven point memorandum to Mendès-France approximated the final terms of the Geneva Accord.[33] But he refused to negotiate with the Communists or to sign the Accord because that would be to condone Communist tyranny. President Eisenhower stated that we would respect the terms of the accord without being a signatory, a stance that Thomas J. Hamilton aptly termed "innocence by disassociation."[34] Nothing was allowed to sully the purity of the chosen people. If Harold Stassen is correct, it was Dulles' disapproval which "prevented the United States from granting diplomatic recognition to North Vietnam after the Geneva Conference."[35] It is clear that he began immediately thereafter to take over the responsibilities of the French in South Vietnam and to build an anti-Communist bulwark there. Recent studies of the Vietnam and Laotian wars and the publication of the Pentagon Papers reveal the pattern of American efforts to encouraged to avoid participation in the forthcoming elections; in 1956, additional American military personnel were introduced in violation of the Geneva limitations.

Early in 1955 this ideology nearly ignited a world war when Communist China began to clear its harbors of the Nationalist blockade centered on the islands of Quemoy and Matsu. They had been temporarily fortified during the Korean War to hinder coastal shipping, and were not included within the defense perimeter in the Mutual Defense Treaty with Chiang in 1954. They had no direct relation to the defense of Formosa or to the security of the "free world." Yet Dulles threatened publicly to use atomic weapons on Chinese airfields in case of an invasion, and the President agreed. Congress passed the vague and sweeping Formosa Resolution and so powerful was the anti-Communist ideology that there were only three dissenting votes. The great disappointment was that none of our allies except Thailand and the Philippines agreed to fight World War III for the offshore islands. The great crusade to convert the world was failing even to attract the "free nations." It was spared the conflagration because China decided to postpone the invasion.

The climax of this first phase of the cold war crises came with the Geneva summit conference of 1955. It had been promoted by none other than Winston Churchill, who had turned away from the crusading ideal after the death of Stalin and a taste of atomic brinksmanship. The conference represented a real opportunity to settle the issues left over from World War II and thus to bring the cold war to an end. The diplomatic historian Frederick Schuman describes the prospects after the truce in Korea, the Indochina settlement, and the Austrian Treaty in 1955: "There was every prospect for a negotiated settlement of the Cold War by the end of that year [1955]. Then something went wrong, and the Cold War resumed." One of the causes was Eisenhower's heart attack, which "left the direction of American policy in the hands of a secretary of state, who, amid his many virtues, was addicted to the vice of opposing any negotiated settlement of the Cold War."[37] Given Dulles' ideology, it is obvious why he should oppose any real settlement in the consultations after Geneva. It would have meant relinquishing his dream of a Christian NATO and a rearmed Germany under the Christian leader, Adenaur. And, as Gerson explains, "under no circumstances would he accept the Soviet power position in Europe, tolerating covert agression and sanctifying wrongs in Eastern Europe and elsewhere."[38] The demands of realism proved incompatible with the tenets of zealous ideology. It was not long until the cold war resumed with more dangerous prospects than before.

The second critical phase in the Eisenhower Administration lasted until the resignation of John Foster Dulles in 1959. With the exception of the refusal to intervene in Hungary, there was probably never a time when the impulse of realism was more conspicuously absent nor the frustration of zealous hopes more complete. To answer the thrust of Soviet influence in the Middle East, Dulles established the Baghdad Pact and sought to coerce Egypt into abandoning its profitable neutralism. He withdrew the promise to support the Aswan Dam project rather than allow Communist participation, whereupon Nasser nationalized the Suez Canal. Refusing to acknowledge or support British and French interests in the canal, the Administration was shocked by their attack on Egypt in 1956 and piously condemned them in the United Nations. Having alienated the Allies, Dulles allowed matters to drift until 1958 when United States marines were sent to Lebanon to protect a Christian ruler from his Moslem countrymen. That such intervention was righteous while the earlier Suez intervention was sinful was a judgment that could be reached only when ideological factors rather than realistic interests were taken into account. The possibility of Communist influences in Lebanon made the difference. In the Dulles theology, defense of national interests was wrong but defense of "principle" was right.

Immediately thereafter pressure on Quemoy mounted and again Dulles led the nation to totter on the brink of a world war. The world might be blown up for zealous principles, but at least it would have the edifying spectacle of seeing the chosen nation in action! The impact on those who presumably needed conversion was characterized by Cecil Crabb, Jr.: "To foreigners, Americans must resemble nothing so much as the sombre Puritan: motivated by high ideals, austere, unshakable in his conviction that goodness will triumph in the end—but at the same time impatient with wrongdoing, sanctimonious and at time, insufferably self-righteous."[39] The same year the Russians made a determined effort to settle the anomaly of West Berlin by a new form of coercion. The issue that could have been settled by negotiation in 1955 once again threatened to ignite a general European war.[40]

By keeping the crusading zeal as the guideline of American foreign policy, the Eisenhower Administration made chronic crises out of issues that could have been settled by compromise. It is questionable whether any administration has evoked more hostility internationally or experienced a more thorough frustration of its stated mission. Zeal and reality were locked in irreducible conflict, yet the chosen nation and its leaders were so righteous and so far from "self-serving" that they were unconscious of the flaw. It was visible to others but never to them.

With the death of Dulles the third phase of the Eisenhower Administration opened. The President asserted himself vigorously to redirect the course of American foreign policy toward negotiation. Openly avowing the goal of coexistence and speaking warmly of neutral nations for the first time, he was cheered by tremendous crowds in India and elsewhere in December 1959. But negotiations required more than good will, and with a zealously oriented administration, no adequate preparations were made on a compromise position for the second summit conference scheduled for May 1960. Fruitless months were used to appease the French and German allies, who preferred national grandeur to a general European settlement. The mishandling of the U-2 incident provided the final blow. Eisenhower's frank acceptance of responsibility, when in fact he had not authorized this particular overflight and knew little of the precise details, was an admirable act of democratic honesty which helped restore his integrity at home. But it forced Khrushchev into a position of negotiation under duress while his nation's sovereignty was brazenly threatened. Eisenhower's statement that such overflights were necessary and would be continued was a flat rejection of international law and place Krushchev in an untenable position with respect to the militaristic forces in Russia. The U-2 incident offers a clear example of the tactics of Zealous Nationalism directly countering the development of coexistence and the enforcement of international law. In any event, the failure of the Paris summit conference was tragic for both East and West. It would be years before a similar opportunity for a major settlement by negotiation would appear.

By 1960 the anti-Communist ideology in America had jelled into the form it would take for the next decade and more. Both political parties had contributed to its elaboration; both had supported its tenets in critical situations. And although sophisticated American leaders would increasingly dissociate themselves from its express terminology, they continued to be guided by its premises. The public was so thoroughly indoctrinated by zealous rhetoric that even when leaders began to dissent in private they continued to play to popular feelings in their policies and pronouncements.

The past decade or so has marked the emergence of a new factor: a rising tide of skepticism and disillusionment about the morality, effectiveness, and motivations of zealous crusading. It arose in direct relation to the increasingly disastrous use of military power. The frustration in Vietnam, more than any other factor, brought home the counterproductivity, the destructiveness, and the inhumanity of Zealous Nationalism. But the frustration was also the inevitable result of attempts to achieve idealistic national goals such as the New Frontier and the Great Society by means of sophisticated new versions of warfare. Wars against poverty alternated with wars against crime. Sophisticated new doctrines and techniques were developed: counterinsurgency warfare and antiriot devices; Alliance for Progress and Peace Corps; flexible retaliation and Vietnamization schemes. But the dilemma deepened with each new development until many Americans have become completely disillusioned with the whole business of Captain America's "fight for right." Presidential inaugural addresses continue to call for a renewal of the old idealism and speak in glowing terms of America's calling to usher in some "generation of peace." But the dogmas of Zealous Nationalism continue to dominate policy decisions. There has been a steady erosion of the belief and practice of realism. Few would deny that the traditions of democratic equality, respect for law, and Constitutional restraint were at lower ebb in the 1970s than in 1960. Despite all talk about realism, the reliance on zealous force to attain millennial goals was more obvious during the Christmas bombing of 1972 than it had been at any time since the Dulles era. Yet even the maximum application of violence is unavailing. Peace seems more distant in 1973 than anyone could have predicted on that cold January day in 1961 when John F. Kennedy sounded the millennial "call to bear the burden of a long, twilight struggle . . . against the common enemies of man: tyranny, poverty, disease, and war itself."[41] Even our most loyal friends concede that our obsessive striving for "peace with honor" betrays some serious hidden flaws.

The Captain America Complex is riven with an internal contradiction. Its schizoid state may appear innocuous on the pages of a comic book. But in the arena of history it has become a menace. It is now at the point where the tension between zeal and realism must be resolved for the sake not only of the good Captain himself but of the world he strives to redeem. To grapple with this dilemma is the goal of the chapters that follow. The major components of Zealous Nationalism require analysis in terms of both their function and their consequences. Their relationship to the democratic legacy needs to be examined. The hope is to penetrate deeply enough into the complex that a purified sense of national mission may yet emerge.

# TRANSFORMING THE ZEALOUS IDEALS

# 5
# CONSUMED BY ZEAL

What is the nature of the zeal that marks American nationalists? How does it lead to violence and self-destruction? Can the American psyche survive without it? These questions, derived from the history of Zealous Nationalism, can best be approached by an analysis of the linguistic and mythic roots of zeal. After the basic phenomenon has been defined, the varieties of hot zeal, cool zeal, and artful zeal will be examined. The sense in which these forms tend to consume both the zealot and his victim will be explored, and the prophetic modification of zeal will be set forth.

## 1

The origins of our term "zeal" clearly reveal its psychological and moral dimensions. According to Norman Snaith, the Hebrew term *qana* comes from an ancient Semitic root meaning "to be dyed dark-red, black," signifying the deep emotion of rage which arouses such color in the face.[1] This fundamental connotation of red-faced rage is implied in the references to the "consuming" of zeal (Ps. 119:139; 69:9) and to the "burning heat" of zeal (Ps. 79:5; Ezek. 36:5 f.; 38:19; Zeph. 1:18). Johannes Pedersen pointed out that zeal could be described as a fire "because it burns in the soul and makes the cheek glow. Yahweh speaks with the fire of his [zeal], it devours the whole earth."[2] Pedersen went on to note the relation of zeal to righteousness. "All righteousness is rooted in him [Yahweh], therefore he defends every breach in it. . . . Yahweh's hatred of sin is in its essence based on the fact that sin is inimical to life. It creates disaster in the soul, but at the same time it is a breach in Yahweh's will, a disobedience which offends against his honour."[3] Yahweh's zeal was therefore a constant state, a function of his righteousness. From this point of departure one can grasp the moral and psychological reality underlying the seemingly disparate aspects of the Hebrew term, which connotes jealousy, envy, rage, and striving.[4] What links these ideas is the reaction of the self to violations of its sense of right. Whenever the norms one accepts are thwarted by an adversary, zeal arises. Jealousy and zeal are thus basically similar inasmuch as the reaction of the lover at the displacement of the beloved's affections resembles the reaction of the moralist at the violation of his principles. In fact, it is an accident of the English language that the two terms "jealousy" and "zeal" are derived from a single Greek root, *zelos*.[5] This has caused considerable confusion, because "jealousy" came to receive a negative connotation while "zeal" remained basically positive. That in the older translations of the Old Testament God was referred to as "jealous" became inexplicable, and that "zeal" itself is morally ambivalent was only rarely grasped.

The prototype of zeal for the Biblical tradition was Phinehas (Num., ch. 25). He broke into the marriage tent of an Israelite man and his Midianite wife to spear them both with one thrust, spurred by his conviction that such intermarriage had violated the purity of Israel and brought about a plague as punishment. The striking thing is that this prototype closes the gap between divine will and human rage. A short circuit occurs by which Phinehas' zeal is flatly identified with Yahweh's. This so absolutizes human zeal that it justifies the elimination of due process of law and breaks across any restraint of social custom. Phinehas does not wait for a proper Hebrew trial but breaks into the taboo area of the trysting tent to act as judge and executioner. The later Priestly tradition affirmed Yahweh's delight at this atrocity "in that he was jealous with my jealousy among them" (Num. 25:11). Phinehas came to be viewed as a prototype of faith, the hero of a long and violent succession of zealots.

The proof of Phinehas' rightness lay in the claim that he "turned back" Yahweh's wrath against Israel, redeeming her from the plague. By claiming this, the Priestly writers of Num. 25:11 formulated a theory that has had a long and deadly impact. It assumed that reverses suffered by the chosen people, whether sickness, famine, or defeat, were due to divine wrath against internal enemies. The traitor within the camp became the source of evil. To rid the chosen people of such internal sources of corruption was therefore to save the nation. The zealot became the redeemer, cleansing the nation by violence so that its triumphant destiny could be restored.

## 2

Three distinctive forms of zeal have been transmitted from the Biblical tradition to the modern world. The first of these, *hot zeal*, is active, direct and violent in its outcome. In the conviction that God desires the annihilation of the wicked, it carries out the bloody task without a twinge of conscience. Its heroes stand in the succession of Phinehas: Samuel, who hacked the pleading Amalekte king to pieces before the altar of Yahweh at Gilgal; Elijah, who slew the prophets of Baal with his own sword on Mt. Carmel; and Elisha, who called for the annihilation of the Moabites.

Hot zeal assumed decisive importance in Anglo-Saxon mentality during the Puritan Revolution with its campaign to cleanse England from the presumed corruption of Catholicism. Under its impetus, altars were desecrated, works of art were destroyed, theaters were closed, and opposing clergymen were lynched. Fiery Puritan preachers, including the extremist "Fifth Monarchy Men," interpreted political resistance and desires for moderation as demonic forms of corruption. Their sermons and pamphlets urged the crowds to turn on one enemy after the other in furious succession. The rationale for annihilation which hot zeal provided was perfectly exemplified by Oliver Cromwell's command to massacre the Catholic survivors in the siege of the Irish town of Drogheda. He insisted that "this was a righteous judgment of God upon these barbarous wretches, who have imbrued their hands in so much innocent blood."[6] Michael Walzer notes the decisive difference between this revolutionary zeal and the spirit of the French Calvinist nobility, held back by a certain nostalgia for the traditions of feudal chivalry: "There was too much regret, an emotion on which Calvinism does not thrive."[7] Hot zeal of the Anglo-Saxon variety was conspicuously lacking in regret, untouched by the plight of the victim and unconcerned about the social aftermath of the massacre.

William Styron has given an illustration of hot zeal in *The Confessions of Nat Turner*. He suggest that moral rage, nourished by reading the Bible, developed in Nat Turner's case into a sense of divine mission to massacre the slave owners in Virginia. It was a rage which banished all regret. The novelist depicts Nat as reflecting for years on the necessity of "pure hatred." After a brutal slave owner forced his two Negroes to fight each other to exhaustion for the entertainment of the crowd, Nat Turner's rage finally overcame its last vestiges of regret and prepared to break forth into hot zeal: "My heart seemed to shrivel and die within me . . . and rage like a newborn child exploded there to fill the void: it was at this instant that I knew beyond doubt or danger that . . . the world of white flesh would someday founder and split apart upon my retribution, would perish by my design and at my hands."[8] When the butchery of the rebellion was over, Nat was asked in his jail cell whether he regretted killing the children along with their parents. "No, sir,' I replied calmly, 'no, I feel no remorse.' "[9] Here is a zeal so nurtured by the tradition of Phinehas that the rage of the self is synonymous with the rage of God, eliminating the hindrances of mercy or due process. A bloody massacre, which in the end consumes the zealots themselves, is the logical consequence.

The definitive expressions of hot zeal in the American experience were John Brown's raids at Pottawatomie Creek and Harper's Ferry. The favorite line of this antislavery fanatic was "without the shedding of blood there is no remission of sins."[10] He felt that the only way for the sin of slavery to be atoned and for the nation to be redeemed was to annihilate slave owners in Phinehas' style. With his four sons and three other followers he dragged five proslavery settlers out of their cabins and hacked them to death. He was convinced that the raid was "decreed by almighty God, ordained from eternity."[11] Consequently there was not the slightest regret on Brown's part concerning the murders he committed. Mrs. Doyle, the wife and mother of three of the men Brown had killed, reported, "If a man stood between him and what he thought right, he would take that man's life as coolly as he would eat breakfast."[12] When national atonement failed to transpire as a result of these deaths, Brown denied participation in the event and planned the raid at Harper's Ferry. In one sense it was a farcical affair, so poorly planned and executed that the anticipated slave uprising could not possibly have occurred. Brown's disdain for rational planning was perfectly consistent with the impulse of hot zeal: if the raid were God's will, He would see to its success. The logic of this position should have led him to infer from the debacle that it had not been God's will after all; but after his dissimulating testimony aimed at avoiding such an inference, he gained the conviction, as Allen Nevins put it, that he had "fulfilled a mighty destiny," and that God "would yet overmaster all opposition to his divine decrees."[13] The note he left with the jailer as he went out to the scaffold restated the zealous creed which would inspire the North in the subsequent Civil War: "I, John Brown, am now quite *certain* that the crimes of this *guilty land: will* never be purged *away;* but with blood. I had *as I now think: vainly* flattered myself that without *very much* bloodshed it might be done."[14]

One indication of the powerful appeal of this ideal was the response it aroused in the North, which culminated in the passionate marching song of the Union armies, "John Brown's body lies a-mouldering in the grave." Preachers like Wendell Phillips eulogized Brown as "the impersonation of God's order and God's law, moulding a better future, and setting for it an example."[15] Ralph Waldo Emerson extolled him as the "man to make friends wherever on earth courage and integrity are esteemed, the rarest of heroes, a pure idealist, with no by-ends of his own."[16] Henry David Thoreau picked up the theme of pure idealism and connected it directly with the Puritan heritage. John Brown was "one of a class of whom we hear a great deal, but, for the most part, see nothing at all—the Puritans. . . . They are neither Democrats nor Republicans, but men of simple habits, straightforward . . . not making many compromises, nor seeking after available candidates."[17] As far as Thoreau was concerned, the gaunt old man on the scaffold embodied an ideal that derived not merely from the Puritans but from Christ himself: "Some eighteen hundred years ago Christ was crucified; this morning perchance Captain Brown was hung. These are the two ends of the chain which is not without its links. He is not Old Brown any longer; he is an angel of light."[18] The connection between Brown and Christ is viewed here, in effect, through the lens of the book of Revelation. An uncompromising grip on the truth in the face of opposition by a corrupt government that must soon be purified or destroyed—that was the link Thoreau had in mind. In formulating his case, Thoreau carried out the decisive task of secularizing the zealous war tradition for the American scene. What stood in the forefront was the emphasis on holding the transcendental truth without political compromise. If one did this, he was justified in short-circuiting due process of law and even the democratic process itself. An image of the violent idealist thus arose from John Brown's grave to capture the imagination of an increasingly secularized America of the next hundred years. The secular idealism is clearly visible in Thoreau's peroration concerning the hot zeal of John Brown:

> He was a superior man. He did not value his bodily life in comparison with ideal things. He did not recognize unjust human laws, but resisted them as he was bid. For once we are lifted out of the trivialness

> and dust of politics into the region of truth and manhood. No man in America has ever stood up so persistently and effectively for the dignity of human nature, knowing himself for a man, and the equal of any and all governments. In that sense he was the most American of us all. . . . He could not have been tried by a jury of his peers, because his peers did not exist. When a man stands up serenely against the condemnation and vengeance of mankind, rising above them literally *by a whole body*—even though he were of late the vilest murderer, who has settled that matter with himself—the spectacle is a sublime one.[19]

A number of crucial motifs, whose religious origins were soon to be forgotten, are inserted here into the mainstream of American popular consciousness. They provide the raw materials for countless detective stories, comic books, cowboy westerns, and commencement addresses: the distaste for the compromises required by the "dust" of democratic politics, the disdain for the institutions of due process of law, the desire for total solutions by holding to pure ideals, the inclination toward violence and its justification on grounds of idealism, and the "sublime" superiority of such an image of manhood. The myth of an idealistic superhero who redeems his community by selfless violence is here set on its path through the American imagination.

The remarkable thing about hot zeal has been its power to inspire establishment and antiestablishment figures alike, to give shape to behavior patterns on both the right and the left in American politics. It provides a common denominator between persons and movements that appear at first glance to be diametrically opposed. For instance, it is the image of heroic battle which Theodore Roosevelt evoked when he declared at the Bull Moose convention, "We stand at Armageddon and battle for the Lord." As Winthrop Hudson has shown, it was used by other national leaders, including McKinley, Bryan, Wilson, and their predecessors in the political arena.[20] Yet at the same time it inspired the antiestablishment Ku Klux Klan which emerged after the Civil War and again after World War I to battle against governmental corruption of the zealous ideal by inclusion of Negroes or foreigners. The heroic dimensions of this battle were eloquently set forth in the film *The Birth of a Nation*. In the case of the KKK, the zealous ideal was explicitly grounded in the Biblical tradition, as Imperial Wizard Hiram Wesley Evans insisted: "We magnify the Bible as the basis for our constitution, the foundation of our government, the source of our laws, the sheet-anchor of our liberties, the most practical guide of right living, and the source of all true wisdom. Furthermore . . . we honor the Christ as the Klansman's only criterion of character. And we seek at His hand that cleansing from sin and impurity, which only He can give."[21] Since these ideals were thought to be consistent with the religious heritage, they provided cleansing, so that a lynching did not arouse guilt: so long as the zealot was selfless, his violence could redeem. As far as the mythic premises were concerned, Roosevelt and Evans were in agreement.

Such agreement extends to wide areas of current popular culture. The comic books, to choose an example as clear as it is crude, consistently picture the superhero as selflessly engaged in combat against agents of wickedness. Captain America is trapped while seeking to rescue an innocent person, and Baron Strucker, the "Ex-Nazi Master of Weapons," gloats: "I've hated you for years. Your fame, your so-called skill—have made me long to destroy you! . . . You were true to form till the end, Captain America! Nobly sacrificing yourself to save another!"[22] But of course the super Captain America escapes and summarily destroys the evil Baron without resorting to due process of law, redeeming the innocent from his clutches.

A widely popular movie, *Dirty Harry*, shares the same premises. The tough police inspector battles the evil extortionist, Scorpio, despite hindrances by a compromising mayor and the seemingly absurd limitations of the Bill of Rights. When Harry's abridgment of the extortionist's civil rights leads to his release, which once again threatens children's safety, the zealous cop declares, "The law is crazy," and sets out on his private crusade to be Scorpio's judge, jury, and executioner. When the gory business is accomplished, Harry makes what Gerard O'Connor describes as "his Great Moral Choice. He stares out over the pond, which the bullet-riddled Scorpio is now polluting, and with utmost contempt, scales the police badge into it. Scorpio and the badge sink. Harry stalks off into the sunset." O'Connor reports the tremendous response this elicited as the "young, sophisticated under-30 audience roars its approval."[23] One has the impression that the same imagery is at work when rock star Mick Jagger arouses his audience with lines like, "Hey, think the time is right . . . For violent revolution."[24]

Here the sublime heroes call their listeners to respond to the high ideal and set off in battle against the forces of evil to redeem the world. Their own purity, in the sense of being untouched by the corruption of the establishment, is as essential to the crusade as it was for Thoreau. As Janis Joplin said, "All we need to do is keep our heads straight and in ten years this country may be a decent place to live in."[25] Those who follow the call, like a nineteen-year-old terrorist interviewed by *Newsweek*, echo the zealous premises quite clearly. "We'll blow up the whole f------ world if it comes down to it. And if our people start getting hassled and busted, we'll . . . kill every pig on the street. . . . We want freedom and peace, not half-truths and bull. . . . Man, you want a message for the people: do what you believe in. . . . Freedom and peace shall follow."[26] Incongruously, these are precisely the same premises accepted by establishment figures who detest these young zealots. Dr. Max Rafferty assures his newspaper readers that if they carry out the war against Communist aggression and subversion and hold to the pure ideals of the American tradition, redemption will automatically follow. When asked by members of a teenage club whether he thought "that U.S. pilots will be filled with remorse when they think of the people they have killed," his answer is straight from the tradition of hot zeal: "No, they will be too busy thinking happily of the millions they have helped save from Communist slavery."[27]

The result of such premises was visible in the war coordinated by Secretary of Defense Melvin Laird. His book, *A House Divided: America's Strategy Gap*, called for dedication to the truths beyond history which derive from God himself and urged that the nation battle for their sake by means of nuclear weapons, if necessary. "We must accept the moral responsibility to use our power constructively to prevent Communism from destroying the heritage of our world civilization. In terms of military strategy, this means closing the strategy gap by a willingness to take the initiative in all areas. . . . While we have the power we must aim at confronting the enemy directly. We can win every such confrontation."[28] The incongruity of these strange bedfellows is nowhere more plainly visible than in the person of Karl Hess, who helped Laird write his book and who coined the Goldwater slogans, "A choice and not an echo," and "Extremism in defense of liberty is no vice." He appeared several years ago as master of ceremonies for a Black Panther rally, having switched from the far right to the far left.[29] In the circle of hot zeal the distance between two extremes is rather short indeed.

## 3

Standing in contrast to hot zeal, which is active, violent and devoid of regret, is *cool zeal*, which is passive, preferring to let others dispatch the victim, and concerned lest the saint be defiled in regrettable course of the battle. While Phinehas and Elisha were prototypes of hot zeal, the books of Daniel and Revelation provide inspiration for the cool variety,

In Daniel the saints never actually put the villains to death. Think of the ending of the familiar tale of Daniel in the lions' den. The conspirators had sought to find something wrong with Daniel, but "they could find no ground for complaint or any fault, because he was faithful, and no error or fault was found in him" (Dan. 6:4). So they devised a scheme to get the king to sign a decree forbidding prayer, which Daniel's faithfulness forced him to disobey. He is cast into the lions' den; when the king finds him alive the next morning, Daniel speaks with all the modesty of the cool saint:

> "My God sent his angel and shut the lions' mouths, and they have not hurt me, because I was found blameless before him. . . ." And the King . . . commanded that Daniel be taken out of the den . . . and those men who had accused Daniel were brought and cast into the den of lions . . . they, their children, and their wives; and before they reached the bottom of the den the lions overpowered them and broke all their bones in pieces. (Dan. 6:21-24.)

The nice thing about this ancient form of massacre was that Daniel himself played no direct part. His God saw to it that the lions did the job.

What the author of The Book of Daniel suggests is that the saint must keep himself aloof from the battle, pure and blameless while other agencies wipe out the evildoers. The premises and the outcome are precisely the same here as in the tradition of hot zeal. Evil is thought to derive from the behavior of certain persons who must be destroyed before the Kingdom of God can be restored. The same pattern appears in Revelation. There, too, the saints keep their robes white by letting divine agencies massacre the wicked. They repose in contemplation of the wicked burning in angelic sulfur pits. Their Roman persecutors and religious rivals will be destroyed, they are assured, but not by their own hands.

We encounter this concept in such materials as the "Battle Hymn of the Republic." Here it is the Lord himself who is seen to be carrying out judgment through the agency of his Northern marching legions. But the fact that the Union soldiers actually kill their enemies is sidestepped in the hymn to fit into the fastidious tradition of Revelation. If death comes to the Union soldier, he is "transfigured" by his Christlike unselfishness; if death comes to the Confederate soldier, he has been cut down by the "terrible, swift sword" of God. Thus a traditional battle song theme—the joy of killing the enemy—

is completely sublimated in cool zeal. It is as if the Lord alone pulls the triggers while the soldiers play the role of faithful and guiltless channels of remote-controlled wrath.

Several curious aspects of the American character are comprehensible when this structure of cool zeal is recognized. One is the compatibility of the widespread pacifist sentiment with warlike behavior. Americans consider themselves a peace-loving people, reared in the tradition of loving the enemy, and long opposed to military traditions. Many Americans feel that war is intrinsically wrong and harbor dreams of its abolition. Yet when war breaks out they tend to conduct it with obsessive relentlessness. John Hay wrote from Paris in 1898 about his attitude toward the Spanish-American War: "I detest war, and I had hoped I might never see another, but this was as necessary as it was righteous. I have not for two years seen any other issue."[30] A pacifist public with a penchant for total war is an anomaly that continues to puzzle foreign observers. But it fits perfectly with the premises of cool zeal, for the nation so inured remains fastidiously pure from base motives like hatred or avarice, while letting the violent process of presumably divine retribution take its course. That such a public could rapidly shift from a predominantly pacifist sentiment to a martial crusade, as it did in World Wars I and II, is thus not a sign of fickleness but a logical consequence. That such a public could regret and condemn the Vietnam War and yet tolerate the most intensive bombing in history for the sake of peace is equally logical.

The concept of cool zeal also offers an explanation for the striking recurrence of the appeal to pure motivation in American war pronouncements. The Spanish-American War was "not a war of conquest, . . . of envy or enmity, . . . of pillage or gain," wrote Watterson in 1898.[31] President Wilson insisted in his Declaration of War message of 1918 that "we have no selfish ends to serve. We desire no conquest, no dominion."[32] President Nixon constantly reiterates the selfless character of the Vietnam War. His long-term goal, as related to Allen Drury, is "first to get this war ended in a way that Americans can look back upon not ashamed, not frustrated, not angry, but with a pride that in spite of our difficulties we have been totally unselfish."[33] Such sentiments are not merely gratuitous exercises in self-righteousness; they are drawn from the ethos of cool zeal with the aim of preserving the purity of the saints in the midst of the apocalyptic carnage.

Finally, this structure may help to explain something of the interplay between manifest destiny and the eradication of the American Indians so eloquently detailed in *Bury My Heart at Wounded Knee*. The doctrine secularizes the apocalyptic wrath and battle themes of Revelation and Daniel, offering a nineteenth-century way to justify genocide as the regrettable price of divinely ordained progress. It was used, for example, by General Carleton after the decimation and subsequent deportation of the Navahos from their ancestral homes in New Mexico in 1864:

> The exodus of this whole people from the land of their fathers is not only an interesting but a touching sight. They have fought us gallantly for years; they have defended their mountains and their stupendous canyons with a heroism which any people might be proud to emulate; but when at length, they found it was their destiny, too, as it had been that of their brethren, tribe after tribe, away back toward the rising of the sun, to give way to the insatiable progress of our race, they threw down their arms.[34]

Shielded by the idea of remote-controlled wrath, Americans found it virtually impossible to assess blame for genocide. When one surveys the long series of massacres reaching from King Philip's War in 1675-1676 to the Battle of Wounded Knee in 1890, individual responsibility was virtually never admitted or alleged. Well-publicized excesses such as the Sand Creek massacre were occasionally condemned, but the responsible policy makers were never brought to trial. By and large the saints felt as guiltless in those engagements as Daniel felt about the fate of his enemies in the lions' den.

But the modern American feels almost as far removed from the doctrine of manifest destiny as he does from the example of Daniel. How then can it be argued that the tradition of cool zeal has a decisive effect on current behavior? I would suggest that it is communicated through a popular culture in which the terminology changes while the mythic structure remains the same. For example, despite the frequent death of the bad guy in cartoons and comic books, there is a striking tendency to relieve the superhero of culpability. Usually the defeated archcriminal or Communist agent dies by some such way as stumbling off a cliff, getting tangled up in the electrical equipment he has cunningly devised, or at the hands of another villain. In one episode of *King, of the Royal Mounted*, the murderer flees from the posse only to be snared in the noose erected to lynch an innocent boy whom he had framed. The superhero, King, states the principle of cool zeal with apt precision: "Looks like fate and justice sort of joined forces."[35] No sympathy is ever expressed for the victim of such fates because in mythic terms they embody the justice of the divine order. Captain America, after witnessing a similar death at the hands of "fate" is heard to remark, "I'm not even sorry, because he certainly deserved it." In those instances where the hero himself dispatches the victim, there are conventions which serve to shield him from moral liability. He always acts unselfishly to defend interests other than his own; the villain is always stereotyped so as to eliminate any possibility of audience sympathy; and usually the villain provokes the duel and in the process breaks the rules of fairness so that his demise is justified.

These motifs and conventions were powerfully synthesized in the American cowboy novels and movies, which have been primary vehicles for communicating the myth of cool zeal. The plot begins with a villain harassing the innocent townsmen, who are of course passive and defenseless, holding true to the impractical command to love the enemy. The ordinary processes of law are pictured as incapable of dealing with this threat to the saints. So redemption appear in the form of the cowboy superhero who rides in from the plains. He is unknown and unexpected, "a savior from the transcendent realm," in the apt description of Peter Homans.[36] The hero withstands the temptations to shirk the unpleasant obligations thrust upon him. He frees victims from the villain's grasp and tries in vain to dissuade the hotheads from engaging in direct battle. When the rash advocates of hot zeal are killed by the ruthless villain, the cowboy is forced into action. In the climactic duel on Main Street, the equivalent of the apocalyptic battle takes place. The villain not only provokes the duel but acts unfairly by drawing first or shooting from ambush. Fate deflects his aim while the hero coolly shoots straight to enact the divine decree. He dispatches the villain without incurring guilt or betraying any objectionable emotions, and rides off into the sunset, returning to the mysterious realm whence redemption comes. His disappearance frees the innocent community from any need to question the violent process by which it was redeemed, and the Edenic state of peace again returns.

In this classic format, the most powerful myth in the Western world since the chivalric tales, the pattern of cool zeal is convincingly communicated. The pacifist ethic of the community is viewed as requiring the purge of villains; the town must be made safe for democracy. But the solution of hot zeal is rejected as overly emotional. Since due process of law is also deemed inadequate, salvation must come from the cool zealot who acts with perfect unselfishness. He is an agent of the transcendent realm, an impassive channel of divine retribution. He is willing to "die to set men free," yet he almost never suffers more than a superficial wound in the battle. So long as he is faithful to his calling, he provides the violent redemption at minimal cost to himself or society. If he is faithful, he always wins, even against the longest odds. The most far-reaching premise of the myth is that faithfulness to the righteous cause provides the sole model for responsibility. The hero is never held responsible for his violent actions as such, but only for remaining unselfishly committed to the ideal in the process. He can kill over and over again without becoming a murderer, so long as bandits or Indians threaten the safety of the saints. In the mythic sense, the God of the "Battle Hymn of the Republic" is pulling the trigger. The gun is an integral part of this myth because it dispatches the victim by remote means. The hero is never soiled by the blood of his victim. The solution provided by divine justice is quick, hygienic, and total.

The consequences of this mythic rechanneling of responsibility are clearly visible in Southeast Asia. When the peace of the "free world" was threatened in the mid-1960s by "Communist subversion," America turned first to mercenary troops and to superheroes such as the Green Berets. It is widely believed that if they had only been given a free hand to shoot the outlaws down on Main Street, Hanoi, the outcome would have fit the mythic expectation. But when conditions hindered victory and the situation worsened, the immensely unpopular measure of sending in a half million ground troops was tried. The result of so direct and massive an involvement of the saints in a dubious war was national division. The tradition of cool zeal had led us to expect more hygienic solutions. As General Lewis Puller said, "What the American people want to do is fight a war without getting hurt."[37] The mythic structure did not provide for hundreds of American deaths per week in so remote and sticky a cause. A large percentage of Americans began to disapprove of the war, not because it was inhumane or unjust but because its intractability threatened the substance of the national myths. But when the Nixon Administration withdrew American ground troops and turned to automated air tactics, resistance to the war melted away. So long as retribution is enacted by remote-controlled means, at little loss to the peaceful community of the saints, it is tolerated. It is viewed as a regrettable necessity, imposed on us by the recalcitrance of our enemies, but fully justified at whatever cost in civilian casualties because of the purity of our motives.

The astounding public reaction over the murder trial and conviction of Lieutenant William L. Calley, Jr., for his part in the My Lai massacre in 1968 was a case in point. Millions of Americans were outraged at the verdict and at least three quarters of those polled approved President Nixon's intervention on Calley's behalf. "The Ballad of Lt. Calley" sold three hundred thousand copies in three days, according to one report.[38] In the June 1972 *Psychology Today*, Kelman and Lawrence described the puzzles this presented to the scholarly community.

> Social scientists were at a loss to explain the widespread disapproval of Calley's trial. Rarely do 70 percent of a national sample agree on anything, especially current political issues; yet here were all sorts of strange bedfellows: hawks and doves, liberals and conservatives, whites and blacks, young and old, rich and poor, veterans and nonveterans. The standard dichotomies did little to predict which groups supported Calley and which did not. Nor could one predict a person's attitude by knowing whether he supported the war and the military.[39]

Kelman and Lawrence found that sixty-seven percent of those polled felt that most Americans in Calley's position would shoot villagers if ordered to do so. The study concluded that submission to governmental authority was the key to the striking severance of individual responsibility from the killings one performed. But this conclusion was belied by the fact that passionate Calley supporters on local draft boards protested by refusing to carry out their lawful duties. Clearly, submission to governmental orders is not the key. Herbert Marcuse suggested on the other hand that the "mad rush away from individual responsibility, the easygoing effort to vest guilt in anonymity is a desperate reaction against a guilt which threatens to become unbearable."[40] But one looks in vain for evidence of guilt feelings either on Calley's part or on the part of those who acclaimed him a hero. Neither of these explanations penetrates to the peculiar shift in personal responsibility in a culture marked by cool zeal. Calley is a typical, impassive killer of the cowboy type. He acknowledged that he did not feel he was killing humans at all. Without personal malice or any other objectionable emotion he was coolly enacting the remote-controlled retribution called for by his national ethos. To condemn him when he was being responsible to his calling was felt to be grossly unfair. It shattered the mythic ideal which excused any killing for the sake of freedom, so long as it was done with decent motives. As one respondent put it to Kelman and Lawrence, "If they are going to train people to be good professional cool killers and send them out to war and tell them they're back of them and put them in an area where they *have* to fight and then let the men down—it's wrong to draft them."[41] It was like hauling the cowboy back from the golden sunset and convicting him for manslaughter after he had been forced into the duel that redeemed the town.

## 4

While both cool and hot zeal are the moral reactions of a self that is deeply grounded in traditional ideals, there is a third form, the reaction of a self that is grounded in the will to power. *Artful zeal* is motivated by the desire for mastery, usually in the form of political advantage. In a calculating manner it seeks the appearance of zealous behavior to win the support of the public. It is unscrupulous in its exercise of power because it is unhindered by respect for life. It emerges in a society that has begun to doubt and to modify the zealous ideals. And although those who practice artful zeal may not be sincere followers of an ideal prototype, there is a Biblical character who perfectly embodies its structure and consequences. His name was Jehu.

The setting for Jehu's purge in 842 B.C. was the struggle between the zealous Yahweh prophets and the Dynasty of Omri, which was incorporating Canaanite elements into the culture of Israel in the north. Elisha the prophet arranged to have the officer Jehu annointed as Yahweh's new king while the legitimate monarch, Jehoram, was recovering from battle wounds in the summer palace in Jezreel. The scene was cleverly arranged to make it appear that an ambassador from Yahweh had selected Jehu (II Kings, ch. 9). The officer mounted his chariot and drove furiously toward Jezreel before King Jehoram could be forewarned. He shot the king with his bow and dispatched his cousin, Ahaziah, the visiting king of Judah, at the same time. Then he went after the old queen mother, Jezebel. She was thrown down from the upper window and trampled to death by Jehu's warhorse. In a laconic description of the remarkable nonchalance which Jehu exhibited in the midst of the slaughter, II Kings 9:34 reports, "Then he went in and ate and drank."

From this point on, the story of Jehu becomes one of atrocity equal to any from Indochina. He arranged to have the seventy sons of Ahab executed, putting their heads in two grisly piles beside the gate of the city. Then he went to work on the rest. "So Jehu slew all that remained of the house of Ahab in Jezreel, all his great men, and his familiar friends, and his priests, until he left him none remaining." (II Kings 10:11.) Several days later, he was traveling north and came upon a caravan in royal attire. Discovering that they were relatives of the slain king of Judah, he "slew them at the pit of Betheked, forty-two persons, and he spared none of them" (II Kings 10:14). It was immediately after this massacre that a revealing encounter with Jehonadab, a reactionary religious leader, took place. Jehu invited him into his chariot with these words: " 'Come with me, and see my zeal for Yahweh.' So he had him ride in his chariot. And when he came to Samaria, he slew all that remained to Ahab in Samaria, till he had wiped them out" (II Kings 10:16). Clearly it was the artful appearance of zeal that Jehu sought. If he had truly been caught up in passion for Yahweh's cause, he would not have been concerned that it be seen by the molders of public opinion. His real goal was to establish a political dynasty, not to achieve some religious purpose, as the slaughter of the Yahwist-inclined family of Ahaziah revealed. His purpose was achieved when a properly impressed prophet produced an oracle legitimatizing his new dynasty: "And the Lord said to Jehu, 'Because you have done well in carrying out what is right in my eyes, and have done to the house of Ahab according to all that was in my heart, your sons of the fourth generation shall sit on the throne of Israel' " (II Kings 10:30).

The remainder of Jehu's actions reveal the same artful capacity. To wipe out the remaining believers in Baal Melqart, the Phoenician deity posed as a fanatical Baal worshiper for a time. He invited likeminded persons to enter the Baal temple with him and convincingly took part in the ceremonies before calling in his troops for the blood bath. At this massacre, as usual, he had a Yahwist fanatic on hand for public relations purposes. But there is a limit to the most artful manipulations, and inevitably the discrepancies between appearance and reality show themselves. After destroying the administrative and economic leadership of the Northern Kingdom, Israel, he was unable to defend the state against the neighboring Arameans. He was defeated in battle after battle, losing substantial portions of his territory in the process, finally placing himself in vassaldom to Assyria to protect his dynasty. Since this involved allegiance to the gods of Assyria, no true zealot could have taken such a step. When one notes that Jehu tolerated local forms of Baalism (II Kings 10:29), there are grounds to agree with those who doubt his sincerity. Owen Whitehouse put bluntly: "He *posed* as a religious zealot."[42] But the long-term consequences of such artful rule are extremely grave. It was Jehu who ushered in the long dark age of Assyrian assimilation, so popularizing violence in the process that the subsequent self-destruction of the Northern Kingdom was inevitable.

It is therefore with considerable foreboding that one notes the beginnings of artful zeal among American leaders, particularly with reference to the Vietnam War. The Pentagon Papers reveal quite clearly the gap between official ideology and actual political goals. While public pronouncements stressed defending against Communist aggression, preventing a domino effect, and honoring our commitments, it was the fear of political consequences that guided policy makers. As Stanley Karnow explained, "Having suffered through the Joe McCarthy era, the Democrats felt especially vulnerable on the Far East issue. After all, they had 'lost China' and pursued a 'no-win' Korean policy. Thus they came to believe that for domestic political reasons they could not afford another setback in Asia. Or as (James C.) Thomson puts it today: 'They thought that they had to hold Saigon in order to hold Washington.'"[43] This political motivation revealed itself over and over again through the highly contrived dissimulations of the Johnson Vietnam policy. As the President himself admitted in justifying the 1965 escalation to his close advisers, "This is a bad year to lose Vietnam to the Communists."[44] The fact is that every year has been deemed a "bad year" to face reality in Indochina because of the feared reaction of a zealous public. This helps to explain what Daniel Ellsberg called the "process of immaculate deception" on the part of the last three Administrations. They consistently disregarded skeptical intelligence reports and knowledgeable opinion about the prospects in Vietnam in the hope that they could postpone the inevitable until after the next election.

There have been differences in recent Administrations in the artful rhetoric used to shield this political goal from public view. President Johnson sought to combine the dove-pleasing style of political realism with hawk-pleasing zealotry. He veiled his decision to escalate the war in realistic-sounding speeches warning against "committing a good many American boys to fighting a war that I think ought to be fought by the boys of Asia to help protect their land."[45] The Pentagon Papers reveal that there was an Administration consensus to enlarge the war as early as the September prior to the 1964 elections but operations were delayed because "the President was in the midst of an election campaign in which he was presenting himself as the candidate of reason and restraint as opposed to the quixotic Barry Goldwater."[46] The abortive but highly publicized peace overtures were likewise "contrived more to placate American doves than to achieve a genuine settlement."[47] When the nation found itself with a large-scale war within months after the election, the rhetoric shifted to the vintage motifs of zeal.

But the art was far too apparent to be convincing. A credibility gap emerged and the President was so severely hampered that he was forced to announce his decision not to seek reelection. The public was unable to accept so wide a war under the aegis of a mixed rationale of realism and zeal. Johnson regained his credibility only after assuming the cool role of savior without political ambitions, relying on zealous rhetoric alone during his last months in the Presidency.

The art of Richard Nixon has been much more successful. He has relied from the start on the premise of cool zeal that the millenial peace can be assured only by a remote control victory in which the saints incur no blame. Within the secure protection of this mythic structure his maneuvering room has been substantial, and the gaps between ideology and reality have not evoked public concern. He has combined bellicose statements about refusing to accept defeat with suitably unselfish protestations about his own lack of political motivation. As he put it in the Cambodian invasion speech, "I would rather be a one-term President than to be a two-term President at the cost of seeing America become a second rate power and see this nation accept the first defeat in its proud 190-year history." When combined with the promises to "end the war . . . to win a just peace . . . [and to] avoid a wider war," the mythic structure was so tight that the public found it irresistible. That the invasion was in effect a widening of the war by taking responsibility for yet another regime, thus avoiding the onus of acceding to a "Communist" victory in Cambodia, was clear for anyone to see. That the President's goal was precisely to become a two-term executive by avoiding such onus was also apparent. But such discrepancies were overlooked by the public. To admit their force was not simply to oppose Richard Nixon but to break with the national myth. The facade was unassailable because its enunciator fit himself so perfectly into the pattern of the unselfish savior. Vice-President Agnew claimed this in connection with the Cambodia speech: "In times of crisis, presidents have always seemed to rise above self interest and politics."[48]

The Vietnamization policy as a whole was a distinctive product of artful zeal. As a military strategy it was absurd from the outset. What rational person could believe that we could force the other side to relent by withdrawing our troops? That we could get our prisoners home by refusing to compromise? That we could improve the faltering morale of a client regime by infusion of more weapons? That we could prevail in an essentially guerilla war by reliance on bombing? The policy made sense only as an attempt to manipulate political opinion at home. This explains the frequent announcements of future withdrawal of American troops all scheduled for completion in 1972, an election year. It explains the constant reports of progress in the face of all the evidence to the contrary. These devices ingeniously disarmed critics at home. But shrewd observers repeatedly pointed out the reelection strategy on which Vietnamization was based. Walter Lippman described the dominant role of Nixon's desire not to "let anybody charge him with having lost the war" and his conviction that "he had to end the war in his first term if he wanted to be re-elected."[49] William R. Frye noted in a January 1972 column that the announcement of the eight-point peace plan was aimed at buying time for building up the Air Force, and that its manner of presentation made certain that the Administration would be justified in continuing the bombing and still give it enough "momentum of popular approval . . . [to] carry the President past November, 1972."[50]

Even Nixon's strong supporters, such as Stewart Alsop, openly acknowledged the primacy of the political motivation. Explaining the dramatic escalation of bombing and mining of harbors in May 1972, Alsop noted the desire on the part of the Administration to avoid allowing the remaining American troops to be caught in a general collapse in South Vietnam: "An American Dunkirk in Vietnam would not only be a defeat—it would be a national disaster that his critics could and would blame directly on the President. The disaster could destroy Mr. Nixon, not only at the polls next November, but worse, in the future's history books. Thus for Mr. Nixon anything—quite literally anything—that can be done to avoid that disaster must be done. This suggests the real unstated reason for the President's decision to hit Haiphong and Hanoi."[51] It is truly remarkable that such political motivation, though openly acknowledged, hardly bothers the public. When the NBC Pentagon Correspondent at that time was asked what the North Vietnamese advance implied for the success of Nixon's policy, he replied: "The Vietnamization policy was a political policy from the beginning. Its success or failure can only be determined in November." No one batted an eye at this self-evident statement. So firm was popular adherence to the mythic structure of cool zeal that to draw inferences from such discrepancies when a leader has played the role of cool savior so perfectly was to cast the myth itself into question.

There was one action, however, which convinced even the true believers that Mr. Nixon's zeal is more artful than real. I refer to the visit to the People's Republic of China, which led so many right-wingers to denounce the President. For years he has preached the dangers of "aggressive international Communism." He had accused John F. Kennedy of being soft on Communism because of his desire to modify the stance toward the Chinese islands of Quemoy and Matsu. He had noted with pride in the third television debate of October 13, 1960, "I continued to hammer hard on the general theme that in the struggle against World Communism we could make no greater mistake than to submit to blackmail—that surrendering a relatively small and unimportant area under threat of war would never satisfy an aggressor but would only stimulate and encourage him to step up his demands."[52] The Chinese Communists, in short, were incorrigibly wicked agents with whom one ought to battle but never compromise. Yet in 1971, in his announcement of the impending visit to China, the President referred to it as "a major development in our efforts to build a lasting peace in the world." It would be, as the final lines of the address claimed, "a journey for peace—peace not just for our generation but for future generations on this earth we share together."[53] Except for the inflated image of the millennial peace, this was the language of realistic coexistence, not zeal. And when the President actually shook hands and ate with Chou En-lai, true believers in the United States were apoplectic.[54] Was this not the same demonic Communist leader whom Dulles, Nixon's erstwhile idol, had refused to greet at Geneva in 1954? Given that agreement to the One China principle, a negotiated settlement of the Taiwan and the Taiwan Straits were prerequisites for the visit, one wonders what led the President to move so far from his earlier stand. James Reston noted that in return for these concessions Nixon gained no practical result other than "a relaxation of tension as an argument for reelection."[55] But what could be more to the point? Having persuaded the zealots of his faithfulness to the cause, what objection should one have that he perform a dramatic gesture to win the support of the realists? Had not Eisenhower achieved his highest peaks in popularity after being cheered in foreign capitals as an emissary of peace? It made perfect political sense. But no convinced zealot would have done it.

This is not to reduce the issue of artful zeal to the simple matter of insincerity. The artful zealot may be fully convinced in his own mind that the cause for which he fights is God's cause. He may feel that his own political mastery embodies the divine will. Only the discrepancies between ideology and behavior offer a glimpse of the real grounding of the system: not in the divine will but in the will to power. The true zealot, whether hot or cold, is absorbed in his cause. He derives his significance not from the exhilarating battle itself, nor from his own triumph in the battle, nor from the political results for himself, but rather from the justice of God. There is a motif in the "Battle Hymn of the Republic" which states this quite powerfully: "Glory, glory, hallelujah, *His* truth is marching on." The transition into artful zeal is marked when a person begins to derive his significance not from God's triumph but rather from the prestige or meaning which thereby accrues for the self. Jehu sought the prestige of a dynasty and used the rhetoric of zeal to establish it. President Nixon has sought the meaning of life in mastering crises, which the Presidency supremely offers. His book, *Six Crises,* reveals that it is not the triumph of some cause which is ultimate, but rather the personal sense of mastery in the midst of the battle. As the following excerpt indicates, it provides him with nothing less than the ultimate meaning of life:

> The easiest period in a crisis situation is actually the battle itself. The most difficult is the period of indecision—whether to fight or run away. And the most dangerous period is the aftermath. It is then, with all his resources spent and his guard down, that an individual must watch out for dulled reactions and faulty judgment. I find it especially difficult to answer the question, does a man "enjoy" crises? I certainly did not enjoy the ones described in this book in the sense that they were "fun." And yet, life is surely more than simply the search for enjoyment in the popular sense . . . But meeting crises involves creativity. It engages all a man's talents . . . A man who has never lost himself in a cause bigger than himself has missed one of life's mountaintop experiences. Only in losing himself does he find himself. Only then does he discover all the latent strengths he never knew he had and which otherwise would have remained dormant. Crisis can indeed be agony. But it is the exquisite agony which a man might not want to experience again—yet would not for the world have missed.[56]

As always, it is "especially difficult" for a man to lay hold of the ultimate meaning in his life. Yet Richard Nixon has done it here with disarming honesty. It is the thrill of mastery in battle, of losing himself in the struggle to be Number One. In the background stands the mythic superhero in a cowboy suit who redeems the community by the battle he always wins. It is natural that such a man would define his Presidency almost exclusively in terms of foreign policy, i.e., ridding the community of its external threats. It is consistent that he would view the movie *Patton* so many times. But the discrepancy with the mythic prototype is obvious. The "six crises" are not matters of happening by beleaguered towns and helping them out by regrettable duels on Main Street. They are all battles for his own prestige. Here is a man who seeks such battles as the "easiest" times in life, the moments of his most creative challenges. These are, in the language of American pietism, the "mountaintop experiences." And it is something less than reassuring to have the possibility of an atomic holocaust at the fingertips of a man who seeks out crises for the sake of mastery, and who identifies the fulfillment of his religious ideals as deriving from his own coming through on top. As the history of Jehu indicated, artful zeal yields a destructive legacy.

## 5

The destructiveness of zeal manifests itself first within the person of the zealot. From Shakespeare's Othello to Melville's Captain Ahab and down to characters such as Adam Stanton in the novels of Robert Penn Warren, this process has been traced by sensitive writers. It is expressed in a single pithy sentence of the psalmist: "My zeal consumes me, because my foes forget thy words" (Ps. 119:139; cf. 69:9). The writer of these lines burns with indignation at the behavior of sinners. What makes their actions so infuriating is the conviction that what they do is against God's law. This short circuit of zeal diminishes the self by the fire of its own rage. No thoughts are admitted to the mind except brooding on the boundless affront to divine justice and picturing the anticipated vengeance. The world becomes divided into the bitter camps of those few who are with the zealot and those who are against him. Neutrality becomes a reproach, prudence a betrayal. The self is thereby isolated, and a sign of its lost equilibrium is the obsessive repetition of the first person singular pronouns. "*My* zeal consumes *me,* because *my* foes forget thy words." The self in effect becomes the sole axis of the universe. In absolutizing its own rage, it assumes a burden far too heavy for finitude to bear. Under its weight the self loses its sense of freedom as well as the openness which is requisite for creativity. It feels driven by necessity to a violent outcome for which alternatives can no longer be envisioned. In short, as the Biblical tradition has always affirmed, idolatry first enslaves and then consumes the idolater. It then destroys everything he touches.

The inner constriction of idolatrous zeal places its stamp on every phase of action. The human values consumed within the zealot himself are destroyed also in the community he seeks to redeem. Despite the myth of a Captain America who always disappears from the scene at the end so that his behavior does not further influence the peaceful community, zealotry leaves ineradicable scars on the society it seeks to redeem. Robert Penn Warren deals with this in *The Legacy of the Civil War.* He notes the change in mentality that resulted from the triumph of zealous exponents of "higher law" such as the Northern abolitionists who "claimed a corner on truth by reason of divine revelation. The man who is privy to God's will cannot long brook argument, and when one declines the arbitrament of reason, even because one seems to have all the reason and virtue on one's side, one is making ready for the arbitrament of blood."[57] Warren cites Stanley M. Elkins' thesis that the sense of responsibility in post-Civil War society came to be "transformed into implacable moral aggression: hatred of both the sinner and the sin." Added to this was the ever more popular longing for the apocalyptic moment, the "total solution . . . to purge in violence the unacknowledged, the even unrecognized tension."[58] Warren refers to this as "higher-law-ism," the principle that one man plus God is the majority and thus can shed blood in his name and for his presumed cause.

One could trace the destructive impact of this "implacable moral aggression" throughout the past hundred years of American history. One could demonstrate in detail the high cost of zeal in such incidents as MacArthur's rush into North Korea in the winter of 1950, which led to four fifths of the casualties in that dreadful war.[59] Its impact upon the unfortunate people of Indochina is so familiar that it needs no reminder. One should also tally the cost of what Arthur Goldberg termed "an appalling, even frightening deterioration in our national standards of morality and law,"[60] as visible in incidents such as the widely applauded dismissal of the Green Berets case in 1969.

Contrary to popular belief, the greatest danger does not lie in the excesses of hot zeal. Our dominant myths condition us to be wary of overt anger and extremism. Much more serious in its potential for destruction on the American scene is cool zeal. The widespread adulation of the cool superhero opens the door to impassive killings with good conscience for the sake of redeeming the community. The killer is misled by the myth to believe that he is responsible solely for pure motives but never for the consequences. As Robert Penn

Warren says, "The man of righteousness tends to be so sure of his own motives that he does not need to inspect consequences."[61] The public seems to assume that fate will take care of the happy ending of the most dubious battles so long as the motives are pure. Given the risks of total war in the atomic age and the automated character of limited warfare, in which the directors and even the agents are so shielded from their victims that regret cannot emerge, a structure of cool zeal has ominous possibilities indeed.

Of the three forms of zeal, however, it is the artful variety which is finally the most insidious. Since it is tied to the drive for power rather than to any transcendent norm of justice, it is impervious to regret. Protected by playing the role of cool saviors, such men are not restrained by public disapproval. Their protestations about innocent motives are sufficient to defend the most blatant misuse of power. Such men will despise Constitutional precedents and make political use of the very religious leaders and traditions which could stand in judgment of them. The only thing they will fear is cracks in the zealous facade. That they will consider newsmen mortal enemies is logical. Every effort must be made to subject newsmen to the will of the government, to protect the vital image from public scrutiny. Lacking the restraints of conscience, democratic tradition, Constitution, or due process of law, such men have a boundless capacity to consume even the most promising of societies.

## 6

Since consuming zeal derives from our dominant religious tradition, its antidote should be sought in that same tradition. We should begin with the central insight of the prophetic message of the Bible, embodied in the First and Second Commandments.[62] Although they do not explicitly mention zeal, they have directed our analysis of the idolatrous character of short-circuited zeal. The First Commandment, that one should have no other gods before Yahweh, calls upon the faithful community to refrain from giving its ultimate loyalty to finite principles, institutions, or myths. In its initial form, the commandment did not require that one deny the existence of such factors, but merely that one cease to hold them as ultimate. The Second Commandment is simply the reverse side of this admonition, namely, that one refrain from worshipping any "graven image" of ultimate reality, whether it be in the form of a visual image or an abstract definition. Both commandments deal with the avoidance of idolatry. They serve to protect rationality and humanity itself by freeing it from bondage to man-made principles, institutions, or ideologies.

The relevance to the problem of zeal should be obvious. If one took these commandments seriously, he would never fall prey to the fatal short circuit between his own rage and divine rage. Zeal would then lack the power to consume, because it would never be able to claim ultimate approval for its definitions of the right or its strategy to deal with what it feels to be wrong. It would take itself less seriously and would respect the restraints of custom and law. Taking these commandments seriously would also serve to protect the community from the arbitrary actions of the self that constantly tends to absolutize its own goals and to infringe upon the lives of others in attaining them.

We would be falling prey, however, to some of the worst habits of the Puritan mentality if we now, having noted the grave dangers of zeal, were to eradicate it completely from American ideology. It is not zeal itself but the absolutizing of zeal which is destructive. Only when the fatal short circuit occurs between human and divine rage does idolatry commence. Short of this barrier, however, zeal is an absolutely essential component of the moral life. If one is committed to love and justice, for example, he must strive for them even though he is incapable of devising their perfect definition or even of making a precise discrimination in their application. The philosopher John Lawrence insists: "Responding to moral imperatives requires acting in a positive manner, but can equally require a commitment to suppress the rejected alternatives."[63] This point was grasped in an interesting but problematic article by the Unitarian clergyman Horace Bridges, published in the *Atlantic Monthly* at the time of American entry into World War I. He wrote of "a duty of hatred, an imperative of conscience prescribing resentment, as unconditional as the very law of love itself; nay, the law of resentment is the necessary complement of the law of love and pardon."[64] Although Bridges went on to define the German war effort in the categories of absolute and bestial evil, which overstated the case, his point is nonetheless valid. There is a duty of hatred, but it remains healthy only so long as one continues to act on the premise that his hatred is not necessarily God's hatred.

To deny the necessity of zeal and to eliminate it from American morals would be to open the door to nihilism or worse. Without zeal for some righteous purpose the American moral sense could disintegrate. It could fall into the apathy that precedes aimless and utterly destructive violence, as Rollo May suggests.[65] Or it could seek only selfish ends, using weaker nations for its own profit and destroying those who insist resist or interfere. The prospects of vast American power, unrestrained by the internal flywheel of its own sense of moral obligation to mankind, are terrifying. We could transform the rest of the globe into a replica of the moonscape now visible in Indochina.

We must grapple with the paradox of zeal, namely, that when it takes itself with ultimate seriousness or betrays its impulse with apathy, it sickens and becomes destructive. To confront this would require giving up our propensity for total solutions and discovering some procedures for muddling through. To face this paradox would be to acknowledge our finite situation and take up the complex tasks that all other nations must face. But there are resources in the more realistic portions of the Biblical message that may guide the development of procedures to keep zeal responsible.

One resource is the approach taken by Jesus concerning the zealous rage which was so popular an aspect of religious and political life in his time. It was widely assumed that righteous zeal was one of the clearest signs of devotion to God and his law. The law forbad the sinful expression of rage and lust but it did not attempt to suppress these emotions. The "evil urge" and the "good urge" were viewed as the spontaneous and uncontrollable heritage of the sons of Adam, and it was pointless to hold a man responsible for anything but his actual deeds.[66] In an environment dominated by myths of Zealous Nationalism, these assumptions provided the perfect justification for idolizing rage. It was very easy to identify one's spontaneous anger as a God-given call to enact judgment on the malefactor. Zealous murders were very much the vogue, and the religious parties in Jesus' time fought and killed each other with ferocious zeal.[67] Over and over again this zeal generated atrocities against Samaritans or revolts against the Romans.

Jesus was dealing with one of the foremost social and political problems of his time when he challenged the traditional attitude toward anger:

> You have heard that it was said to the men of old, "You shall not kill; and whoever kills shall be liable to judgment." But I say to you that every one who is angry with his brother shall be liable to judgment; whoever insults his brother shall be liable to the council, and whoever says "You fool" shall be liable to the hell of fire. (Matt. 5:21 f.)

If anger was subject to divine judgment, two important consequences followed: it was not automatically identifiable with divine zeal as the tradition encouraged one to believe; it was a matter for which men were to be held responsible. Both the short circuit of zeal and the resignation to Adamic urges were countered here. Men could no longer assume that their anger was identical with that of the divine judge, so that anything they did would automatically be approved. Killing in God's name might turn out to be murder. Furthermore, the wording of Jesus' statement carries a clear reminder of one of his basic theses, that the enemy is a "brother." To "insult" him or to call him "Thou fool!" is to lose sight of shared humanity and to prepare the way to annihilation. The remarkable advice Jesus gave elsewhere to "turn the other cheek" and "walk the second mile" was aimed at recognizing precisely this essential brotherhood. To love the enemy and pray for him who despitefully uses you (Matt. 5:44) was the logical climax of this new doctrine of responsibility. It redirected zeal to a healthy concern for justice in relation to the life of one's enemy.

It is important to note that this approach is a far cry from that suggested by Bible interpreters schooled in the tradition of cool zeal. Jesus does not say, "Be not angry! Repress zeal! Be a nice boy!" Generations of well-meaning Christians have misunderstood Jesus' statement in this manner. He explicitly does not say it is wrong to be angry, but rather "everyone who *is* angry . . . shall be liable to judgment." These are not in any sense the same thing. The one is a call to repression, which ends up in hideous forms of remotely enacted wrath, disguised by hypocrisy; the other is a call to mature responsibility not only for the moral rage itself but also for its actions and aftermath. Jesus was not in the slightest concerned, as the tradition of cool zeal has been, with preserving the image of the self from unfortunate emotions; rather, he was concerned with preserving the health of the self and protecting the neighbor from zealous behavior.

For zeal to be responsible, it must acknowledge the limitations of its moral vision and still dare to act in prudent faith. Only when zeal is fixed steadfastly on transcendent justice, which stands forever beyond the limitations of human achievements, can it remain both effective and humble. The critical need is for a pilgrim zeal, striving for the lasting city but never arriving; moving forward with courage and prudence, but never overrating the results; and respecting persons because of their intrinsic value in the eyes of divine righteousness. Such pilgrim zeal may be glimpsed in the life and thought of Abraham Lincoln and in some of the best of American literature. What we must do is make use of these resources and transform America's zeal before it is too late.

# 6
# THE GRAND CONSPIRACY

In his statesmanlike account of the origins of the Vietnam War, Louis J. Halle describes the impact of the conspiracy theory on American thought. It led American planners to misunderstand the nationalistic thrust of Ho Chi Minh and his movement, to link them prematurely with the Chinese Communists against whom they were seeking to maintain their independence, and to take over the abortive French efforts to sustain a pro-Western regime there. "From the beginning the West was governed by the myth of a single conspiracy for world conquest under the direction of a satanic band in the Kremlin to whom all who called themselves Communists, the world over, gave blind obedience."[1] Since the mid-1950s, we have discovered how little the Russians actually were able to control events in allied countries. The split between Russia and China, preceded by the independence movements in Communist countries of Eastern Europe, gave the lie to the conspiratorial premise. Nevertheless, we committed ourselves to the civil war in Indochina on false premises and were unable to disentangle ourselves even after signing peace agreements.

What is the source of this conspiracy theory, which has had such pervasive effects on the American mind and American policies? What answer does it provide to the question concerning the source of evil in the social realm? How does the theory operate and what relation does it have to Zealous Nationalism? What relation does it have to such cold war motifs as the domino theory, the defense posture based on enemy capabilities rather than political probabilities, and the unwillingness to compromise on international issues? In providing tentative answers to these questions, we can set the stage to show the relevance of Jesus' campaign against the conspiracy theology so popular in his time.

## 1

The negative connotation of "conspiracy" and its use in explaining the origin of misfortune are closely related to the development of Zealous Nationalism. In the Phinehas tradition one discerns beginnings of a conspiracy theory in which the actions of a few evil members of the chosen people evoke the wrath of God (Num., ch. 25). It could be "turned back" only by the elimination of the source of corruption. But in a cultural situation in which the ultimate source of evil was thought to be Yahweh himself and where no demonic counterforce to Yahweh was thought to exist, a fully developed conspiracy theory of evil could not arise. Israel's traitors occasionally associated themselves with her enemies, as in the case of Phinehas' antagonist who married a Midianite woman. Yet it was disobedience to Yahweh's law on the part of Israelites themselves that brought down wrath upon them. In this sense human responsibility for evil was affirmed in the early period of Israel's thought.

It was only after the exile, during the period of Persian domination (538-323 B.C.), that the basis for a full-blown conspiracy theory began to appear. This was the period when dualistic thought patterns, probably influenced by the Zoroastrian religion of Persia, began to infiltrate the theology of Judaism. God was seen to be opposed by a demonic counterforce, surrounded by legions of evil angels who stirred up opposition on earth against the agents of righteousness. In the Persian empire, where the majority of Jews lived for this two-hundred-year period, Ahura Mazda, the god of light, was thought to have called the emperor to wage war against the god of darkness and a conspiratorial throng. External and internal enemies of the empire were assumed to be the pawns of this demonic force. History was the battleground between the armies of good and evil. It was precisely during this period that the idea of a devil and his demonic army of spirits began to appear in Judaism. And in this milieu there emerged for the first time a conspiracy theory of evil, virtually in its modern form, in The Book of Daniel.

In the stories of Daniel and his friends, Shadrach, Meshach, and Abednego, evil is presented as deriving neither from the great empire that held Israel captive nor from the sin of the chosen people themselves. The foreign emperors were pictured in a benign light, even at times as the servants of Yahweh, and faithful Jews had no compunction in serving their administration. As for the heroes, the author of this Old Testament book took great pains to picture their innocence. They faithfully served both the empire and the laws of God, refusing the corrupting food and drink of the palace yet doing their duty honestly without hope of personal gain. They prayed three times a day, kneeling in the direction of Jerusalem. There was no evil in them. They did not sin even inadvertently, since they came from families that taught them the details of the Jewish law. For as the author insisted, they were of the Jewish "nobility, youths without blemish, handsome and and skilful in all wisdom, endowed with knowledge [of the Torah], understanding learning, and competent to serve in the king's palace" (Dan. 1:3-4). Unafflicted by the foibles that were thought to have marked earlier heroes of the Israelite faith, such as David, these paragons of perfection were not thought susceptible to the tragedy that befell most men. The author of Daniel pictures evil as a result of the conspiracy of evil men. For example, after Daniel had been made prime minister under King Darius in the story, the "presidents and satraps" began to oppose him. Finding it impossible to discover "any ground for complaint," they worked out a plot and came "by agreement to the king" (Dan. 6:4-6). They set forth the suggestion that no one in the empire should make a petition to anyone but the king himself. The king signed it with the naiveté of one who was as untouched by evil as Daniel himself. When Daniel was caught praying at his usual time he was apprehended and thrown to the lions. Thus evil came to the perfect man.

But of course it could not really harm him, because he was so righteous that the lions would not touch him. He survived the night in the lions' den; the next day the conspirators were themselves thrown in to be devoured. A decisive element in the conspiracy theory was that the good guys always come out unscathed—a theme that worked about as well during the time Daniel was written, when the faithful Jews were being slaughtered by Antiochus Epiphanes, as it has ever since. But when precisely the same plot transpired in the case of Daniel's three friends, and they survived in the fiery furnace "without a hair singed . . . nor any smell of burning" (Dan. 3:27), a myth was born. It was the myth of the Grand Conspiracy.

The myth received extensive elaboration in the apocalyptic books written between the second century B.C. and the New Testament period. The idea of fallen angels, who disobey God out of jealousy, emerged to explain the origin of Satan. The creation stories were reinterpreted to emphasize that it was Satan's voice which beguiled Eve and led to the fall of mankind. The older Hebrew conception of evil as originating with willful human disobedience was dismantled, and man came to be viewed as the pawn of demonic or angelic forces. Determinism came to alter the traditional ideas of human freedom and responsibility. History was viewed more and more as the battleground between cosmic forces of good and evil, and men were called upon to take sides in the ineluctable war. By the time of the Roman period the demonic forces were seen to have taken over the world empire itself. In the apocalyptic materials found at Qumran, the "sons of light" were called to prepare themselves for the battle against the "sons of darkness" who conducted on earth the policies of "Belial," prince of demons (I QM 1:1-5). Against whatever odds, victory would be inevitable, for God would not allow the conspiracy against his justice to prevail.

The classic form of the myth of the Grand Conspiracy is set forth in the book of Revelation. Evil is explained as emanating from Satan, who inspired the heretics within the church; the opposition from the side of the Jewish synagogues, called "Satan's synagogue" by the author (Rev. 2:9; 3:9); and the persecution from the Roman Empire, the "beast" from Satan's deep (Rev., ch. 13). These institutions tempt the faithful to false worship and kill them when they retain their integrity. Posed against Satan's horde is the heavenly army of God, repeatedly entering battle until evil is annihilated. History moves inexorably from the primeval battle between Michael's angelic army and the Satanic horde (Rev. 8:2 to 11:18) to the current struggles between the church and the bestial empire (Rev. 11:19 to 15:4). The stages of these battles are seen as predestined by God, so that the seer can reveal to his audience ahead of time the sequence of the catastrophes. Seals are opened and bowls of wrath are poured out in orderly succession. There is no doubt about the ultimate goal of world history: it will be the final destruction of the demonic Grand Conspiracy and all who serve it.

The solution to the problem of evil will be the victory of the lamb. As Paul Minear's commentary points out, the terms "victor" and "victory" dominate each major section of Revelation.[2] The saints alone will enjoy the fruits of the victory. As Rev. 2:26 f. (Minear) indicates, they will have the pleasure of keeping the subsequent world forcibly under their control: "To the victor who keeps my works until the end, I will give him power over the nations, and he shall rule them with a rod of iron, as when earthen pots are broken in pieces." This is spelled out in Rev., ch. 20, where the saints reign with Christ for the millennial period while Satan is chained in the pit "so that he might seduce the nations no more till the thousand years were over" (Rev. 20:3, Minear). There remains one final battle in which Satan and his cohorts will be destroyed and thrown into the lake of fire. Then in the heavenly Jerusalem, with evil completely banished, the saints will rule triumphantly forever. The total solution to the problem of evil is thus affirmed in the end as accessible to the people of God: "The victor will inherit all these things." (Rev. 21:7, Minear).

The other key assumptions in the Grand Conspiracy are related in Revelation to this grandiose scheme of victory over evil. If the saints are to rule, they must be perfectly righteous. As ch. 14 describes the hundred and forty-four thousand saints, "No lie was found in their lips; they are faultless" (Rev. 14:5, Minear). The stereotype of the enemy is equally radical. The agents of Satan are utterly lacking in human qualities. Even after fearsome punishment they remain incorrigible idolators, murderers, sorcerers, and fornicators (Rev. 9:20 f.). Since they are irredeemabe, their destruction is the single aim of God and his saints. Although the saints are not directed to take up the sword, lest they besmirch their white robes, they cry out for annihilation: "How long until you [God] judge and avenge our slaughter by the earthdwellers?" (Rev. 6:10, Minear) That the entire world may be destroyed in this slaughter is a delightful prospect for the saints (Rev. 16:19-21).

Those who came to accept this vision of the Grand Conspiracy and its ultimate destruction in the apocalyptic battle would be willing to accept the prospects of such a battle at any appropriate moment. That the world must be destroyed for the source of evil to be cured was a perfectly logical conclusion.

## 2

The books of Daniel and Revelation offer a fully developed conspiracy theory of evil. To understand the impact of this theory, it is essential to distinguish between its main characteristics and Prophetic Realism. I shall begin with its interlocking premises, then move to its consequences, in order to demonstrate its appeal to those schooled in the tradition of Zealous Nationalism.

The traditional doctrine of universal, willful sin crucial to Prophetic Realism maintains human responsibility for evil. In the creation story in Genesis, the human desire to be "like God, knowing good and evil" (Gen. 3:5) in some absolute sense, led to eating the forbidden fruit and brought in its wake the poisonous residue of alienation and violence. In contrast, the conspiracy theory assumes that evil originates in the demonic realm and is not the fault of humans at all. For a fully developed conspiracy theory it is essential therefore to posit the existence of a devil, a cosmic counterforce to the divine will. This counterforce must be equipped with vast and cunning powers. It must be capable of infiltrating the web of historical experience, luring its willing and unwilling agents into its wicked design. One must imagine a vast network of historical and angelic agents of this malevolent design. Individual agents may indeed believe that they are acting righteously, but the person with insight into the Grand Conspiracy knows better: they are nothing but the unwitting tools or fellow travelers of Satan.

The conspiracy theory also demands a break with the traditional Biblical doctrine of human freedom, an essential component of personal responsibility. The prophetic premise is that those addressed by the divine word are capable of changing, of repenting so as to avoid the disaster that might otherwise overtake their sinful behavior. This must be replaced by a deterministic doctrine if the conspiracy theory is to reach its full development. Since humans are merely the pawns of cosmic forces, their particular background and personal aims in life need not be considered. Evil persons must be destroyed because they are the extension of the demonic force; it is never assumed that they act out their own desires for mastery or justice. Likewise the saints are not fully accountable for their deeds because they are being used by God. The good or evil they do, such as acquiescing in the destruction of the world, is God's doing, not their own. Human responsibility is limited to the matter of faithfulness to the force whose pawn one has become.

The prophetic tradition views humans as involved in the tangled web of their own sins, social alienation, and international pressures, in which the best they can hope to achieve is a modicum of justice by the grace of God. In contrast, the conspiracy theory believes in a total cure for the problem of evil. It will be effected by the violent elimination of the Satanic agents. This may be accomplished by God himself or one of his mysterious agents, or it may require the work of an army of the saints. But there will be no muddling through. Evil, like a problem of plane geometry, is susceptible to a perfect solution.

History is thus the arena of cosmic warfare. Its plot is never visible in the struggle of the actors on the darkling plain, but only in the forces of good and evil that loom over the battlefield. The complex knot of historical causation, so baffling a puzzle to the historian, can be cut with one stroke of the sword. It is the Grand Conspiracy of Satan that gives shape to history. Only when the apocalyptic battle itself is fought can history reach its climax and be dissolved in the golden light of the eternal Jerusalem. There the saints will live forever in perfect peace, no longer harassed by the agents of wickedness. In the meantime, the responsibility of the saints is not to guide history creatively or to take steps for human betterment, but simply to be faithful to God's side in the cosmic struggle. It matters little whether their zeal is hot or cool; the important thing is that right should triumph, though the world itself be destroyed in the process.

The conspiracy theory eliminates the possibility for pragmatic assessment of historical or political factors. The one who is privy to the Grand Conspiracy knows ahead of time. Her only interest in details relates to ascertaining the stages in the predestined course of history. The peculiar motives of individual actors and the variations in national or individual temperament are irrelevant in assessing probabilties for the future. Power factors play no role. Though a handful of the saints be surrounded by foes, their ultimate triumph is assured. They will gladly participate in the apocalyptic battle because they already know its outcome: after the incineration of the world, they will inherit the heavenly Jerusalem.

The conspiracy theory also eliminates the need to improve the institutions of government. The saints in Daniel are perfectly content to work for the Persian empire so long as it exists, since after the demise of the last earthly empire, they will directly rule the earth. How they will carry out this rule is never considered ahead of time, either in Daniel or in Revelation, because complex institutions of due process of law and division of responsibility will be unnecessary once the world is rid of the source of evil. In the meantime, why concern oneself with striving for justice in the empire by institutional reform? Even the most radical reforms cannot thwart the power of the Grand Conspiracy! And once it is destroyed in the apocalyptic battle, only the saints will be left, and surely they will need no institutions of law and order. Once the world is made safe for democracy, the saints will take care of themselves in perfect harmony.

Finally, the conspiracy theory eliminates the possibility of compromise. With the world divided between the forces of God and Satan, no neutral space remains. To agree to live in harmony with those who are against God is to break faith and join the demonic ranks of the Grand Conspiracy. There is nothing worse than coexistence with evil. As the angel said to the church of Laodicea in Rev. 3:16, "Because you are . . . neither cold nor hot, I will spew you out of my mouth." The danger of neutralism, of course, is that it beguiles the saints to weaken their preparedness for battle. It is one of the most treacherous devices of Satan. As for the compromises required in the democratic political system, they are unspeakably filthy. Preferable is a system where the saints exercise absolute power and do not have to give up their faith by compromising.

These premises and consequences interlock to produce a complete world view, with a precise definition of good and evil, an explanation of their origins, and a knowledge of the historical process by which they battle one another for supremacy. It offers the true believer a completely satisfactory explanation for the presence of adversity in the experience of the chosen people. Once its premises are admitted, it is a logical and appealing ideology. It assures a chosen people of its perfect virtue and its right to an unproblematic existence in a world without evil. It gives meaning to the present dark moment in history and sustains the resignation of the saints to whatever destruction unfolds in the course of the battle. Above all, it provides the assurance of a perfectly happy ending. That it is idolatrous from beginning to end does not seem to occur to the saints. After all, did they not learn of the Grand Conspiracy from the Bible itself?

## 3

The impact of this conspiratorial theory on American thinking was visible from the outset. We have noted this from the English Reformation down to the American Revolution and beyond. As Bernard Bailyn has shown, there was a widespread conviction among American leaders that they were facing a demonic conspiracy in the court of George III. The curious fact was that a virtually identical premise was held by the English court itself. With both sides struggling against the presumed influences of the devil's Grand Conspiracy, neither would pull back from the brink. War became inevitable.[3]

When the perfect society anticipated by the saints failed to appear after the Revolution, the conspiracy theory offered ready explanations. One thinks of the remarkable series of hysterical campaigns and political battles that mark American history. In the 1820s it was the anti-Mason movements. As a secret organization, the Masons were perfect targets for the accusation of involvement in the Grand Conspiracy. The controversy started when William Morgan, who had written an anti-Masonic tract, was abducted and presumably murdered in upstate New York. Four persons were found guilty of kidnapping him and got off with light sentences, but no evidence for murder was actually found. Nevertheless, there was a popular feeling that the Masons had gained revenge and were in control of the courts and the Federal Government. Anti-Masonic newspapers and clubs sprang up all over the North. Anti-Masonic candidates were elected to local and state offices. Several states even passed laws to require secret societies to make annual public reports so that conspiracy could be kept within bounds. The movement played a decisive role in the national election of 1832, and it was several decades before the feeling died down that the Masons were conspiring to subvert and control the Republic.

With the Irish immigration of the 1830s, the conspiratorial accusation shifted to the Roman Catholics. Native American parties sprang up to counter the presumed threat to the republic. They imagined that Romish plots were aimed at subverting the public school system and ultimately taking over the nation in the service of the pope. The decades through the 1850s saw the emergence to prominence of the Know-Nothing Party, which demanded the exclusion of all non-native Americans from political life. The idea was that since evil was brought in from the outside by foreign agitators, one could purify the Republic by having nothing but Americans in control. Ex-President Fillmore ran as the Know-Nothing candidate for President in 1856. Samuel Morse, the inventor of telegraphy, wrote a book entitled *Foreign Conspiracy Against the Liberties of the United States.* It is a curious attestation to the omnipresence of the conspiracy motif that after the demise of the Know-Nothing Party around 1856, its enemies crowed about their triumph over a dreadful conspiracy. Indiana Congressman George W. Julian concluded afterward that the Know-Nothing movement had been "a horrid conspiracy against decency, the rights of man, and the principle of human brotherhood."[4]

Recent studies of the struggles between the North and the South in the decades before the Civil War indicate the importance of the conspiracy theory on both sides. David Brion Davis' book *The Slave Power Conspiracy and the Paranoid Style*[5] notes that the Northerners interpreted Southern power in the Senate, passage of runaway slave laws, and blockage of northwestward expansion as a vast conspiracy to impose slavery onto the entire nation. The Southerners in turn were obsessed with the thought of abolitionist conspiracies both inside and outside the South, aimed at getting control of government so as to impose rule by blacks. Both sides thought Satan was maliciously guiding the behavior of their antagonists. This contributed to the secession in 1860, when the Republican Party, sympathetic to the abolitionist cause, gained power. As Eric Foner's study of Republican ideology has shown,[6] Southern fears were not entirely groundless. For the Republicans determined to stop what they considered a conspiracy of Supreme Court, Administration, and slave interests. As historian William W. Freehling noted in a recent review, the paranoia on both sides was fed by the actual political possibilities: "What historians, no less than psychiatrists, must remember is that monstrous fears feed on monstrous realities."[7] But to view these realities as the product of some demonic conspiracy, which could only be cleansed by violence, was to thrust the struggle out of the purview of the democratic political system and onto the bloody battlefields of the Civil War.

A more recent example of the conspiracy theory of evil was the "Red Scare" of 1919-1920. Having made the entire world safe for democracy, the nation sought after the armistice to return to "normalcy." It was shocked by labor unrest and a series of bombing incidents that now appear to have been staged by various groups and persons who were unconnected with any general conspiracy. But Attorney General Palmer and his chief of investigation Flynn were certain that these events were part of a gigantic plot to overthrow capitalism and establish a Communist type of government similar to that currently emerging in Russia. Unprecedented raids by government agents netted several hundred radicals and labor organizers, some of whom were summarily deported without trial. Hundreds of others were detained and savagely beaten by mobs and policemen before it was determined that they were completely unconnected with any subversive activity. The celebrated Sacco and Vanzetti case was a direct product of this atmosphere. And long after the Red Scare and its excesses were over, the legacy of an "underlying fear of radicalism and the proclivity for intolerance" remained to influence American politics.[8] It resulted in the emergence of dozens of patriotic societies that took up the task of rooting out Bolshevik conspirators from churches, schools, colleges, and labor unions. It encouraged the passage of restrictive immigration laws, for as General Leonard Wood summed it up, "We do not want to be a dumping ground for radicals, agitators, Reds, who do not understand our ideals."[9]

The consequences were even more serious when a similar hysteria broke out in the 1950s. After the defeat of the Nationalists in China and the emergence of the Iron Curtain in Europe, the frustration of American hopes was explained by what Eric F. Goldman called the "Great Conspiracy." The premise of this theory was that the "hated developments could all have been prevented. . . . The rise of Communism around the world did not result from long-running historical forces; the red advances came from the Alger Hisses, who had contrived to bring them about."[10] Senator Joseph McCarthy rose to give the most coherent statement of this theory, charging in his June 14, 1951, speech before the Senate that Secretary of State George Marshall had been party to "a conspiracy so immense, an infamy so black, as to dwarf any in the history of man . . . .

[a conspiracy directed] to the end that we shall be contained, frustrated and finally fall victim to Soviet intrigue from within and Russian military might from without."[11] Despite the groundlessness of such charges, there was an enormous readiness on the part of the American public to receive them. There was an evangelical fervor to the pro-McCarthy rallies in those years, endorsed by many clergymen. Enormous cunning was ascribed to the demonic enemy within and without. Communist triumphs were all assumed to have been precisely planned and directed from headquarters in Moscow. A pro-McCarthy magazine, *Counterattack*, blacklisted a popular television singer because a Communist paper had listed her as a supporter of their candidate for councilman in New York; such proof was unequivocal because the Daily Worker is very accurate; they never make a mistake."[12]

That such statements were patently ridiculous detracted nothing from their power to convince or from their destructive consequences. Un-American activities committees began their search into the private lives and beliefs of citizens in brazen disregard of civil rights. Antisubversive laws were passed and loyalty oath campaigns were inaugurated which severely crippled key governmental agencies like the State Department, not to mention state universities and other institutions. Outstanding specialists in Far Eastern affairs both in the Government and outside were harassed or fired from their positions, producing a gap in experience and wisdom that contributed to the subsequently disastrous American policies in Asia. Police and intelligence agencies were fundamentally altered by the conspiratorial fever, producing for the first time in American history a pattern of surveillance of American citizens that still runs substantially outside public control. J. Edgar Hoover gave voice for years to this counter-conspiracy zeal, linking organizations of dissent or mere political opposition with the demonic Communist plot. As late as 1968 he was testifying before the Commission on the Causes and Prevention of Violence that "communists are in the forefront of civil-rights, anti-war, and student demonstrations, many of which ultimately become disorderly and erupt into violence."[13] Hoover even placed wiretaps on the phones of Dr. Martin Luther King, Jr., in the conviction that the campaign for racial equality must have been Communist-inspired.[14] Such government harassment is a much more dangerous departure from democratic principles than anything a Communist conspiracy could have accomplished. It reveals the incompatibility of the conspiracy theory with American ideals and procedures.

In the literature of the John Birch Society and Billy James Hargis' "Christian Crusade," the complete panoply of these assumptions comes to expression. The Communist conspiracy which they oppose is explicitly linked with Satan. Hargis insists: "It is apparent upon examination that Communism cannot be of human origin, for human beings are of themselves incapable of total corruption. Only Satan could inspire in human beings complete dedication to utter folly, unspeakable horrors, and total untruth. Only Satan can be the inspiration for Communism. . . ."[15] In contrast, America is stereotyped as the "Christian country, led by the Spirit of the Living God."[16] Attempts at coexistence are "simply the first stage in the building of a world government of the Anti-Christ."[17] The entire system is rendered invulnerable to criticism by the flat identification of Hargis' viewpoint with that of God himself. "Those of us who have been in this fight against Communism know beyond a shadow of a doubt that what we do is of God, and those who oppose this conservative effort are not fighting us—they are fighting God."[18]

With this idolatrous structure of certainty in the Grand Conspiracy, the most preposterous accusations are made and the most unlikely explanations are offered. Without batting an eye the John Birch Society could claim that Dwight D. Eisenhower was an undercover agent of the Communist movement. The mythic premise was stated by Robert Welch:

> Communism is never anything but a drive for power or position or glory or wealth on the part of the Insiders at the top. . . . These insiders impose the components of Communist tyranny on a people and on the world, subtly, skillfully, deceptively, and with patient gradualism. . . . This is why nothing else that you do to oppose collectivism or immorality or revolutionary vandalism really matters, unless you expose the Conspiratorial drive behind them.[19]

What makes the nonsense plausible is simply the conspiracy premise itself. Evidence is not required; indeed, it could not be provided, if everything is really controlled by the mysterious beings "at the top." The power of the message derives from the fact that it offers a consistency and internally logical treatment of the conspiracy myth at a time when the established authorities have been forced to swerve from it under the impact of reality.

It needs to be observed, however, that a similar conspiracy pattern manifests itself in the language of the New Left. Rather than Communism as the agency of the Grand Conspiracy, it is the military-industrial complex, whose mysterious tentacles reach into every area of government and daily life. In place of the pseudeo-Christian terminology of the far right, it uses the well-worn maxims of Marxist ideology. But history is still viewed as the battlefield between mysterious "systems" and "complexes" of good and evil, and men are still called upon to take up the role of violent saviors who will destroy wickedness by the "revolution," which is sure to be victorious. The saints are still viewed as pure and undefiled as those in Revelation, albeit because of their lack of material self-interest rather than their adherence to some religious code. The wicked are still viewed as irredeemable and thus doomed to annihilation. As one of the advocates of this "solution" solemnly assured me, to execute everyone whose income is above ten thousand dollars per year when the revolution comes would not be murder. It would be an act of justice. The relish over such prospects matches the relish of the saints in Revelation over the sinners burning in the eternal fires.

The impact of such thinking on campus discourse is almost fatal. With zealots on both sides seeking not the discovery of new truth but the destruction of grand conspiracies, the possibility of an open forum is virtually nil. This has been the case particularly in relation to the Vietnam War. The President's Commission on Campus Unrest in 1970 noted the "chilling effect on rational academic discourse" which such conspiracy thinking had caused:

> As opposition to the war grew and the war continued to escalate, explanations of America's involvement in it became more radical. From having been a "mistake," the war was soon interpreted by radical students as a logical outcome of the American political system. They argued that what was most objectionable was not the war itself, but rather "the system" that had entered, justified, and pursued it.... The university, too, came to be seen as a part of "the system," and therefore it became a target—as distinct from an accidental arena—of antiwar protest.[20]

Educators were unprepared for this massive outpouring of counter-conspiracy zeal, because they were convinced that the era of ideology was long since past and that the secular mind-set would naturally be free from the evangelical heritage of America's past. What had actually occurred was a translation of the conspiratorial model into secular terminology. Americans differed violently in the terms and details, but for the most part they were not free from the conspiratorial premises themselves.

**4**

If blame is to be assessed in the tragic involvement in Indochina for the past quarter century, neither a conspiracy of the right or one of the left should be singled out. It is the conspiracy theory itself which should be blamed. A case can be made demonstrating that if it were not for the widely accepted premises of the conspiracy theory, we never would have drifted into so ill advised a war in an area strategically so insignificant. As Kahin and Lewis have pointed out, we initially encouraged the Vietminh independence movement and sought to dissuade the French from reestablishing a permanent colonial rule there after 1945.[21] The publication of Ho Chi Minh's correspondence with President Roosevelt indicates the extent to which the Vietnamese themselves hoped for the application of American principles of self-determination. It was only after the fall of Nationalist China and the rise of the conspiratorial cold war mentality that we began to support the French. Kahin and Lewis write:

> Major support for the French was not given until mid-1949, when communist rule was established in China. . . . In accordance with these new American priorities, France's position in Vietnam was now described in terms of the Free World's stand against communist expansionism, and Washington ceased to perceive the war in Vietnam as primarily a local colonial conflict. Now linked to the Cold War, Vietnam was regarded as an area of strategic importance to the United States.[22]

Ho Chi Minh's long-term goals were lost sight of in the sudden belief that he was the cunning agent of a demonic campaign. Hans Morgenthau has described the crucial significance of this "demonological conception of the world in which the United States is pitted in ineluctable conflict against other nations of incalculable power and infinite cunning. . . . Our involvement in the Vietnam war is similarly justified by this demonological conception of the world which assigns to the United States the mission to defend the Free World against aggression and subversion from the Communist conspiracy."[23]

Having made this fatally conspiratorial assessment of the Vietnamese independence movement, it was logical that we would take up the task of the French after their collapse in 1954. The United States refused to sign the Geneva Accord and established instead the Southeast Asia Treaty Organization in the fall of 1954 to protect the rest of Southeast Asia from "Communist aggression." As Dulles said:

"There is no reason to believe that this effort [of Communist expansion] will stop of its own accord. If it stops, it will be only because something stops it. That something will either be violent resistance or a moral resistance so solid that to oppose it would evidently be futile."[24] Since the devil's Grand Conspiracy aims at nothing less than domination of the entire world, one knows its aim ahead of time and takes steps to counter it.

This facet of conspiracy thinking came to be known as the domino theory. As the Pentagon Papers reveal, it was "the basic rationale for American involvement" from the start. It was first formulated by the National Security Council in February 1950. "The neighboring countries of Thailand and Burma could be expected to fall under Communist domination if Indochina is controlled by a Communist government. The balance of Southeast Asia would then be in grave hazard."[25] The Security Council paper of January 1954 repeated this dire prediction that if "any single country" is "lost" to Communism, the rest of the dominos would likely fall, starting with the rest of Southeast Asia, then India and Japan, ultimately endangering the security of Europe itself.[26] That the vastly different countries and movements in Asia could be decisively influenced by a single event or that the various religious and nationalistic impulses were somehow reducible to a single factor could be believed only by those who had no detailed knowledge of the multifarious peoples and cultures of Asia. But it required no evidence! The Pentagon Papers state this unequivocally: "The domino theory and the assumptions behind it were never questioned"[27] from 1949 until the disastrous American military involvement of fifteen years later. Only the powerful influence of the myth of the Grand Conspiracy can explain the adherence to this improbable dogma by Dulles, Eisenhower, Rusk, McNamara, Bundy, Johnson, and Nixon.

The mythic certainty is illustrated by a conversation between country singer and composer Merle Haggard and a fellow musician who shares Haggard's former enthusiasm for the great crusade:

> "Well, one thing's for sure," said Fuzzy, a veteran of the Korean War who fervently believes in "Okie" and "Fighting side." "If we don't hurry up and stop 'em over there, pretty soon we're gonna be fighting 'em in Bakersfield. Right there at the Kern Canyon, by God."
>
> "Fighting who?" said Haggard, straight-faced.
>
> "The damn Communists, that's who."
>
> "They interested in Bakersfield?"
>
> "Aw, you know what I mean, Merle."
>
> "Ain't no rice there."

> Fuzz's sap was rising. "Naw, it's that 'domino theory.' If we don't stop 'em in Vietnam, they'll take the rest of Asia. Then they'll take Australia, Hawaii and the whole world."
> "Where'd you read that at?" said Haggard.
> "I didn't *have* to read it. By God, I *know*."[28]

Given the mythic certainty of the domino theory, it is little wonder that American intelligence organizations provided so little in the way of realistic guidance for policy makers. For the most part, intelligence reports simply reflected the myth itself, overlooking evidence to the contrary. Louis J. Halle pointed out this chronic shortcoming, which affected not only the conduct of the Vietnam War but American foreign policy as a whole from 1949 on: "The tacit assumption that the intelligence experts in Washington made, when they set themselves to interpret the vast arrays of data before them, was that of a conspiratorial movement."[20] With such an assumption, alarming but ultimately misleading reports continued to bombard American leaders, spurring them further and further into the quicksand of an unwise war. The myth of the Grand Conspiracy produced a vicious cycle of self-delusion in which the best resources of a sophisticated intelligence system simply confirmed what had been a false position from the beginning.

The myth plays a particularly decisive role in the official thinking of the Armed Forces themselves. Lewis H. Lapham recently described "military theology" as a closed system of moralistic tenets quickened by a conspiracy theory of evil. "The Army also resembles the medieval church, preserving what every good officer believes to be 'the true American virtues' in the midst of a decadent temporal society riven by disillusion and despair."[30] The definition of good and evil includes a traditional, puritanical code of personal ethics, but its living core is the conviction that there is a Grand Conspiracy, which the Armed Forces feel they are fighting, and which manifests itself in every adverse criticism. In his visit to Fort Knox, Lapham noted that the officers

> liked to refer to the Louisville *Courier-Journal* as *Izvestia;* at the Pentagon it is fashionably humorous to refer to the *Washington Post* as *Pravda*. Even Walter Cronkite, the kindly and conservative man who oversaw the departure of the first astronaut, recently has fallen from grace. At dinner that evening in the garden at Fort Knox, I remember General James V. Galloway naming him as a member of the conspiracy. A colonel's wife laughed and said, "You don't mean that, Jim, . . . not Cronkite." The general nodded. "Brinkley, of course," the

woman said, "and Huntley and Howard K. Smith . . . but not Cronkite." "Cronkite too," Galloway said.[31]

The certainty which this mythic perspective provides in assessing the probable behavior of our antagonists was revealed in a statement by General Thomas S. Power:

> Soviet rulers are not like the leaders of other nations with whom one can reason and conclude agreements to be approved and honored by the people whom they represent. . . . The military aspects of the Communist threat represent just one phase of the most insidious and gigantic plot in history.[32]

And the Chinese, according to Power, "once they have succeeded in building up a sufficient stockpile of nuclear weapons and delivery vehicles . . . will doubtless embark on a major and sustained campaign of aggression against their neighbors."

At point after point it seems apparent that the mythic certainty has prevailed over all evidence to the contrary. When political and military leaders so blindly follow such counsel into one debacle after another, one is tempted to pose Jesus' sarcastic question: "Can the blind lead the blind? Will they both not fall into the pit?" In this case it is the peculiar blindness of claiming to see everything. Under the influence of the myth of the Grand Conspiracy, reality disappears from view and the nation is advised repeatedly to enter mad crusades that can lead in the long run only into the pit of destruction itself.

## 5

We must turn at last to the resources of Prophetic Realism to counter this destructive blindness. Since Jesus' contemporaries were on the verge of precisely such a crusade, his efforts to counter the premises and consequences of conspiratorial theology may be particularly relevant. As noted earlier, several of the nationalistic movements in Judaism were convinced that the source of evil lay in the influence of foreigners, and particularly in the rule of Rome. From the beginning of Jesus' ministry, his departure from the widespread premises of the Grand Conspiracy was noticeable. His opening sermon in Nazareth reversed the expected sequence of the kingdom of God in relation to the destruction of evil. He announced "good news to the poor . . . release to the captives . . . recovering of sight to the blind," and liberty for those who are oppressed (Luke 4:18) as coming "today," before the apocalyptic battle against the source of poverty, slavery, blindness, and oppression was fought. The audience was surprised and irritated, only to have Jesus reiterate the point that foreigners such as those in Sidon and Syria would enter the kingdom before the Jews themselves (Luke 4:24-28). He barely escaped being lynched by his own townsmen at this suggestion that the hated Gentiles would be accepted by the messianic kingdom rather than be destroyed in its coming (Luke 4:29 f.). Were these not the same peoples whom Deuteronomy and Daniel had targeted for annihilation, and whom the zealots aimed to massacre as members of the Grand Conspiracy?

This radical break with the popular myths of his time Jesus worked out in a fundamental fashion in the temptation experience early in his ministry. That experience was apparently related later to his disciples in parabolic form. Here the devil was pictured as a tempter who set the seductive motifs of the Grand Conspiracy before him as strategies for ushering in the kingdom. Jesus' first temptation was to use divine power to eliminate the evil of poverty. To "turn stones into bread" would be to fulfill the paradisiacal conditions the zealots envisioned after the destruction of Satan's hordes, who now were thought to be taking food from the mouths of Jewish children. Jesus rejected this as a demonic urge to transcend the human situation. The problem of life is not overcome by eliminating evil but by living in the midst of it by faith in God's word: "Man does not live by bread alone, but by every word that God utters" (Matt. 4:4).

Jesus' second temptation was to gain assurance in advance about the income of his ministry. To throw oneself down from the pinnacle of the Temple to test whether the angels will "bear you up" is to have precisely the sort of certainty that the Grand Conspiracy seemed to offer. This too is judged as a demonic distortion of the finite situation man has in relation to God's future: "Scripture says again, 'You are not to put the Lord your God to the test' " (Matt. 4:7). The ideals of the great crusade against the sources of evil, in which victory is assured in advance no matter what the odds, are crumbling here under the impact of divine reality.

The final blow was struck when Jesus rejected in the third temptation the theocratic dream itself, the rule of the entire world by the saints after the demise of Satan. To fall prey to such a dream was equated with worshiping the demonic. "Once again, the devil took him to a very high mountain, and showed him all the kingdoms of the world in their glory. 'All these,' he said, 'I will give to you, if you will only fall down and do me homage.' But Jesus said, 'Begone,

Satan! for it is written, "You shall do homage to the Lord your God and worship him alone." ' " (Matt. 4:8-10)

This is the most penetrating and comprehensive rebuttal of the theology of the Grand Conspiracy which is available to us. Jesus has exposed its subtle distortions of God's will into a graven image of man's dreams, its flagrant violation of respect for God's open future, and its pretensions of being virtuous enough to carry out God's rule on earth. But most shocking of all, he has denoted as demonic not the presumed source of evil in the form of foreign conspiracies, but rather the very belief in the theology of the Grand Conspiracy itself! The mystique of evil, which has fascinated true believers from Daniel to the John Birch Society, has here been deftly set aside and replaced with a realistic appraisal of the moral depravity of humankind itself. What is demonic is not some alien conspiracy against the good but rather the religious perversion of the good by those who presume to act on God's behalf.

The main lines of Jesus' subsequent ministry all radiate from this decisive starting point. Each of them stands in stark opposition to modern as well as ancient forms of conspiracy theology. Rather than wait for some violent process to cleanse the world of evil so the saints could inherit the kingdom, he openly celebrated its presence in a world where evil still remained. To these festivities he invited sinners and outcasts, even Roman collaborators and their archenemies, the zealots and zealot sympathizers, whose alienation was overcome by the indirect process of celebrative love. The common stereotypes were attacked in the brilliantly designed parables, which evoked new visions of humanity and common sense from his listeners. His attack was so thoroughgoing that he refused to be addressed with the honorific title "Good Rabbi." "Why do you call me good? No one is good except God alone." (Luke 18:19.) To fall prey to the conspiracy theory's myth of perfectly good saints is to claim for man what is rightfully due only to God. And if this realistic insight were accepted by the pious defenders of the "free world" and "Christian America," the self-righteousness that is essential for the conduct of the conspiratorial foreign policy would dissolve.

As for the idea of the demonic itself, it is clear that Jesus refused to take it with the obsessive seriousness of fellow religionists then and now. He used the dualistic language of his time but refused to ground his thinking on anything but the reality of God. He taught his disciples to live in relation to the Father alone and thus to leave the solution to the problem of the demonic in God's hands. A line from the Lord's Prayer is a case in point: "Lead us not into temptation but deliver us from the evil one" (Matt. 6:13). While humankind is pictured as capable of avoiding demonic temptation, it is incapable of saving itself from the power of the demonic itself by futile crusades; God alone is capable of such deliverance. Thus the human race is set free to live in the midst of evil possibilities without becoming so obsessed in the effort to transcend its finite situation that it destroys itself and the world. In this sense Jesus interpreted his healing ministry, conducted in the style of first-century exorcisms, as a means of setting persons free from demonic compulsions and opening to them the possibility of a restored life in relation to God. "If I by the power of God cast out demons, then is the kingdom of God come to you." (Luke 11:20.) It adds up to the practical annulment of the demonic as a ruling factor in human life. This thought is expressed in his ecstatic pronouncement concerning the impact of the healing ministry, "I saw Satan fall like lightning from heaven!" (Luke 10:18).

The acceptance of this interpretation of Jesus' ministry would cut the nerve of conspiracy thought, which ascribes the dominant role in history to the demonic and then takes up demonic methods in the crusade. It would allow one to incorporate Jesus' realistic assessment of the demonic potential of the religious impulse itself. It was Peter's preference for the zealous rather than the loving approach to the problem of evil in Israel that elicited Jesus' harsh command, "Get behind me, Satan!" (Matt. 16:23). He warned against religious leaders who wear the peaceful clothing of sheep, "while underneath they are ravenous wolves" (Matt. 7:15). He reserved his fiercest denunciations for the religious establishment itself for so encouraging self-righteousness that its converts become "twice as fit for hell as you are yourselves" (Matt. 23:15). To accept this would also enable one to adopt Jesus' political pragmatism. "Or what king will march to battle against another king, without first sitting down to consider whether with ten thousand men he can face an enemy coming to meet him with twenty thousand; if he cannot, then, long before the enemy approaches, he sends envoys and asks for terms." (Luke 14:31 f.) One would also acknowledge the wisdom of Jesus's refusal to chart the future kingdom by some conspiratorial design: "But of that day and hour [of the kingdom's final coming] no one knows, not even the angels in heaven, not even the Son; only the Father." (Matt. 24:36) Politics would then evolve into the prudent business of responding to reality rather than attempting to mold it to suit our tastes. Rather than making cataclysmic efforts to reshape the world, we could settle down to the task of gradually humanizing it.

The change in perspective would be particularly fruitful with regard to the coexistence of various racial, religious, and economic groups in one democratic society. So long as they are imbued with the impulse of the Grand Conspiracy, they will be locked in lethal combat with each other, precisely as they are in Northern Ireland, with each side seeing the devil behind the other's barricades. The only hope is to take the realistic point of view that evil and good are so inextricably mixed in mortals that precise solutions are impossible and consequently that existence under law is essential. It is the perspective of the prudent landowner in Jesus' parable of the wheat and the weeds (Matt. 13:24-30). The weeds in this parable are probably the poisonous darnel, which looks identical with wheat while in the early stages of growth.[33] The weeds are admittedly evil, but the parable casts doubt on man's ability to make a precise separation. The conspiratorially oriented audience would have been drawn into the parable by the cleverly repeated motif that "an enemy" was responsible for the bad seed. Their natural response, both in first-century Israel and in twentieth-century America, was to tromp out in the field with the servants and rip the offending weeds out by the roots. The counterproductivity of this approach is convincingly stated by the landowner: since the weeds and the wheat look so much alike, the crusade will destroy them both (Matt. 13:29). God alone can separate precisely between good and evil; humans must devise means to live together in the meantime.

It is time Americans rigorously separated themselves from the pretension of the Grand Conspiracy. It is as incompatible with the democratic process as it is with the message of Prophetic Realism. To act on conspiratorial premises in the name of Americanism and Christianity is a classic instance of wolves in sheep's clothing. No matter how convincingly they bleat, the end result of their crusade is bloody annihilation. All one must do to be convinced is look closely at the results of such mythic thinking—in the leveled city of Jerusalem, in the bloody alleys of Belfast, and in the shredded jungles of Vietnam.

# 7

# THE GOOD GUYS AND THE BAD GUYS

Radical stereotypes are the logical corollaries of the conspiracy theory. They form images of perfectly good saints locked in battle with perfectly evil villains. This division of the world into Good Guys and Bad Guys is an essential factor in the cold war in general as well as of the Vietnam War in particular. Neither struggle would have occurred as it did without such stereotypes. Would the average American have been greatly alarmed if the world had been divided in 1945 between us and the Canadians or the Norwegians or the Swiss? Would we have been willing to resort to the destructive tactics we have used in Indochina if we had visualized our antagonists as white, Christian saints? Thus to explore the process of stereotyping is to grapple with one of the essential components of our current national dilemma.

Stereotyping occurs in many cultural traditions, but it is shaped differently by complex psychological and historical factors in each case. Therefore, the place to begin the analysis is not with stereotyping in general but with the ideological sources of American nationalism, namely, in the Biblical tradition as appropriated by our Puritan predecessors. After briefly tracing the historical development, I propose to describe the images of the Good Guys and the Bad Guys prevalent in the recent past. The impact of these images on our behavior will be dealt with in detail: the encouragement of reflex action in foreign policy, the justification of military annihilation, the encouragement of official dishonesty for the sake of a public image, the erosion of the ideals of democratic equality and due process of law, and finally the use of stereotypes in justifying violence. At that point we may be in a position to grasp the contribution of the realistic tradition in the Bible to the task of humanizing the stereotypes that make zealous conflict possible.

## 1

Contrary to what one might expect, the early phases of Biblical history did not manifest a particularly striking tendency toward stereotyping. There was sufficient provocation in the early tribal warfare, the experience of slavery in Egypt, and the long struggle with the Canaanite city-states, but for some reason highly consistent stereotypes did not arise. In the Song of Deborah (Judg., ch. 5), for example, both the chosen people and their enemies retained their essential humanity, despite the passionate excesses of zealous warfare. This helps to explain how the Israelite tribes could have lived in relative harmony so intermixed with the city-states for hundreds of years. It throws light on the relative ease with which David later incorporated these foreign population groups into his empire, some of them becoming well-known exponents of Israel's faith. The early history of Israel is rife with examples of foreigners whose noble behavior belied the traditional image of Israel's enemies. Uriah the Hittite, the husband of Bathsheba, clung vigorously to the standards of Israel's zealous warfare even while at home (II Sam., ch. 11); Ruth the Moabitess put aside the enmity of long warfare to migrate to Israel with her bereaved mother-in-law; and Job was admired for his wisdom, although he came from Edom, that usually despised area of resistance against Israel. The tribal enmities, however primitive and ferocious, did not eliminate the possibility of exceptions.

This was really quite an amazing state of affairs, given the long tradition in the early Yahwist faith of resistance against foreign elements. It was not until the seventh century B.C. that the situation changed to make more rigid stereotypes possible. Deuteronomy developed the earlier prophetic critique against Canaanite religion into a comprehensive rationale for the national decline. It was supposedly due to God's wrath at the widespread acceptance of foreign religion and culture by Israel. The solution that Deuteronomy proposed was to wipe out the corruption by centralizing cultic activity in Jerusalem and eliminating the foreigners. The command was to destroy the "Hittites, Girgashites, Amorites, Canaanites, Perizzites,

Hivites and the Jebusites. . . . The Lord your God will give you victory over them. Your part is to exterminate them, never parleying with them, never pitying them (Deut. 7:1 f.).

This program was a decisive step toward rigid stereotypes of the enemy. To be sure, Deuteronomy did not encourage a parallel stereotype for the Jews themselves. Since "of all nations you are the smallest" (Deut. 7:7), there was no reason to boast, except in the power of Yahweh. Deuteronomy, with its exhortation to sincere worship and social justice, seemed to assume the very real possibility that Israel might fall short of her calling. But it nevertheless called for the annihilation of many of the groups that had been incorporated into Israelite life in the earlier period, stereotyping them as the source of corruption. Although this could not be carried completely into effect in the short decades between the Deuteronomic reform and the fall of Jerusalem, it decisively shaped subsequent religious trends. Under the pressure of the Babylonian exile, the impulses toward racial purity and avoidance of foreign contamination became more and more central. By the time of the Restoration of Ezra and Nehemiah in the next century, the maintenance of racial purity, even at the price of breaking up marriages with foreigners, became a religious obligation. With the written law defining the obligations of religion in an exclusive sense, the world came to be divided between the Jews and the Gentiles—foreigners whose very touch would corrupt the faithful. The realistic vision of Israel as a finite and partially sinful people began to give way to a stereotype which was a reverse image of the enemy.

The stereotyping process culminated in the books of Daniel and Revelation. Here the saints are entirely pure and their antagonists entirely corrupt. Daniel is spared by God because he "was found blameless before him" (Dan. 6:22). The term used here measures perfection by the standard of cultic purity; he who has not violated the commandments is "blameless" or "untainted" from any source of corruption. The question of proper or improper motivation does not arise to cast doubt on this neat framework of perfection.

The word "saint" is frequently used in Revelation as a technical term to depict radical separation from corruption. A typical statement of this conception is the description of the heavenly Jerusalem after the banishment of all sources of corruption: "Into it will come nothing unclean, nothing corrupt, nothing false, only those included in the Lamb's book of life" (Rev. 21: 27). In such passages, a legalistic and predominantly cultic definition of perfection is assumed. The saints are those who refuse to worship the corrupt "beast" of Rome (Rev. 20:4), who "have not defiled themselves with women" (Rev. 14:4), and who "keep the commandments of God and the faith of Jesus" (Rev. 14:12). They are those in whose mouths "no lie was found, for they are blameless" (Rev. 14:5). Matching the purity of their behavior is the white robe the saint in Revelation wears, and the author explicitly links this to legal obedience: "Now the fine linen signifies the righteous deeds of God's people" (Rev. 19:8). The author connects this purity with passive endurance of persecution rather than with active resistance, again with the concern not to besmear the saints with the blood of their corrupt victims. But this does not in any sense rule out the saints' explicit hatred of their enemies. They cry out before the throne of God for vengeance against their persecutors (Rev. 6:10) and rejoice in the thought that after the apocalyptic victory the agents of Rome will be tortured in eternally flaming sulfur pits where "the smoke of their torment will rise for ever and ever" (Rev. 14:11). Obviously this definition of saintly purity has nothing to do with replacing the motivations of hatred with those of love. If the saints keep proper distance from "corruption," they have neither flaws nor sins.

Matching this stereotype of the saint is that of the wicked. They are inevitably foreigners in The Book of Daniel—persons who do not conform to the strict laws of righteousness in the Torah. But there is as little interest in their actual motivational structure as there is in the case of the saints themselves. They are introduced simply as enemies and rivals who inexplicably oppose the saints. Daniel 3:8 is typical: "It was then that certain Chaldeans came forward with malicious accusations against the Jews."

In the visions of Dan., ch. 7, this evil stereotype is extended to the great enemies of the author's past and present, each of which is depicted as a grotesque beast. The worst of all is the "fourth beast" representing the reign of Antiochus IV who was persecuting the Jews at the time Daniel was written.

> And a fourth beast I saw last, fiercer, and stranger, and more powerful yet. It had great teeth of iron, ready to crush and to devour, and those it spared it would trample down with its feet . . . and out of its head grew ten horns. Even as I watched them, a new horn grew up in the midst of the others, and three of them must be plucked away to make room for it; eyes it had, this new horn, like a man's eyes, and a mouth that talked very boastfully. (Dan. 7:7 f.)

This last horn is interpreted in Dan. 7:21 f. as Antiochus, who made "war against the saints, and prevailed over them, until the Judge appeared, crowned with age, to give them redress, and their turn came to have dominion." By characterizing the enemy as bestial, several things are accomplished. The destructive impact of the empires is explained because they are inhuman from the start and there can be no sympathy when such bestial entities are destroyed in the end. This may relate to the seemingly inexplicable behavior of Daniel's rivals, allowing the reader to see that their conspiratorial behavior is a natural consequence of their bestiality. At any rate an enormously significant development has taken place here which allows insurmountable stereotypes to develop. For if one's political enemies are actually beasts for whom wanton destruction is natural, there is no hope except for their annihilation.

Revelation, ch. 13, develops this theme further by characterizing the government of Rome as follows: "And the beast that I saw was like a leopard, its feet were like a bear's and its mouth was like a lion's mouth" (Rev. 13:2). It utters blasphemies and makes "war on the saints," deriving its capacity to perform "great signs" from the fact that it exercises the authority of the Satanic "dragon." The source of bestiality is therefore precisely defined as demonic, which makes the stereotype even more rigid than in The Book of Daniel. All of the author's enemies are grouped under this rubric, even though many of them have no function in the Roman government. "But as for the cowardly, the faithless, the polluted, as for murderers, fornicators, sorcerers, idolaters, and all liars, their lot shall be in the lake that burns with fire and brimstone." (Rev. 21:8) These persons, including those Christians whom the author regards as heretics,[1] are viewed as incapable of repentance, even after the punishments described in Rev., chs. 8, 9, and 16. If such people will not see the light even after having been "bombed back into the stone age," then one can only conclude that they are incorrigible and deserve the final sweep into the lake of fire. What other solution is there for the bestial servants of the dragon?

## 2

The connection between these stereotypes and their modern counterparts should already be apparent. One need sketch only briefly the style of their transmission. The Puritans were so deeply imbued with Daniel and Revelation that the use of such terminology became habitual. Alexander Leighton wrote that although his Puritan colleagues desired peace, they must recognize the bestial quality of their rivals. "But we must understand with whom we live in this world, with men of strife, men of blood, having dragon's hearts, serpent's heads."[2] With this kind of stereotype the only solution was that of violence. So, Leighton continued, it behooved the saints to "work with one hand and with the other hold the sword." As this spirit manifested itself on American soil it was quickly matched by an equally rigid stereotype of the purity of the saints. They alone carried on the faith betrayed in England; they alone ruled as the saints were destined. After the American Revolution this feeling of superiority over European forebears assumed remarkable proportions. John Adams' letter to Thomas Jefferson on Nov. 13, 1813, claimed nothing less than millenial sainthood for Americans: "Many hundred years must roll away before we shall be corrupted. Our pure, virtuous, public spirited, federative republic will last forever, govern the globe and introduce the perfection of man."[3]

How were such paragons to live in a world of sinners? The answer was they could not. And those who clung most ferociously to their own stereotype of virtue were willing to declare eternal war on those who fit their stereotype of wickedness. One thinks of William Lloyd Garrison's blanket condemnation of Southern leaders: "They ought not to be allowed seats in Congress. No political, no religious co-partnership should be had with them, for they are the meanest of thieves, and the worst of robbers. . . . We do not acknowledge them to be within the pale of Christianity, of republicanism, of humanity."[4]

That the enemy is not human and therefore deserves annihilation has been one of the most frequently repeated legacies of Daniel and Revelation. During World War I the Germans were pictured as bloodthirsty "Huns," completely devoid of human attributes. An advertisement in *The American Magazine* pictured some American troops during World War II praying with their chaplain "that the people back home will understand that here in this green hell the enemy is not a man but a devil . . . [that] we fight for the right . . . of all men to live and grow in a world where every man may keep forever free from hatred, greed, and tyranny—his home—his country . . . and his God. Amen."[5] Here are both sides of the stereotype in their essential form, set in the context of apocalyptic warfare to make the world "forever" safe for the saints. The enemy is demonic, and the saints are perfectly pure, no matter what they may do in the battle. These images have been presented in so many movies, stories, comic books, and newspapers that they have etched themselves firmly in the national consciousness. Although the identification of the enemy may change through the centuries from Cavalier, to

Royalist, Englishman, Rebel, Yankee, Indian, Spaniard, Hun, Nazi, Jap, or Gook, the form of the stereotype and its apocalyptic solution remain constant. Even in the counterculture which rejects the traditional roster of American enemies, the form remains. The stereotype is applied to the establishment, the military-industrial complex, the university or business administration, or to the capitalistic system.

The interchangeable identifications of the Bad Guys and the Good Guys suggest that a well-defined stereotype has been established in the American mind. A. Dale Tussig made a start at discerning the structure of this system in an article entitled "Education, Foreign Policy and the Popeye Syndrome." In the Popeye comics, Bluto is the Bad Guy who picks the fight and virtually destroys the hero by his unfair tactics. Thrust into extremity, Popeye eats a can of spinach, which Tussig suggests may itself be symbolic of that which is unpleasant but "right and moral"; he then uses the same unfair tactics to dispose of his foe.[6] Tussig sets forth the pattern of this stereotype which justifies the hero's violent action, i.e., "the threefold combination of the villain's established evil character, the fact that he attacked first, and his use of dirty and immoral tactics, not only justifies the hero's fighting back, but his complete and total subjugation or annihilation of the villain."[7] This is a helpful start which can be taken up in a more exhaustive sixfold pattern derived from our analysis of Daniel and Revelation.

*a.* The most decisive aspect of the contemporary stereotype is the *identification* of the person or movement with one side of the cosmic struggle between good and evil. Dualism of the late Biblical variety is essential for such mutually exclusive categories as cowboys vs. Indians, cops vs. robbers, Terry vs. the Pirates, Popeye vs. Bluto, GI Joe vs. the Gooks, or Captain America vs. the Enemy. The reader or viewer is tipped off immediately by conventional motifs as to whether a given character belongs to the good or the bad side. The villains are pictured in bestial or demonic fashion and the hero in supremely human fashion, along moralistic rather than heroic lines. Often it suffices merely to state which side a person or movement is on. I was amazed to observe during my years as faculty adviser of one of the largest College Young Republican clubs in the Midwest how crucial such an identification was in the ambiguous political infighting of local and state conventions. The first question in any conflict was: Who are the Good Guys and the Bad Guys? Who are the white hats and the black hats? That these primitive categories from the older cowboy movies could still play a decisive role in the thinking of intelligent college students revealed the power of this dualistic legacy. The designation of good or evil defines both the character of the sides and the inevitable outcome. When cosmic identification is abandoned, the stereotypes lose both their exclusiveness and their power.

*b.* The next traits relate to the behavior of the Good Guys and the Bad Guys. The former is marked by a *defensive* stance and the latter by an *offensive* stance. Decisively shaped by the tradition of cool zeal, the Good Guy stereotype always includes a passive, peace-loving pattern of initial behavior. Popeye never picks a fight, but is forced into it against his will by the most extreme provocation. The cowboy redeemer often rides into the beleaguered town without his pistols, having resolved never to use force again. In contrast the Bad Guy is always pictured as the aggressor. Like the Satanic enemies of Daniel and Revelation, he "makes war on the saints," and always "prevails" for a time. By this offensive behavior it is clear that he does not desire peace at all. He loves war for the pleasure of destruction, and this bestial-demonic trait makes it impossible in the long run to tolerate his existence in a world of passive saints.

*c.* While the behavior of the Good Guys is *clean*, that of the Bad Guys is *dirty*. Although the definition of such behavior is influeenced by the idea of "fairness," it is clear in the popular presentations of the myth that cleanness in the Biblical sense of "untainted" is the more basic category. The white robes of the saints in Revelation shimmer in the background. The hero is pictured wearing a "white hat," neatly shaven, dust-free, and clean living. The villain is portrayed as careless in his dress, filthy in his personal habits, and unprincipled in his fighting tactics. Fairness and unfairness are subsumed under the category of cleanliness, and one always knows by external observation how the two sides will conduct themselves in the inevitable battle. The importance of clean appearance plays a decisive role in associating racial or cultural types with the Bad Guys. Indians, blacks, Orientals, and swarthy Europeans tend to be stereotyped on sight. If cleanliness is next to godliness, then darkness must be devilish.

*d.* Finally the behavior of the Good Guys and the Bad Guys is marked by opposite relationships to the law. The one is *law abiding* and the other is incorrigibly *lawless*. The hero is usually pictured as respecting lawful authority, as politely fulfilling the written and unwritten laws and customs of the community, and as deeply revolted by the lawlessness of others. The villain usually flaunts the laws and customs in an open manner, provoking audience displeasure as much by his demonstration of disrespect as by serious violations. But the plot of the western or criminal story inevitably demonstrates the outcome of such an attitude in the form of murder, robbery, extortion, or kidnapping. It often develops the motif that the Bad Guys even refuse to abide by their own laws, such as the agreed-upon division of the booty. This points up the incorrigibility of the lawless in a manner quite reminiscent of Revelation. The petty moralism of pietistic religion is frequently more prominent than respect for actual due process of civil law. The cowboy hero, for example, is typically pictured as drinking alcohol unwillingly if at all, as refraining from gambling, and as resisting the advances of the flirting maidens. The villain, on the other hand, breaks all the pious laws by drinking with intoxicated delight, by obsessive gambling, and by lecherous behavior toward the always unwilling maidens.

e. The final traits relate more to attitude than to behavior. While the Good Guys are stereotyped as being *faithful* to the ideals, the bad Guys are pictured as being so incorrigibly unfaithful that they *refuse to repent*. This is a rather complex attitudinal pattern on both sides. The villains tend to be pictured as completely unprincipled. Even when they promise to "go straight," they prove unable or unwilling to resist the temptation of easy stealing or murder. They are given opportunities in each story to change their ways, and their inevitable refusal to do so prepares the audience to welcome their demise. As in Revelation there is no exit but death for those who refuse to repent.

For the heroes and heroines, faithfulness implies the courage to oppose the villains on grounds of principle alone. They never seem to seek or enjoy the accolades of the community, and in the classical tales, they never ride off with their sexual partners. In the taking courage episode before the final confrontation with the Bad Guy, the cowboy or detective decides to be faithful to himself and what he believes right, without regard to the inevitably cowardly attitude of the crowd. Having so resolved, he becomes curiously immune to criticism if he happens to break one of the ideals or laws in the battle. This is where Popeye's can of spinach fits in. His initial desire is to be passive, but when he receives the clear call to battle he must faithfully but regretfully obey. He then becomes a channel of divine justice and whatever he does to win the battle is tolerated. Spinach symbolizes quite effectively the unpleasant obligation to redeem the community through violence as well as the implicit promise of strength so that victory is inevitable. Just as in the book of Revelation, to be faithful causes one to suffer, but it also qualifies one to be the victor in an apocalyptic battle in which no holds are barred.

On this basis the stereotype combines such seemingly contradictory elements as a perfectly clean and basically passive hero, committed to lawful obedience, carrying out his highest form of faithfulness by violating cleanliness, law, and passivity. The dramatic transition from cool to hot zeal is the marrow of the myth—from Clark Kent to "Superman," from Bruce Wayne to "Batman," and from Dick Grayson to "Robin."

*f.* The Good Guys must maintain their *humility* even in face of the *arrogance* of their antagonists. As noted above, they must be faithful without exhibiting ulterior motives such as the desire for prestige, for gratitude, for personal gain or even for personal satisfaction. They must derive no pleasure out of killing the Bad Guys—the can of spinach is proof against that. In the period of waiting for the duel, they must exhibit no overconfidence. Like the saints in the apocalyptic tradition, their trust must not be in themselves but rather in the cosmic source of justice. Humility therefore involves the avoidance of any objectionable emotion or motive; it manifests itself as coolness, a sense of being utterly detached from the battle even in the midst of it. In contrast the Bad Guys are presented as arrogantly confident of victory, trusting entirely in themselves and overbearing in their demeanor. They consistently set themselves above others, bullying the townspeople and taunting the weak. They appear to act from purely selfish motives. In contrast to the cool Good Guys, they lose control of their emotions in an objectionable fashion. In a Puritan culture, that in itself is the epitome of arrogance.

These six features of contemporary American stereotypes of good and evil interlock automatically so that when one of them appears, the others are presupposed. They produce a reverse image by which one tends to compare himself favorably with every adversary. They provide the set of conventions by which characters in comics, movies, books, and politics are identified as belonging either to God or the devil. They are so deeply rooted in the American mind that reality itself is obscured.

## 3

These stereotypes played a decisive role in the cold war and continued to do so in the Indochina conflict. They led us to interpret the Russian position in Europe after 1945 in overly aggressive terms, although it is now clear that their major goal was to prevent a recurrence of the disastrous invasions of their territory that had so frequently issued from the West. The stereotype led us to view the independence movements in various former colonies as intrinsically dangerous and unwisely to take sides in civil wars. Once a movement or person received the stamp of the Bad Guy stereotype, our policy would become what Ernest May called "axiomatic." We would deal with foreign countries up to the point that they manifested the traits of evil, and then we would throw the book at them. They were viewed as outlaws and no punishment was considered harsh enough.[8] The axiom was the stereotyped definition of absolute good and evil, with its consequent solution of apocalyptic violence. Once the axiomatic response took place, a process of self-fulfilling expectations was manifested, whereby the nation so treated reacted with hostility. Our belligerent policy toward an "evil nation" provoked responses that served to confirm in our minds the incorrigibility of the enemy.

A sad example of the axiomatic response was our China policy. Having made a stereotyped assessment of the virtues of the competing sides in the Chinese civil war, we became certain that Satan had triumphed in the Communist victory in 1949. We refused to recognize the new regime or to open normal diplomatic relationships. We interpreted every action from the Korean War to the occupation of Tibet or to the Indian border dispute as originating from Chinese aggressiveness. We then proceeded to encircle China with American military bases and to harass her border provinces with mercenary troops and subversive activities. We encouraged the Nationalist regime on Formosa to sponsor raids, espionage and blockades of Chinese harbors. Quite naturally the Chinese responded with hostility, and although this took only verbal form for the most part, it was interpreted as confirmation of the demonic stereotype.

The power of the stereotype went so far that we assumed China was somehow responsible for the situation in Indochina and that the Vietnamese were merely puppets. As Lieutenant General James M. Gavin noted in an interview.

"In '54, '55 and '56 when we first considered going into Southeast Asia . . . we agreed among ourselves in the Pentagon, the planners, that we were really going to war with China."[9] The public now has access to a much more realistic picture of Vietnamese antagonism against China and maintenance of their own nationalistic goals of independence, but this only serves now to underscore the power of the stereotype to obscure reality for so many years. As Allen S. Whiting, of the Center for Chinese Studies at the Unversity of Michigan, put it in testimony before the Senate Foreign Relations Committee at the time of the Chinese atomic capability scare: "I see no basis in fact or theory for attributing a significantly higher likelihood of irrationality to Chinese as compared with Russian decision-makers. . . . The preponderant weight of the evidence shows that the Chinese leadership to date has used force beyond its borders with a consistently deliberate control to minimize the risks."[10] Whiting went on to warn against the self-fulfilling expectation of evil behavior as manifest in our desire to erect an antiballistic missile defense against the Chinese. It would not be "a guarantee against Chinese irrationality or miscalculation but rather may actually be a further goad to Chinese assumptions of our malevolence and permanent enmity."[11] By assuming that Chinese atomic capability would lead inevitably to atomic aggression, we could act in such a way as to provoke it.

Louis J. Halle has noted in this connection a consistent pattern of American miscalculations because capabilities rather than actual intentions were taken into account by military strategists. For example, in the summer of 1950, after the Korean invasion, we decided for the first time to intervene with our own forces in the Chinese civil war by positioning the Seventh Fleet between the mainland and Formosa. The military advisers of President Truman convinced him that China might decide to invade Japan: "This argument was plausible only in terms of the principle that military preparations must be based on a possible opponent's capabilities rather than on his intentions. For a variety of reasons it was virtually inconceivable that the new regime in Peking would actually undertake the conquest of Japan, but the fact was that it would have the capability of doing so."[12] The hidden premise of such thinking was the demonic stereotype of the Chinese. One assumed that they would practice aggression if given a chance. Their capability was identified with their intentions because they were felt to be depraved. Like the Bad Guys in the cowboy westerns, the Chinese were expected to break all laws within their capability, so long as the Good Guys did not restrain them.

The stereotypes of the Good Guys in Asia were equally effective in separating American policies from reality. Chiang Kai-shek and Syngman Rhee were pictured as loyal members of the "free world" despite the fact that their regimes were anything but democratic. They both had systematically destroyed their political opposition and stamped out free speech in their countries. In the course of time their dictatorial policies came to be repudiated by the vast majority of their countrymen. Yet they were sustained by the United States because they were on the right in the apocalyptic battle. John Foster

Dulles responded to some critical remarks by the diplomat George V. Allen, who had studied the behavior of these two leaders: "Well, I'll tell you this. No matter what you say about them, these two gentlemen are modern-day equivalents of the founders of the church. They are Christian gentlemen who have suffered for their faith. They have been steadfast and have upheld the faith."[13] The stereotype of the saints derived from Revelation is visible here. Minor faults might exist, but keeping the faith in the battle ranks one among the elect. If Chiang Kai-shek and Syngman Rhee had done this, then they were pure by definition and their behavior was above scrutiny.

The sixfold typology of the Good Guys and the Bad Guys provided the appeal in the speeches defending the Indochina war, especially in the years 1968-1972.[14] The public responded to Presidential claims that the North Vietnamese were "international outlaws," involved in "aggression across an international border," using dirty tactics like "indiscriminate shelling" of "civilian population centers," violating "the treaties they had signed in 1954," demonstrating the spirit of "intransigence," and making "arrogant" demands. The picture of the Good Guys in those speeches was equally gratifying. Our side seeks only to "win the kind of peace that will last," engaging in bombing for the sake of "protective reaction," offering the fairest and "most generous peace terms," respecting "scrupulously" the neutrality of Cambodia and Laos, and holding firm to faithful "resolve" while engaged in a "selfless cause." With the use of such motifs a public that was skeptical of the wisdom of the war, suspicious about the virtue of our allies, and utterly weary of hearing Vietnam reports, was induced to support its indefinite extension. The amazingly positive public reaction reveals the grave dangers such primitive conceptions still contain, not only in leading us into an endless succession of unwise crusades against ostensible Bad Guys around the world but also, as the following section will show, in eroding the democratic heritage.

## 4

The adverse side effects of stereotyping are often viewed as separate phenomena, unrelated to the process of behaving according to cultural myths. I would like to suggest that several alarming tendencies in current American life are the natural by-products of Good Guy/Bad Guy thinking.

First, there is the growth of official dishonesty. From the secret Lansdale sabotage operations in North Vietnam in 1954 to the Gulf of

Tonkin incident of 1964 and down to the raids on villages and dams in North Vietnam, the public was misled, misguided, and misinformed.[15] The facts which were long since known by the enemy have been classified as secret so that the public would not discover what has occurred. The misleading news reports derived from slanted briefings by military authorities became so habitual that they lost their power to arouse indignation. But this was more than merely the power of habit. It was an indication of the power of stereotypes. For the goal of official lying is almost always to preserve the image of the Good Guys. Behavior inconsistent with the defensive, clean, law-abiding, faithful, and humble stance demanded by the stereotype must be denied or hidden.

During the Johnson Administration one read routine reports such as the following: "American field commanders in Vietnam also have been instructed to play down in their public statements all U.S. Military actions which appear to be offensive rather than defensive."[16] One recalls the elaborate pattern of official lying at all levels during the Green Berets case, in an effort to avoid the image of Bad Guy behavior. Joseph Kraft noted in this connection "the casual willingness of the government to cover up, to lie. . . . In its final denouement, the Green Berets case emerges as a giant whitewash. The decision to dismiss charges drew an official veil of secrecy over what looked like an act of premeditated murder effected by eight American soldiers against a man vaguely suspected of being an enemy agent." Kraft traced in some detail the web of lies at every level of government, apparently all aimed at sustaining the stereotype of the Green Berets as Good Guys.[17]

The difference between this case and countless other episodes was that the public discovered the pattern of official lies rather quickly. Only belatedly did it discover the pattern of bombing the villages of Laos, which began secretly in 1964 and was secretly escalated by President Nixon in 1969. Despite official disclaimers, first-hand reports by airmen indicated that hundreds of villages were destroyed by napalm and anti-personnel bombs. While the public was given the impression that bombing had diminished in Indochina as part of the Vietnamization policy, by the spring of 1972 the bombing tonnages in Laos were double what they had been in the previous Administration.[18] Special Forces soldiers have testified that "they fought in Laos while Presidents Johnson and Nixon were insisting that the U.S. had no combat troops in Laos."[19] Senator Stuart Symington reported in 1970 that "under the veil of what was officially termed 'armed reconnaissance,' American fighter-bombers, as far back as 1964, began to attack Communist ground targets and troops—and therefore inevitably civilians—in northern Laos; and American air effort in that area has grown continuously since that time."[20] The rationale of such secrecy is obvious, and it has nothing to do with denying vital information to the enemy which already knows exactly what has occurred. It has a mythic rationale: Good Guys do not conduct a barbaric war against a neutral country.

Elaborate measures have been taken to make such deception possible, not simply in Laos but in Cambodia and Vietnam as well. The Administration barred reporters from accompanying American troops or planes. It succeeded in eliminating interviews of active pilots. It turned over the handling of newsmen to South Vietnamese officials, who were notoriously sensitive about any adverse reports, and reliable news slowed to a trickle. After dozens of reporters were killed in their independent efforts to get the news, more and more agencies contented themselves with distributing the official releases. As reporter Fred Branfman noted: "Put all these tactics together—don't let reporters see what's happening, lie, and classify—and you get a hidden war. Today we're faced with a war straight out of George Orwell, an automated air war waged halfway across the globe by a tiny elite through a very conscious and deliberate news management which prevents the people at home from knowing what's going on."[21]

One of the most amazing features of this policy of deliberate deception was its forthright quality of moral conviction. Week after week in the summer of 1972 the public was assured in the most solemn tones that we were not bombing villages or dikes in North Vietnam, although there had been almost daily first-hand reports by newsmen from various nations of such attacks. The steady conviction behind the official denials revealed a mythic structure of assumed truth which was being maintained against all evidence to the contrary. These were not mere journeyman lies. They were idolatrous lies, advanced with the complete conviction that they represented the higher truth. For if the stereotypes of the Good Guys and the Bad Guys, on which the defense of the Vietnam strategy rested, were really true, then any contrary evidence must be false. Whether a democratic system of government can survive the erosion of integrity and the public disillusionment that such idolatry produces is a very open question.

This leads to a consideration of the second adverse side effect of stereotyping: its impact on the political process. Our system is based on the idea of the consent of the governed. Its function depends upon widespread acceptance of certain ground rules and a large degree of trust. Rather than relying on coercion, it has functioned with the willing cooperation of its citizens. What happens to such a system when citizens discover that successive Administrations have lied to them, have committed atrocities on their behalf without public approval, and have manipulated the national ethos to their own political advantage? The answer now lies before us. A whole generation of young people appears to have lost faith in the democratic process. Some have become disillusioned with the possibilities of peaceful social change. Others are infatuated with the tricks of image manipulation. Large numbers are now refusing to cooperate with the democratic ground rules or to trust those who have been elected to positions of responsibility. The password, "Never trust anyone over thirty!" was a fair index of what occurred. In response to the breakdown of democratic behavior, governmental bodies have turned increasingly to means of coercion. It should not require the gift of prophecy to see where such trends can lead.

Given the usefulness of the stereotypes in winning elections, politicians have often been loath to confront the actual issues. With relatively few exceptions our Presidential campaigns have been waged by image-making. And in 1972 the process seemed simply to repeat itself. There was an effort to stigmatize the opponent as a Bad Guy and to convince the public that the Good Guy should win. The resultant smear campaigns and public-relations lies kept the public from grappling with the policy questions on which their judgment was required. This is of course nothing new. William G. McLoughlin has noted that the "moralistic and pietistic temper has always inspired our political life. There has scarcely been an election in American history since 1796 which was not conducted as a fight begood and evil for the power to steer the ship of state toward the millennial harbor."[22] The long-term effects of such campaigns are anything but democratic. With the candidates presenting mythic stereotypes, the questions on which the electorate's judgment ought to be rendered are submerged. These questions are then decided outside the electoral process. Many bright young people observe such trends and conclude that democracy is incapable of providing justice in the modern world. Since their thinking is often as dominated by stereotypes as their elders', they sometimes conclude that salvation will come only when their own pure generation comes to power.

One of the immediate threats to the democratic system is the emergence of cynical image manipulators who skillfully juggle the popular stereotypes to sell their candidate. Joe McGinniss has given us a graphic picture of this process in *The Selling of the President 1968*.[23] Richard J. Whalen has noted the results of this process in that government comes to be "seen as an extension of campaigning. The name of the game is to manipulate the market, those remote, statistically defined populations outside the bubble." The chief of state is insulated from the public like a monarch surrounded by a court of sycophants. It has made the White House into what Whalen termed "the soundproof, shockproof bubble."[24] This is alarming not only because of its insulation from reality but also because the larger issues of government—justice, equality, and the common good—are lost from sight, and a chronic incapacity to confront the truth comes to infect not only the candidate but the public as well.

A third negative side effect of the stereotypes is their tendency to erode due process of law and the principle of democratic equality. The moment people get stereotyped as Bad Guys, they are marked for destruction. As threats to the order of the saints and as agents—whether knowingly or unknowingly—of the demonic realm, they tend to be viewed as lacking the rights of citizenship. Their lives can be taken without the use of the normal processes of law. Civil rights are designed for the Good Guys who are intrinsically peaceful, and not for the incorrigibly lawless types who threaten the system.

American minority groups have long experienced the effects of this stereotyping. The long and sordid history of lynching, raping, and abusing blacks is a case in point. And contrary to the usual opinion in the North, this has not been a tendency peculiar to the former slave states. One should not overlook the antiblack laws in Midwestern towns, forbidding Negroes to stay overnight within the city limits. One should not lose sight of the fact that the black settlements in the farm areas of the North after the Civil War were for the most part harassed out of existence, their citizens denied equal protection before the law. Was it not in Omaha, Nebraska, where Malcolm X's father was lynched? The theme was as clear for the blacks as it was for the Indians and many other minority groups.

For the most part this denial of equal rights to persons stereotyped as Bad Guys has been exercised by private citizens rather than the law enforcement agencies themselves. Admittedly the record is spotty, with many incidents of prison brutality and unfair trials. But the Constitutional heritage, with its provision of equal rights in the amendments, has been a bulwark against the popular tendency to treat citizens according to the stereotypes. Supreme Court decisions on the basis of those amendments have progressively developed procedural barriers against prejudicial behavior on the part of law enforcement officials. What is lacking is forthright leadership on the part of the executive branch of the Government in defending such procedures and carrying them out in pursuance of Constitutional obligations. We have witnessed instead the systematic frustration of such equal protection for the sake of winning public approval. In violation of their oath of office, Presidents have turned away from the task of enforcing the law of the land in order to play politics with the stereotypes. This presents a danger to the democratic system out of all proportion to the previous denial of equal rights on the part of zealous private citizens. When the vast powers of the modern state serve the popular stereotypes, who is to protect the citizen against the sort of systematic denial of rights manifested in Nazi Germany?

This erosion of democratic equality is linked with explicit calls to place the Bad Guys in concentration camps or otherwise sever them from the body politic. One expects such calls from the radical right or left, but it is a new situation in American politics to hear them from the national Administration itself. Richard Kleindienst urged in 1964 that "if people demonstrated in a manner to interfere with others, they should be rounded up and put in a detention camp." He specifically suggested that Bad Guys who seem to oppose the democratic system should not be given equal protection of the law. "Is there a legitimate interest in favor of our modern ideological criminal in today's world that is deserving of protection?" he asked an audience at the Pentagon on May 1, 1969.[25]

This kind of call to replace the institutions of equal protection before the law with those of crusading dictatorships finds enthusiastic support on the part of a zealous public. A newspaper editorial in 1968 called for the use of "whatever means necessary" to turn back "the fringe of humanity that feeds on disruption. . . . If destructive passions can be aroused by the strident invocations of the Stokely Carmichaels and H. Rap Browns, then those voices should be removed legally from the great forum of this nation's agony of social debate."[26] As if to encourage this sort of sentiment, President Nixon actually attempted to stir up violent reactions from crowds of presumed Bad Guys so that the zealous public would draw the proper conclusions. When he confronted the crowd of demonstrators outside the San Jose municipal auditorium in November 1970, Nixon climbed up on his limousine and inflamed the crowd with the peace sign with both hands. "That's what they hate to see," he told his party.[27] The conclusion the public was intended to draw was clearly delineated by Vice-President Agnew in the wake of this incident. He told a Belleville, Illinois, audience that it was "time to sweep that kind of garbage out of our society."[28] If the Administration ever accomplished that goal, it would mark the end of a democratic society. The stereotypes of the Good Guys and the Bad Guys would have devoured our Constitutional heritage.

## 5

Given the destructive potential of stereotyping, why is it so difficult to overcome? Surely it has long been apparent that it leads to violence, that it counters the precious heritage of democratic equality, and that it has led us into unwise wars. Educators in particular have long been aware that stereotyping disguises reality and incapacitates the mind to make impartial and pragmatic assessments of evidence. Yet experience indicates over and over again the resilience of the stereotypes, their capacity to resist any argument or evidence to the contrary. Particulary in the several decades when ideological conceptions of Good Guys and Bad Guys have come to dominate the discussion in American universities, educators have been baffled by the seemingly intractable irrationality of their conversation partners. No matter how much data was amassed to disprove popular stereotypes, their power seemed to remain. The same observation holds with regard to the decisive molders of the Vietnam policy. The wisdom of our best-informed specialists in Asian affairs rebounded harmlessly when directed against the stereotypes. This experience led many advocates of more realistic forms of thinking into headshaking despair. "What more can be done?" asked critics such as Senator William Fulbright, who labored for years against the stereotypes and their violent expression in American foreign policy.

The mistake is to consider stereotyping a purely intellectual problem, a habit of the mind which can be altered by the infusion of contrary evidence. In actuality it is a religious problem. The American stereotypes of good and evil are idolatrous belief structures, held not by superficial levels of the intellect but rather by the tenacious resources of the whole self. They are essential aspects of Zealous Nationalism, offering the believer a clear and morally defensible sense of the identity and solution to evil and an equally clear and gratifying sense of self-righteousness. To give them up is to acknowledge the guilt of the self and the sinful qualities of one's national or peer group history. It is to enter the dangerous and ambiguous realm of relative judgments on every level, with no hope of absolute certainties and every prospect of incriminating mistakes. On the intellectual level alone it is preposterous to think that such advantageous structures would give way under the mere infusion of contrary evidence. Consequently, the liberal tradition in America, hostile toward theology, naive about the tenacity of belief of structures, and superficial in its grasp of human nature, has been helpless in facing what it recognizes as one of the decisive components of the national mood.

In the realistic tradition of Biblical thinkers, however, there are some brilliant strategies designed to grapple with the hold of idolatrous stereotypes. In taking the religious tenacity of the stereotypes fully into account, these strategies avoid the frontal attack which is inevitably futile. To use Kierkegaard's expression, they "wound from behind." They usually begin by seeming to take the viewpoint of the stereotype with full conviction, drawing the idolator into the line of argument or action, and then exploding the stereotype from within. They lead the conversation partners to advance on their own assumptions beyond themselves, to the point where the stereotypes suddenly appear absurd or immoral, so that they progress beyond the shadowy land of mythic images into the human daylight. Their goal is nothing less than the humanizing of men and women by leading them to be free from the grip of idolatrous stereotypes.

The first strategy is what I would like to call *ironic transposition*. It was used by Amos with powerful effect in his sermon at Bethel, the royal cult center of Israel in the North at the time of the national expansion under Jeroboam II. The Northerners had explained their successes and justified their treatment of their enemies with the stereotypes of God's righteous and elect people defeating their unrighteous foes. Rather than directly attacking these brutal stereotypes, Amos used them in ironic fashion to condemn Israel's enemies for precisely the same kinds of crimes which Israel herself had committed (Amos 1:3 to 2:3). Only after Amos had the nationalistic audience fully on his side did he transpose the images to give a sudden fresh insight into the impact such stereotyped behavior had already made on Israelite life (Amos 2:6-16).

In the New Testament era, Jesus made use of this transposition technique, combining it with the ironic humor of his parables. In one incident a man burst onto the scene with a demand so abrupt and imperious that it bespoke the presence of the typical first-century stereotypes: "Master, tell my brother to divide the family property with me" (Luke 12:13). The Jewish law encouraged the holding of family property in common, the elder brother directing affairs and dividing the living with the younger. Lacking a legal remedy and apparently finding cooperation with the dominant older brother intolerable, this man was so obsessed with the rightness of his cause and the injustice of his brother's hold that he did not even precede his demand with an explanation. Jesus responded at first with a question phrased to adopt the imperious questioner's stereotype of himself as "good." "My good man, who set me over you to judge or arbitrate?" He then told the crowd: "Beware! Be on your guard against greed of every kind, for even when a man has more than enough, his wealth does not give him life." This remark would not seem at first glance to be directed against the questioner, because from his perspective his brother's greed had caused the problem. But the emphasis on "greed of every kind" and the antithesis between wealth and life served to juggle the stereotype of absolute right and wrong with its obsessive solution. Then Jesus launched into the story of the "rich fool" (Luke 12:16-20), which would have moved the crowd to laughter but served at the same time to transpose the stereotype. The questioner and the crowd would see in the "rich man" a stereotype of the wicked materialist, like the older brother. The rich man's obsessive conversation with himself and his ridiculous behavior of pulling down his barns to build "bigger" ones would strike them as funny. At the very moment the rich man completes his plan he is surprised by death, which comes as abruptly as the whistling man in tall black hat and evening clothes disappeared down the manhole in silent movies. And since he considered no one but himself in the story, who is to inherit his money? His relatives. But the story achieves more than relief of a tense situation by laughter. The questioner is brought to laugh at precisely the same obsessive behavior in which he himself has just engaged! His laughter helps break the stereotype and enables him to see the illusion concealed in his own desire to be sole manipulator of his portion of the estate. This ironic transposition made it possible for him to live with his all too human but basically insoluble dilemma.

A second strategy is to *stretch the stereotype* of the Good Guy, extending it along the lines of its natural development so that its grotesqueness can be glimpsed. To be effective it must avoid polemical grossness but precisely utilize the religious ideals of the audience so that they are enabled to identify themselves in a positive manner from the outset with the stereotype which is to be stretched.

It is clear that Jesus is using this technique in the parable of the Pharisee and the tax collector (Luke 18:10-14). Joachim Jeremias has shown that Jesus offered in the figure of the Pharisee not a caricature but the epitome of the religious ideal common to first-century Jewish piety. The audience would initially identify itself with the Pharisee, who "went up into the temple to pray." Most moderns have entirely missed this point. In the proper fashion of Jewish prayer, the Pharisee does not claim he has earned his superior status. "God, I thank thee that I am not like other men, greedy, dishonest, adulterous, or even like this tax collector. I fast twice a week, I give tithes of all that I get." By thanking God for his virtue, he affirms God's grace with conventional humility. Even the comparison with others would not strike the audience as boastful, because the traditional Eighteen Benediction prayer thanks God that one is not a "Gentile . . . a woman . . ." or some other person unable to assume the burden and blessing of the whole law. Jesus merely stretches the natural lines of contemporary piety in mentioning the morally depraved types. But the trap is already set; whereas the comparison models in the conventional prayers are those who cannot obey the whole Jewish law, the models for the "greedy, dishonest, adulterous" could just as easily include Jews such as the Pharisee himself. The subtle stretching of the paradigm of virtue reveals immediately that it is not the blessing of the law which is central for this man, but rather the status of being better than the "rest of men."

The comparison with the tax collector likewise stretches the stereotype of the good man. The audience, hostile to the agents of the Roman government, would easily applaud the inclusion. Yet the terrain of the popular piety is getting trickier, because presumably the Pharisee was praying to God. Why is he looking around at the tax collector? Although the audience would still identify with the Good Guy stereotype, they would be aware that something was amiss. But the description of the Pharisee's prayer moved even farther in the same direction. To "fast twice a week" and "pay tithes on all that I get" were the extremes in piety. They were points that most people recognized as the height of piety, but at the same time resented having imposed upon them by the Pharisees. The listeners who had identified themselves with the Pharisees were thus led subtly into issues that had infuriated them as unreasonable burdens which only the rich and leisurely had time to fulfill. Suddenly the discrepancy with the Pharisee's protestation that he was really not like rich men—"greedy, dishonest"—begins to jar the mind. It is made even more offensive by the repeated "I . . . I . . . I . . ." The audience suddenly grasps the essential fact: although his prayer is couched in the elaborate disguise of conventional piety, this Pharisee is not praying.

He is boasting!

This insight is immediately confirmed by the contrasting picture of the tax collector. He prays in the simple and humble manner prescribed by the prophets and psalms. He acknowledges his human failures and relies entirely on God's mercy. Here is the true form of piety which the Pharisee had elaborately feigned in his prayer! The piety of the Pharisee, initially accepted as normative by the audience, now appears truly grotesque.

The final line of the parable simply applies the hammer to the structure which is about to explode from internal tension. "I tell you, this man [the tax collector] went down to his house justified rather than the other." He alone was accepted by God. Given the cultural assumptions of the time, the listeners have to agree. They are led to see the grotesqueness of their *own* stereotypes of the Good Guy and to see that the hated tax collector actually is capable of model piety. In being stretched to their logical conclusions, stereotypes which would have resisted any frontal assault have been exploded from within, and the listeners are enabled to see the human realities which the stereotypes only disguised.

A third strategy is closely related with the parable just considered: *to humanize the Bad Guy*. This too must be done skillfully, lest the critic fall prey to suspicion of disloyalty by picturing an enemy as a person of virtue. It must be a fully believable and natural story or process, by which the audience is led on its own assumptions to break with past stereotypes of enemy behavior. Depicting a tax collector as a model of Biblical piety achieves such an end, even though it mainly serves in the story to provide the clarifying counterpoint to the Pharisee's hypocrisy.

A more explicit use of this strategy is Jesus' classic story of the good Samaritan (Luke 10:29-37). The background of the vicious stereotype of Samaritans as incorrigible heretics and miscegenists is an essential premise of this story, lifting it above the level of a moralistic example, as it is so often understood. When the lawyer asks the question that elicits the story, the issue of cultural stereotypes is really under debate: "And who is my neighbor?" (Luke 10:29.) This raises the question whether the command to love the neighbor as oneself relates to enemies, Gentiles, and heretics, a matter which most of Jesus' zealous contemporaries answered in a fiercely negative fashion. Neighbors like the Samaritans are not to be loved but rather liquidated as hindrances to the coming of God's kingdom. Instead of attacking this vicious stereotype directly, or placing the demand to love Samaritan neighbors on the unwilling lawyer, Jesus devises a parable that strikes at the root of the problem. It pictures a Samaritan not as the recipient of neighborly love but rather as a humane agent of such love. This is set up with extraordinary care so as to convince rather than to offend. A Jewish traveler from Jerusalem to Jericho is attacked by bandits and left "half dead" along the barren and dangerous road. When two religious officials "passed by on the other side" without providing assistance, a situation of urgent, lifesaving necessity arises to elicit the sympathy of the hearers. The extremity of the circumstances and the resentment against the callous officials prepare the audience to approve assistance from an otherwise unacceptable source: the Samaritan. To receive such help in an emergency is not morally offensive to the believer in the stereotype, whereas to render such help to a Samaritan violates the obligation to carry out zealous murder. The story decisively undercuts the stereotype which presumes the Samaritans to be bestial, unfeeling, cruel louts.

The indirect impact of the story is specifically made by Jesus' question to the lawyer at the conclusion of the story: "Which of these three do you think was neighbor to the man who fell into the hands of the robbers?" The lawyer answers, "The one who showed him kindness!" And Jesus concludes, "Go and do as he did." The question shifts here from "Who *is* my neighbor?" to "Who acted in a neighborly fashion?" The shift makes sense because to answer the first question directly would require a futile attack on the stereotype. Jesus' question in contrast evokes the irresistible recognition that the Samaritan indeed fulfilled the commandment of neighborliness. The decisive premise of the stereotype must therefore be discarded by the audience; how can all Samaritans be bestial if this one man showed such mercy? Even the sophisticated lawyer must acknowledge this much, though he still cannot bring himself to use the word "Samaritan" in his reply to Jesus. The parable enables him to begin shedding the blinders of the stereotype and acknowledge the humanity of the antagonist.

A fourth strategy was developed by Jesus utilizing nonverbal as well as verbal means to *celebrate coexistence* between enemies. The crucial requirement of this method is the effective expression of unconditional acceptance. When two persons who are antagonistic because of stereotyped expectations of hostile or bestial behavior feel completely accepted by a third party, they will act toward him or her with their guard down. If the trust is deep enough, they will be able to extend such openness to each other. But since the stereotypes have such resistance to direct confrontation, indirect means such as sharing in a festivity or a new common cause are the most effective agencies of reconciliation.

Both in his circle of disciples and in the joyous celebrations of the presence of the kingdom, Jesus used such means to astounding advantage. Contrary to the customs of the times, he invited disciples to join him and thus achieved two components of this strategy. He communicated a sense of his acceptance of them in the invitation, but he also was able to make certain that his circle was not merely a gathering of like-minded persons. From various sides of the ideological struggle, Jesus chose men who had acted out the stereotyped roles which made coexistence impossible. Matthew the tax collector, a hated Roman collaborator, was called to be a fellow disciple with Simon the Zealot (Luke 6:15)[29] and Judas Iscariot, whose very name implied membership in the zealot underground.[30] Jesus led these men into fellowship with hated tax gatherers such as Zacchaeus (Luke 19:1-10), as well as with haughty Pharisees (Luke 14:1-24), despised outcasts, and even prostitutes (Luke 15:1; Matt. 21:31; Luke 7:39). These were groups which opposed one another with the fury that ideological fanaticism provokes. They were constantly attempting to destroy each other, and each justified his brutality with the faceless stereotype of the demonic enemy who must be destroyed for the kingdom to come. The experience of celebrating together the presence of the kingdom served to overcome these barriers with amazing effectiveness.

Jesus instructed his followers to employ their creative impulses to restore a spirit of coexistence with persons who had acted in hostile fashion. In Matt. 5:38-41 he advises them not to "resist" persons stereotyped as "evil." This implies not giving back in kind, if the Greek expression is taken fully into account. It is not the passive acceptance of evil so often inferred. The examples make it clear that spontaneous gestures to restore relations between coequals are envisioned. When the insulting backhand strikes one "on the right cheek," one should ignore the insult and express willingness to begin again. When the hated Roman legionnaire forces one to carry his pack the compulsory mile, perhaps one might go beyond the legal obligation and treat him as a fellow human being with a heavy burden, rather than as an enemy. The element of spontaneous celebration of coexistence predominates in these examples; Jesus is not in any sense setting up pacifistic rules. The key element is to reach through the mask of the stereotype and treat the "enemy" as a person worthy of concern and personal relationship. Such nonverbal gestures can do more to break down destructive stereotypes than the most closely reasoned argument.

A final strategy is to retain or develop *institutions of coexistence*. Structures of law and custom which allow competing groups to interact peaceably and adjudicate their conflicts are constantly in danger of being discarded by a zealous public. The fact that such institutions treat ideological opponents as equals may be infuriat-ing to the parties themselves, but it is absolutely essential in preserving a modicum of domestic tranquillity and affirming the limitations of the stereotypes. Thus the exponents of Prophetic Realism from the time of Amos to the historical Jesus displayed a marked interest in such institutions. One thinks of Amos' affirmation of the validity of international codes of behavior in the sermon at Bethel, of Isaiah's vision of the international tribunal of justice, and of Jesus' unpopular stand in support of institutions of Roman justice. In the latter instance, to advise his hearers to pay taxes to Caesar undoubtedly was viewed as blasphemous by the zealots, but it fit precisely with his concern to overcome the violent stereotypes which were leading his generation into a disastrous crusade.

Jesus' concern for institutions of coexistence was revealed in the cleansing of the Temple, the incident which led directly to his execution. The moneychangers and sellers of sacrificial animals had moved their operations into the Court of the Gentiles as a convenience to the Jewish pilgrims, who usually had to buy their sacrifices in the stalls on the hill opposite the Temple. In addition, the populace of Jerusalem had begun to use the gates on either side of the Gentile court as a shortcut into the city. With the court transformed into a noisy bazaar, dignified worship by Gentile pilgrims was impossible. An institutution designed for both Jews and Gentiles was being callously distorted by behavior which was explicable only on the premise of the vicious stereotype of the Gentiles as irredeemable. As the account in Mark, ch. 11, reveals, Jesus made use of the hostility of the zealous Passover crowd against the Sadducee Temple authorities in throwing their agents out of the Gentile court, but he did so with a rationale which the crowds certainly did not have in mind. "And he taught, and said to them, 'Is it not written, "My house shall be called a house of prayer for all the nations"? But you have made it a den of robbers.' " (Mark 11:17.) The citation from Isaiah proclaims the ideal of the Temple as an institution of coexistence, a place where all the nations would come to worship. To retain such an institution could contribute to the healthy recognition that stereotyped enemies stand as equals before God.

These strategies may offer current critics of American stereotypes some raw materials for their endeavor. It is a task which should engage the vital energies of an entire generation of artists and teachers, ministers and civic leaders. Avoiding the futile methods of the past and grasping the essentially idolatrous structure of popular stereotypes, they are called to help overcome the stereotypes which have shielded reality and led to brutality. This can only be accomplished by those who love people enough to respect the moral conviction which undergirds the stereotypes, and who understand them enough that the hidden capacities for sympathy and justice can be brought to the fore. We need the resources of the film makers, the novelists, and the artists whose genius is to create new images of humanity. We need the wisdom of community leaders to defend and develop institutions of coexistence such as the Constitution and the Declaration of Independence. We need the courage of religious leaders to incorporate enemies into their fellowships and to develop the means of tolerant cooperation. One can only pray that they will work with such effectiveness that we may be brought to confront reality before it is too late.

# 8

# TO CONVERT THEM OR DESTROY THEM

Why is the hideous face of violence so appealing to Americans? That one can even pose this question is an index of how far we have come since the assassination of John F. Kennedy two decades ago. When it was followed by the assassinations of Martin Luther King, Jr., and Robert F. Kennedy, the riots of the 60s and the bombings of the 70s, more and more people began to raise this question. Presidential commissions probed the problem and a flood of important studies began to appear. The awareness began slowly to dawn that H. Rap Brown was right when he made the assertion which scandalized many of his fellow citizens, that violence was "as American as apple pie." The hostile reactions to Brown's statement revealed something of the shape of our dilemma. While we are revolted at the violence of others, our ideology seems to condition us to consider our own violence benign. The conviction was nicely put by the line in the Dick Tracy comics at the time of the Robert Kennedy assassination, "Violence is golden when it's used to put evil down." On these grounds many concluded that social change was impossible without violence, while others maintained that President Nixon had no choice but to "bomb them back to the peace table." With an appeal as pervasive as this, it no longer suffices to condemn violence in others. We must somehow penetrate to the source of its peculiar appeal.

I propose to approach the problem of violence from the side of its positive rationale. Starting with the idea of righteous violence as a means of redemption and conversion, I should like to elaborate the appealing mystique of violence. The popularization of this mystique in American history will be sketched. Then the critical resources of Prophetic Realism will be applied so that the contrast between unconditional love and violence as the means of world conversion can be grasped.

## 1

That violence can be redemptive is affirmed in one of the oldest pieces of Hebrew poetry, the Song of Miriam, which celebrates the triumph over the Egyptians at the time of the exodus:[1]

> Sing to Yahweh, for he has triumphed gloriously,
> Horse and rider he has thrown into the sea!
>
> (Ex. 15:21.)

In sweeping the Egyptians into the sea, Yahweh saved his people from slavery and demonstrated his glory and power both to Israel and to onlooking nations. The community is exhorted to celebrate this act of redemption through song. There is a note of ecstatic enthusiasm here which concentrates on Yahweh as the agency of magnificent, redemptive violence. In the later elaboration of the song these motifs, implicit in the archaic fragment, are explicitly stated, revealing the connections between violence and redemption, destruction and conversion (Ex. 15:11-16). Yahweh's violent warfare achieves the "salvation" of his people, which in this context means emancipation from the Egyptians. In having "redeemed" them, he demonstrates his "steadfast love." From the very start of the Israelite tradition, therefore, violence is the means to set men free! Yahweh's glory is visible in his terrible "deeds" and "wonders." He is praised as a "man of war" (Ex. 15:3) who triumphs over the foes of his people, demonstrating his superiority over the other gods (Ex. 15:11). Yahweh's capacity to destroy the enemy is connected with a primitive form of conversion. The neighboring peoples tremble because their gods are unable to protect them from Yahweh's martial power. They behave quiescently as the Israelites move into their territories. Their acknowledgment of Yahweh's power is a form of conversion, for in the primitive context, to worship a god is to affirm his superiority over other forces and to assure oneself of safety in his sphere of power.

In the context of the song it is not violence as such but righteous violence which has the capacity to redeem and convert. The violent desires of the Egyptians are stigmatized as boastful, bloodthirsty, and predatory (Ex. 15:9). This immoral form of violence is frustrated by Yahweh's blast of wind which drives the waters over their heads. One frequently encounters this critical attitude toward private or foreign violence in Biblical material. The Hebrew form of the flood story emphasizes the moral justification of worldwide destruction because of the violence which has spread over the earth in the wake of the fall of Adam and the rise of violent civilizations. "Now the earth was corrupt in God's sight, and the earth was filled with violence. . . . And God said to Noah, 'I have determined to make an end of all flesh; for the earth is filled with violence through them.' "

(Gen. 6:11-13.) Here is divine violence aimed against human

violence: one in the service of righteousness and the other in the service of "corruption" motivated by human pride. This moral structure is typical and is stated succinctly in Ps. 11:5: "The Lord tests the righteous and the wicked, and his soul hates him that loves violence." The dilemma here is that God is envisioned as hating violence though he is violent himself. Violent men are to be destroyed with violence because violence is hateful in the hands of men perceived as evil. Not until the maturing of Prophetic Realism was this dilemma resolved, but for American civil religion, the redemptive capacity of righteous violence still predominates.

Given the prevalence of the conspiracy theory of evil, destructive violence is usually associated with the evil realm. In Ps. 58 the agents of the foreign gods enact the violenct decrees of their vicious idols. In order for Yahweh's righteousness to prevail in the cosmic struggle, the psalmist demands the most bloody forms of annihilation.

> The righteous will rejoice when he sees the vengeance;
> he will bathe his feet in the blood of the wicked.
> Men will say, "Surely there is a reward for the righteous;
> surely there is a God who judges on earth."
>
> (Ps. 58:10 f.)

Here is the mystique of righteous violence in its mature form. The issue is not merely between Israel and her political rivals, but between Yahweh and false gods (Ps. 58:1 f.). Since the agents of the gods are incorrigible, filled with "the venom of a serpent . . . like the deaf adder that stops its ear" against the truth (Ps. 58:3-5), violence is justified. Harvey H. Guthrie has pointed up this dimension of cosmic incorrigibility: "Vague as to *who* the 'wicked' are, the psalm ascribes *what* they are to causes lying beyond their own ability to decide or to set their venemous course. . . . The sovereign of the cosmos himself must intervene if effective remedy is to be realized."[2] The cosmic level of the struggle between God and the demonic constitutes the mystique of violence. The believer "rejoices" in the bloodshed, because the righteousness of the cause overcomes any revulsion.

In Ps. 58 the motif of conversion is again present, even though the enemy itself is too incorrigible to be converted. The last verse of the psalm suggests that "men" in general will be convinced of Yahweh's righteous judgment on the earth when he prevails against the resistance of the other gods. Despite the improbable effectiveness of this kind of missionary rationale, it typifies the tradition of Zealous Nationalism.

This conversion motif is visible in the crude expectation of the prophet Zephaniah that all sinful nations will be punished so they will repent and be converted. Since they are recalcitrant, the prophet envisions that Yahweh will enact his will to "gather nations, to assemble kingdoms, to pour out upon them my indignation, all the heat of my anger; for in the fire of my jealous wrath all the earth shall be consumed. Yea, at that time I will change the speech of the peoples to a pure speech, that all of them may call on the name of Yahweh and serve him with one accord" (Zeph. 3:8 f.). Whether anyone would really be converted by this indiscriminate orgy of zealous violence, or whether indeed there would be anybody left to convert —these are questions which apparently do not trouble the prophet. It is an archetypal form of the idea that one has to destroy the city to save it! The form which conversion is to take is stated more clearly here than elsewhere. If the heathen are to change their language and learn to pray in Hebrew so as to serve Yahweh "with one accord," conversion is clearly a matter of cultural assimilation. A powerful impulse comes to light here, one that is directly related to the "fire of zealous wrath." When a particular moral or cultural stance absolutizes itself in zeal, as in the vision of Zephaniah, it thrusts itself violently upon its adversaries. The desire is either to convert or to destroy the presumed agents of evil; if this version of truth is absolute, every one else's must conform. From this premise, to convert *is* to destroy!

In the ancient Semitic custom of the "ban" or "devotion" of spoils to Yahweh one sees the basic similarity between conversion and destruction. At the conclusion of a battle the priests would order the booty and prisoners placed under *herem*, to be destroyed or dedicated to God. This is evidenced in the Biblical account of the destruction of Jericho (Josh. 6:17-21). The rationale of *herem* was that in conquest the evil realm belonging to the sphere of the rival god was appropriated by the chosen people. Since it would defile their purity and erode their strength to take over such objects, the objects had to be decontaminated.[3] Some objects had to be burned, others purified, and others devoted to the holy treasury, depending on the degree of toxic threat. The critical point is that coexistence with the alien realm was thought to be impossible. The choice was to destroy or to convert by radically altering the threatening features. In either case the duty was to eradicate the distinctive marks of the alien sphere. The appropriation by one of the Israelites of a part of the Jericho booty so eroded Israel's strength that the next battle resulted in defeat. Only when the source of corruption was located and the offender's entire family was extirpated could Yahweh's wrath be averted and victory be assured (Josh., ch. 7). Since this entire story is highly idealized—Jericho having actually been destroyed long before Israel's conquest of Canaan, as archaeologists have discovered[4]—it presents a pure statement of the ideology. It provided an ideal precedent not only for Jewish behavior in the later period but also for Puritan and American zealotry. An analysis of the grievances that have led to the emergence of the black and Indian power movements reveals the implication of this ideology: in Zealous Nationalism conversion has been tantamount to cultural annihilation; to convert is simply another way to destroy.

One final motif needs to be set forth: the capacity of righteous violence to bring peace. It plays a role in the story of Achan, the looter of Jericho. With his punishment and the dedication to Yahweh of his booty, Israel was delivered from her enemies. "Then Yahweh turned away his burning anger." (Josh. 7:26.) The same motif appears in the story of Phinehas, who in a similar situation averted Yahweh's wrath by lynching Zimri and his Midianite wife. The tradition had Yahweh declare, "Behold, I give to him my covenant of peace . . . because he was zealous for his God, and made atonement for the people of Israel" (Num. 25:12 f.). The future priesthood of Phinehas and his descendants would be granted prosperity and respite from opposition, just as for Israel as a whole the averting of Yahweh's wrath would signify the return of success. "Peace" in this ancient tradition had a wider and more material sense than in modern usage. It connected "the state of wholeness possessed by persons or groups, which may be health, prosperity, security, or the spiritual completeness of covenant."[5] If such wholeness were being ruined by alien corruption, to destroy corruption was to restore peace. A similar logic was implied in the many statements linking a successfully completed war with the idea of peace.[6] To prevail over the enemy was to gain peace, for the threat to the well-being of the community would thereby be averted. The precedent was established here for the long tradition of seeming double-talk, which typifies Zealous Nationalism: wars for the sake of peace, destruction of enemies to guard the peace, and ultimately as in Revelation, the violent destruction of the entire world so that the peace of the saints could be secured.

To summarize, Biblical zeal offers an astounding mystique for violence, which makes it seem plausible that righteous violence could redeem God's people, demonstrate his superiority over rival forces, and even convert the world. This mystique clarifies the proximity of destruction and conversion, and it justifies the most appalling atrocities against alien persons and objects. Violence could even produce peace. With an appeal of this magnitude, it is logical that the grounds for violence so often seem self-evident. It also follows that a culture schooled in this tradition will exhibit extremely high levels of violence in both its traditional and its collective behavior.

## 2

This Biblical tradition of redemptive violence was popularized in Western culture by the Crusades. It was then taken up by the Reformation in England. As Michael Walzer has shown, Puritanism developed the crusading impulse of the Old Testament to the logical extreme. Puritan divines visualized God as a God of violent justice and they called upon their people to carry out his purposes in history:

> A warlike God made warlike men . . . "Above all creatures [God] loves soldiers," proclaimed a Puritan preacher . . . "above all actions he honors warlike and martial design." "Whoever is a professed Christian," declared another, "he is a professed soldier." . . . As there is permanent opposition and conflict in the cosmos, so there is permanent warfare on earth. "The condition of the child of God," wrote Thomas Taylor, "is military in this life." The saint was a soldier—but so was everyone else; Puritans did not recognize noncombatants. "All degrees of men are warriors, some fighting for the enlargement of religion and some against it."[7]

The rationale of such warfare was to destroy the agents of wickedness and thus usher in the era of redemption promised by Daniel and Revelation. Not only would Puritan violence be redemptive, it would convert the world. When God had destroyed evil, root and branch, the last resistance to the truth would disappear. But evil must be totally annihilated. To say that even women and children were combatants, agents of the force of evil, was to prepare the way for the unrestrained application of *herem*.

From this Puritan outlook it is possible to draw direct lines to the peculiar mystique of violence in America. Senator William Fulbright suggested this in his thoughtful speech, "Violence in the American Character," written in the wake of President Kennedy's assassination: "The Puritan way of thinking, harsh and intolerant, permeated the political and economic life of the country and became a major secular force in America."[8] He pointed particularly to the impact of the Puritan dogma of absolute good and absolute evil, which tends to rationalize violence. When the saints feel called upon to take up the task of overcoming such evil, their missionizing is marked by intolerance, and their warring takes on the harshness of the Old Testament ban.

The implicit connections between zealous mission and zealous warfare come sharply to the light in the accounts of American missionaries. Winthrop Hudson has shown the interlocking character of foreign missions and world redemption, citing Rev. Heman Humphrey's sermon of 1819 at the ordination of the first missionaries to Hawaii.[9] Here he compared the mission enterprise to Israel's conquest of Canaan. "As the nation of Israel was then militant, so is the church now. As the land of Canaan belonged to Israel in virtue of a divine grant, so does the world belong to the church. And as God's chosen people still had much to do before they could come into full and quiet possession of the land, so has the church a great work to accomplish in subduing the world 'to the obedience of Christ.'" Humphrey went on to describe the fortuitous circumstances which made it appear proper to conquer the heathen for Christ. He challenged "our American Israel" to take up this great task, and the terminology evoked images of a war against wickedness. The missionaries were to look upon themselves "as soldiers in this important expedition. You have set your faces towards Hawaii as part of the 'promised land' which remaineth 'yet to be possessed.'" Mission in this context amounted to cultural annihilation, with the alien sphere of the false gods first purified and then assimilated. This was a grandiose conception of world redemption, with the expectation of world peace when the chosen people come "into full and quiet possession of the land." Mission was simply an alternate form of warfare.

This zealous rationale appears with striking frequency in the writings of missionaries and theologians who were widely influential in shaping the sense of American destiny. John Eliot, the first missionary to the American Indians, who helped to found the Society for the Propagation of the Gospel in New England, wrote tracts concerning the "wars of the Lord against the Anti-Christ."[10] Timothy Dwight, president of Yale during the Revolution, described the triumph of America over the "savage nations," with mission and national destiny combined.[11] During the entire colonial period, the main motivation for mission was the "glory of God," which would be advanced when he triumphed over Satan's realm.[12] Samuel W. Fischer used similar motifs in his sermon before the American Board of Missions in 1860, entitled "God's Purpose in Planting the American Church." God's purpose was to spread the mission throughout the world: "to form men, to give laws to nations, and to interpenetrate the souls of missions with the truth as it is in Jesus." He interpreted the growth in American power "the power that subdues and moulds other minds by a law as certain as that which bids the flowers open," as given by God. It would make possible the fulfillment of America's destiny to "lead the van of Immanuel's army for the conquest of the world."[13]

The definitive statement of mission and manifest destiny was made by Josiah Strong, the Secretary of the American Home Missionary Society. The English-speaking peoples were being prepared by God to enter the competition with other races for the control of the world. The Christian mission would serve to destroy the cultures of inferior and corrupt peoples and incorporate them into the dominant culture of the chosen race. Now that the westward expansion was completed in America, the new stage could begin: "the final competition of races, for which the Anglo-Saxon is being schooled." American's "peculiarly aggressive traits calculated to impress its institutions upon mankind" will inevitably dominate the world. The result would fit the Darwinian formula: "Can anyone doubt that the result of this competiton of races will be the 'survival of the fittest'? Nothing can save the inferior race but a ready and pliant assimilation... The contest is not one of arms, but of vitality and civilization."[14] Strong's writings gave decisive impetus to that sense of manifest destiny which justified campaigns to convert or destroy the adversaries. There was an "Old Testament fierceness" in this doctrine, to use the description of Hans Kohn. He cites the Democratic politician and journalist John Louis O'Sullivan, who wrote in 1847: "The Mexican race now see in the fate of the aborigines of the north their own inevitable destiny." As Kohn put it, "They must be either amalgamated and assimilated or they must utterly perish."[15]

The prevalence of such ideas in more recent times and the basic congruity between zealous mission and zealous annihilation were strikingly illustrated in a conversation Langdon Gilkey reported in *Shangtung Compound.*[16] Gilkey was interned in a Japanese prison camp with a mixed group of businessmen and missionaries, several of whom were discussing how Japan should be treated after the war. The less "religious" members of the group agreed that, while the Japanese were cruel and aggressive under the present circumstances, the best thing to do after the war was "to try to forget this whole business and to bring them back into the world of civilized and peaceable nations as quickly as possible." The fundamentalist missionary Baker disagreed with furious urgency: "Why they're all pagans there, and filled with all kinds of immorality. In fact, they're hardly human at all—look at the way they behave! No, I don't feel any responsibility to them as brothers. If our world is to be ruled by righteousness, we must rid it of these unrighteous groups as best we can. There's no question but what we should crush them completely in order to weaken them permanently as a nation. If necessary, I'd even say we ought seriously to consider depopulating the island." One might be inclined to dismiss this genocidal sentiment as extreme and atypical, except for the fact that it fits the tradition so precisely. It reveals the basic connections which are disguised by more sophisticated spokesmen. The mystique of violent redemption, either by mission or by war, leads in extremity to just such sentiments.

As the history of the mission to the American Indians reveals, the mystique produced more than mere sentiments. From the beginning the goal of many missionaries was to destroy the Indian cultures and to replace them with Christian civilization. When the Indians resisted cultural annihilation, they were consigned to *herem*, beginning with the Pequot Massacre of 1637. Captain John Underhill defended this episode by referring specifically to the application of the ban in the Old Testament:

> It may be demanded, Why should you be so furious? But I would refer you to David's War. When a people is grown to such a height of blood, and sin against God and man... then he hath no respect to persons, but harrows them, and saws them; and puts them to the sword, and the most terriblest death that may be. Sometimes the Scriptures declareth women and children must perish with their parents. Sometimes the case alters; but we will not dispute it now. We had sufficient light from the word of God for our proceedings.[17]

The rationale of the massacre, in short, was precisely the same as the rationale for mission. The bloodthirsty savages had to be radically decontaminated for inclusion in the kingdom of the saints, and if they refused, annihilation was the logical solution. As one looks over the rationale for the Protestant mission to the Indians, as Robert Berkhofer has done in his *Salvation and the Savage*, this radical effort at cultural annihilation comes to the fore. Berkhofer writes: "Only a detailed examination of these efforts in terms of the missionary mentality will persuade the reader how no custom was too picayune for censure and change and no demand too sweeping and drastic in the missionaries' attempt to revamp aboriginal life in conformity with American ideals."[18] That such efforts were counterproductive from the start should have been obvious. But in the tradition of Zealous Nationalism, reinforced by Biblical precedents, conversion and destruction went hand in hand in self-evident fashion. If resistance to the mission necessitated the application of *herem,* it was the fault of the Indians and not of the saints.

## 3

The mystique of violence has imparted a distinctive shape to American wars. These in turn have been decisive bearers of the mystique into a secular era. In this century at least, Americans have not had to learn it from reading the Old Testament or listening to missionary sermons. They have absorbed it from the traditional presentation of American history, in which the decisive dates are not the births or deaths of political leaders but the beginnings and endings of great crusades. They have endorsed it by experiencing wars to redeem the world for the Four Freedoms, or to defend the "free world" against those who would impose dictatorships on their innocent neighbors.

Ever since the Mexican War, the goal of redemption of the world through violence has been taken up by Americans. The historian Ray A. Billington picked up this motif in connection with his discussion of the attitude of manifest destiny:

> Every patriot who clamored for Mexico's provinces would indignantly deny any desire to exploit a neighbor's territory. The righteous but ill-informed people of that day sincerely believed their democratic institutions were of such magnificent perfection that no boundaries could contain them. Surely a benevolent Creator did not intend such blessings for the few; expansion was a divinely ordered means of extending enlightenment to despot-ridden masses in near-by countries! This was not imperialism, but enforced salvation. So the average American reasoned in the 1840's when the spirit of manifest destiny was in the air.[19]

That violence against Mexico could produce "salvation," or that "enlightenment" could be enforced, was of course absurd. But this crusade helped prepare the way for that of the 1860's. Harriet Beecher Stowe reminded her readers "that prophecy associates in dread fellowship, the day of vengeance with the year of his redeemed." Hollis Read asserted in 1861 that the war would break up "Satan's empire," shatter false traditions, and usher in the Golden Age for the entire world.[20] Late in the war a similar note was struck by a New York preacher, Marvin R. Vincent: "God has been striking, and trying to make us strike at elements unfavorable to the growth of a pure democracy; and these and other facts point to the conclusion that he is at work, preparing in this broad land a fit stage for the last act of the human drama, the consummation of human civilization." Vincent went on to put the rhetorical question: "Who shall say that she shall not only secure lasting peace to herself, but be, under God, the instrument of a millennial reign to all the nations?"[21] Shaped by the mystique of violence, a war for political ascendancy between two sections of the country became a redemptive battle to set the whole world free.

The concept of redemptive violence was translated increasingly into secular terms in the latter part of the nineteenth century. Albert K. Weinberg has traced the rise of the idea of "humanitarian coercion" prior to the Spanish-American War. Leaders began to suggest that "all previous American history had prepared for the realization of the beneficence of force."[22] Underdeveloped countries would have to be brought forcibly into democratic civilization. Theodore Roosevelt wrote in 1895 that force would also be beneficial in reinvigorating the American spirit. "This country needs a war," but the weaklings and "anglo-maniacs" opposed the redemptive process, favoring the cowardly route of peace at any price.[23] Violence would not only restore the morale of the chosen people, but as many persons hoped, would shatter the last vestiges of tyranny in the western hemisphere. It would usher in the new age of freedom.

In the two world wars the mystique of redemptive violence came to full expression. Antidemocratic forces were seen to be threatening the peace of the saints. The belief was that righteous violence could hold them at bay and permit the emergence of democratic governments. President Wilson called for the application of "force, force to the utmost, force without stint or limit, the righteous and triumphant force which shall make right the law of the world and cast every selfish dominion down in the dust."[24] With the victory of this crusade, the impetus was irresistible to make World War II into a redemptive campaign as well. President Roosevelt's Declaration of War message called for a campaign of total victory so that America would never again be threatened by treachery or tyranny. The belief in the power of violence to transform the world was expressed in the prayer he cited in his United Nations message:

> The spirit of man has awakened and the soul of man has gone forth.... Grant us honor for our dead who died in the faith, honor for

> our living who work and strive for the faith, redemption and security for all captive lands and peoples.... And grant us the skill and valor that shall cleanse the world of oppression and the old base doctrine.... And in that faith let us march toward the clean world our hands can make. Amen.[25]

This belief was appropriated by President Truman in his message of April 1945 calling the nation "to live up to our glorious heritage" by bringing the war to total victory. "America will continue the flight for freedom until no vestige of resistance remains.... America will never become a party to any plan for partial victory [for it would] jeopardize the future security of all the world." The country should "lead the world to peace and prosperity...to a cleansed world."[26] Here is the distinctive shape of the violent mystique, phrased in the secular terms which are now the natural mode of expression for American civil religion. The world is to be redeemed by the total destruction of the enemy; lasting peace is to be secured by the application of violence; the whole world is to be converted to freedom by the successful crusade.

One feature of the zealous mystique, however, is minimized in these idealistic calls to battle: the application of the ban. With the prevalence of cool zeal, which leads Americans to prefer fastidious detachment from the process of annihilation, a portrayal of the dreadful means of achieving "unconditional surrender" was avoided. Newsreels could show dramatic scenes of bombs dropping from the airplanes and the billowing explosions they produced, but no one described in detail to the American public what it was like to be a defenseless civilian during these attacks. Practically no public debate took place on the fateful decision to aim the bombing raids at residential areas as well as military installations. The enemy was to be demoralized by the application of the modern form of *herem* and thus forced to surrender. A *Reader's Digest* article of 1943 entitled "Bomb Germany—and Save a Million American Lives" sets forth the rationale which has subsequently become a dogma. Destroying Germany's cities would "make it impossible for the enemy to supply his armies in the field and can bring about his collapse from within." With an all-out air campaign the war could be won in six to nine months. With such inflated hopes, no discussion of the moral issue of killing civilians was offered. The article simply noted that "public opinion in America is turning strongly in favor of the Air Plan, just as it has turned in England—for it is the people's own lives that are at stake."[27] To save the lives of the saints and at the same time bring a quick peace was a rationale so allied to the traditional mystique that moral objections could scarcely arise. If the new form of violence is universally redemptive, why *not* use it universally against the enemy, including women and children?

The increasing power of the mystique can be measured against earlier standards of behavior in war. In World War I, Americans had been outraged against German war tactics in violation of neutrality and the Geneva Convention. The sinking of civilian vessels on the high seas by German submarines had been a cause of our entrance into the war. American servicemen had avoided killing civilians and had treated prisoners, by and large, according to the laws of war. But now they were taking up with no qualms a strategy of bombing residential areas with hideous new weapons such as incendiary bombs. Once the war was over, Americans disregarded the official Air Force studies which concluded that mass bombing of residential areas had been a mistake; it had raised rather than lowered the enemy's will to resist; and it had been ineffective in slowing down war production. The dogma developed that bombing cities had won the war, or at least decisively shortened it. So in subsequent conflicts the dogma of redemptive bombing held sway. Down to the present moment, the application of *herem* from the air is the favorite American means of warfare, despite its ineffectiveness and its barbaric level of civilian casualties. Although Americans would admit it is ridiculous to attack flies with dynamite, somehow it appeared self-evident that millions of tons of high explosives were the appropriate means to settle a civil war in an Asian jungle.

The power of the mystique to silence the moral and practical objections to mass bombing may also be measured against the behavior of allied peoples. The British preceded us in the use of mass bombing but apparently never came to view it as redemptive. For example, revenge for the German bombing of English cities and a demonstration of power to Russian allies appear to have played major roles in the decision to bomb Dresden, one of the most barbaric acts of the war. In British explanations of the policy one always senses the consciousness that it was a bad business. And in subsequent years they seem to have lacked the curious propensity to see *herem* from thirty thousand feet as the appropriate tactic in every campaign. They refused to use bombs at all in the nine-year guerrilla campaign in Malaya, a situation analogous to Vietnam. One hears no demand that they use mass bombing to free blockaded districts of Northern Ireland. Despite their own casualties the British have kept the level of force commensurate with the situation. This is not a function of some higher moral capacity on the part of the British, but rather a sign that they no longer fall prey to the mystique of violence. They experienced once what it meant to follow the Puritan dogma that every woman and child is a combatant, and they are not now inclined to believe it again.

There is something distinctly American about the belief in the efficacy of bombing. The fervor with which it is defended indicates that it is a belief structure rooted in the civil religion itself. When critics attack the belief with arguments about morality or practicality, they inevitably encounter the response that atomic weapons against Hiroshima and Nagasaki "saved a million American lives." This is the standard teaching in the school history books and it leads frequently to the belief that, had we used atomic bombs in Vietnam, we could easily and cheaply have won the war. Actually, Japan was on the verge of surrender when the awful bombs were dropped. An armistice was precluded by the demand for "unconditional surrender"; the Japanese government had been moderated for more than a year under pressure from realists who desired a compromise peace. "Unconditional surrender" was understood to mean disestablishment of the Emperor cult, central to Japanese culture. Since the peace feelers were rebuffed by official Allied circles, the war lingered on. It is doubtful it could have continued long even without atomic bombs. In noting these factors, diplomatic historian Louis J. Halle points out the strange lack of rationality in the American attitude, as well as the ironic fact that the August 1945 surrender was conditional after all, the status of the Emperor remaining unchanged.[28] The bombing of the two Japanese cities, with an appalling loss of noncombatants, was in these terms unnecessary, but since American strategists assumed that the enemy was demonic, they were convinced that Japan would not submit before total destruction. Specialists in Japanese culture were not even consulted in connection with the atomic bomb decision. The ideology alone sufficed. If violence is redemptive in a world of demons, then total violence must be irresistible. A self-fulfilling prophecy was thus set in motion to confirm the dogma for a subsequent generation: the enemy which had presumably been recalcitrant was suddenly brought to terms; the war was won by the marvelous new form of *herem*; therefore the ultimate violence of atomic weaponry is the best means of achieving peace.

With this distinctive American dogma, the path into the atomic age was already determined. Doctrines of massive retaliation preoccupied the postwar leaders, particularly those most committed to the zealous cause. Americans reacted with amazement against realists in other countries who lack enthusiasm for redemptive violence. That the world should be destroyed for the sake of our principles seemed self-evident to us, while others decided it might be better to be "red than dead." Such an attitude seemed highly immoral to Americans. The mystique had rendered us incapable of comprehending even our allies. With the same ideological blindness, we plunged into the arms race without the slightest hesitation and produced an arsenal of ludicrous proportions. A usually prudent and economy-minded public, still traumatized in other regards by the Depression experience, supported the expenditure of uncounted billions on the machinery of modern *herem*. The gap between prudent necessity and actual investment was and is so overwhelming, and the lack of public debate on the matter so amazing, that devotion to ideology alone can explain it. It reveals the religious conviction of a people as vividly as do the long-forgotten pyramids in the jungles of Central America, testimony to the power of primitive obsessions.

Confirmation of the religious as opposed to the pragmatic motivations can be derived from an astounding fact noted by the strategic arms analyst Sidney J. Slomich. The United States, rather than taking "advantage of the relatively good political climate of the middle fifties" by reducing the enormous arms expenditures, "plunged, instead, into the awesome orgy of nuclear missile building."[29] In 1972 we saw a repetition of precisely the same variety of ideological madness when the Defense Department announced plans to develop a first-strike missile capacity in the very wake of the agreements reached in the strategic arms limitations talks (SALT), which should make such steps unnecessary. The conclusion that Slomich drew in 1968 is even more valid today: "There is something awry when societies reject politics and ethics and look for salvation to weapons of mass destruction." What is really awry, I would submit, is the mystique of violent salvation itself.

## 4

The consequences of violent ideology, when popularized by publicly sponsored crusades, are extremely grave. They far surpass those of individual lawbreakers whose violence is aimed at personal advantage. Violence that is "socially critical," to use John

Lawrence's category, is carried out by the sophisticated resources of the nation-state.[30] Its forms of warfare or repression can destroy not just an individual victim but whole peoples and lands. The widespread concern about the problem of violence in America today should not direct itself exclusively against the lawbreaker but should include the much more critical agencies of government and ideology. I should like to develop this thesis in two directions. First, there is the violent propensity of the zealous government itself. It revealed itself in the cruel and senseless war in Indochina, in the potential destructiveness of an overly militarized foreign policy, and in the brutal treatment of prisoners, minorities, and the poor. Second, popularizing violence as a means of redemption and conversion has unintended consequences. Individuals take up the violent mystique to gain justice for themselves against their neighbors. An entire society gradually becomes brutalized by the lust for blood. The democratic and religious heritage of the inviolability of the person begins to melt away. Torture and murder become the accepted means of achieving justice. There is a close relationship between such trends and the violent mystique itself. But the odd thing is that the believers in the mystique, convinced that their violent acts enact righteousness fail to notice the connection. Divine justice is perceived solely in the context of their violent campaigns, never in the social aftermath. The believers become alarmed at the unintended consequences and judge them to be the evil work of certain enemies, who of course must be destroyed for violence to cease. When a similar rationale grips the dissenters as well as those in positions of power, the stage is set for a country to destroy itself. Any culture therefore which propagates the mystique of violence bears within itself the seeds of its own destruction.

To penetrate the idolatrous structure of the mystique is an achievement of formidable scope. It is especially difficult for one who believes in the religious heritage, for popular religion tends to be entirely subordinate to the mystique itself. And it is doubly difficult to achieve during the complex process of social disintegration and ominous power politics. During such a period the popular religious leaders tend to preach the frantic message one hears frequently today, interpreting the decay as a sign of inadequate devotion to the zealous ideals and calling the faithful to one last crusade against the wicked.

Yet this penetration was accomplished in the eighth century B.C. by the prophet Hosea in relation to his own culture, at a time in which the process of social disintegration was in full swing and the threat of national annihilation at the hands of the Assyrians was acute. Hosea's insights into the cause and shape of violent decay are highly appropriate for our current situation. I propose therefore to use some of his powerful oracles to throw fresh light on the roots of current social and political problems.

The first Hosean theme to be considered is the relationship *between the violent mystique and social disintegration:*

> You have plowed iniquity,
> you have reaped injustice,
> you have eaten the fruits of lies.
> Because you have trusted in your chariots
> and in the multitude of your warriors,
> therefore the tumult of war shall arise among your people,
> and all your fortresses shall be destroyed,
> as Shalman destroyed Beth-arbel on the day of battle;
> mothers were dashed in pieces with their children.
> (Hos.10:13f.)

This agricultural image evokes an inexorable process of cause and effect. It exactly reverses that which was assumed in the popular religion. Both the "injustice," involving "a dimension of violence" in the difficult Hebrew original,[31] and the prevalence of "lies" are seen as the direct result of having "plowed iniquity" into the soil. The violent crusades, purges, assassinations, and conquests perpetrated by Northern zealots in the name of the religious mystique were directly responsible for the disintegration. In the next verse,[32] the militant aspect of public policy is specifically attacked. Led on by the mystique of violent redemption, leaders had come to "trust" in their military arrangements. Acting out that trust, they drifted inevitably into wars which were as brutal as the massacre in Beth-arbel, a notorious incident in that time.

The relevance of this thesis should be obvious. Should it be surprising that, having sponsored the most violent kinds of crusades against its enemies in wanton disregard for the value of human life, America is reaping violence for itself? What is more logical than that those trained to be killers of ostensible Bad Guys should find it appropriate to achieve their own private justice by similar means? And what happens when citizens discover that the crusades for freedom and justice actually serve the political goals of corrupt leaders? What is the "fruit" of such "lies"? It is the propensity for further violence: assassinations, fraggings,burnings of cities, stoning of police and firemen, riots in the streets, and brutality in the homes.

The moral cause and effect are as inexorable in the realm of foreign wars as they are domestically. Can we deny that a sort of "trust" in the prowess of modern "chariots" has catapulted us over and over again into military interventions, even in situations where it was inappropriate from the start? Does Hosea's oracle not throw the truthful light on our interventions in Nicaragua and the Dominican Republic, as well as many of the several hundred other small and large engagements in our history? And are we not already experiencing a foretaste of the inexorable price of such crusades? The "mothers dashed in pieces with their children" in Stuttgart and Tokyo, in Hamburg and Yokohama, have their counterparts in Seoul and Hanoi, and who can assure us it will not occur in Chicago? The fifty-five thousand American dead in Indochina, killed as senselessly as the citizens of Beth-arbel, are but a sample of what the "trust" in atomic weapons might one day produce. Our strategists may talk as glibly as they please about .the fifty to one hundred million American casualties in a potential atomic exchange, but that cannot evade the question of where responsibility will lie. It will not be with unscrupulous enemies, in all probability, or with internal traitors, but with us who blindly trust in our "chariots." We go to the brink in that "trust" and may be surprised when we drop over the brink.

The tone of direct accusation in Hosea's oracle should shock us as much as it did his fellow countrymen. Like us, they were convinced that the world had to be made safe for the chosen people and that the sole threat to the peace came from the enemy. They were as certain as we that the security risk lay in the enemy's army and not in their idolatrous trust in their own. And they were certain that proper preparedness and righteous interventions would keep war away from their own neighborhoods. "It is better to fight them in Vietnam than in Long Beach," we solemnly assured one another. But that we ourselves may be the source of the disorder—that is unthinkable! We are the chosen people, are we not, the selfless defenders of the free world? How can peacemakers be responsible for wars? Without the penetrating accusation of a Hosea, it is doubtful whether any would come to a more realistic appraisal. In the violent consequences of the mystique is the punishment that such evasion brings upon itself.

The aspect of divine justice within the plowing of crusades and the reaping of violence is announced by Hosea in the shocking terms possible. He hears Yahweh say:

I am like pus to Ephraim,
and like bone rot to the house of Judah.
(Hos. 5:12.)

In suggesting this sort of translation, James Luther Mays observes that the "comparisons were drawn to the extreme limit, but their boldness is meant to reveal how God in hiddenness is already at work, sapping away the vitality of Ephraim and Judah through the very actions which they initiate and execute. The debilitating effect of their policy is not to be thought of as separate from the effect of his presence in their history."[33] Here is the thesis of Hosea in its most unforgettable form. If he is right, the moral decay of our society today is not an indication of how far we have strayed from the zealous ideals, but rather of how much our enactment of those ideals has brought God's judgment against us. Divine justice is visible in the very social disintegration our crusades have wrought. It may be seen in the riots and drugs which sap the strength of our crusading armies. It is visible in the poisonous breakdown of respect for life and in the rotted blocks of tenement houses in our burned-out cities. In all these signs of demoralization and sickness God is acting to carry out an inexorable justice against those who fall prey to the mystique of violence.

If Hosea's thesis is valid, it follows that there must be a *repudiation of the zealous myths.* As long as a society is awed by the violent deeds of its heroes and leaders, it will tend to follow their example. If the popularization of violence is the means by which disintegration occurs, then it must be exposed and stopped. Hosea makes a daring attempt in this direction when he condemns the most thoroughgoing zealot of them all, the founder of the dynasty in power. Jehu carried out the religious purge with the full support of the zealots of his time. He was the heroic warrior whom the dynasty and the public sought to emulate. He mercilessly killed the wicked Jezebel and enacted the ban against other enemies of the state. His vigor in chariotry and skill with the bow were models for the bold men of Israel. It must have seemed both blasphemous and treasonous, therefore, when Hosea condemned the mythic ideal of *herem* on the plain of Jezreel and predicted Yahweh's repudiation of the nation for emulating it:[34]

And Yahweh said to him, ". . . I will punish the house of Jehu for the blood of Jezreel, and I will put an end to the kingdom of the house of

> Israel. And on that day, I will break the bow of Israel in the valley of Jezreel."(Hos. 1:4f.)

The audacity of this attack on the mythic ideal of the current regime may be grasped when one remembers that both the prophet Elisha and the zealot Jehonadab enthusiastically supported Jehu's purge. Hosea is pitting himself against the dominant religious ideals of his time—and ours! His words reveal a concern about the bloodshed in the massacre and the consequences of popularizing militarism, symbolized by the "bow" which would one day be broken.[35] It is important to note that this prediction of the shattering of Israel's military establishment was fulfilled when Tiglath-pileser swept over Israel in 733 B.C. Having followed the mythic ideal into the senseless war with Assyria, Israel had to suffer the consequences. By attacking the myth, the prophet aimed at freeing his people from its idolatrous grasp before it was too late.

Do we Americans not need a similar shattering of violent myths? Can we expect our children, raised on a steady diet of violent cartoons and brutal murder stories, to grow up less infatuated with solutions in the style of Jehu than Israelite children were? Is it reasonable to hope that the continued popularization of crusades through school history books will produce an outlook which eschews violence? And what judgment is to be rendered on the present-day admirers and followers of Jehu in our government? Can they be held guiltless in having led the public into the application of *herem* against women and children in Vietnam, Cambodia, and Laos? Can the effects of popularizing violence be stemmed if such men continue to win our admiration? We have devoted far too little attention to the matter of public responsibility for the myths by which we live. When the distinctive myths of a culture are predominantly violent, as ours are, and when that culture begins to disintegrate from acting out the myths, it is time to stop quibbling over whether social scientists can agree on percentages of causation. It is time to take responsibility as parents and private citizens, textbook writers and media specialists, teachers and ministers, to repudiate the myths of Jehu.

One logical consequence of the mystique of violence, in Hosea's view, was the *popularization of crime and brutality*. In the following oracle he visualizes Yahweh as charging his people with forsaking the truth of religion in their violent crusades and with violating the commandments concerning respect for persons. Crimes of violence are the logical products of misunderstanding obligations to God, and because of such violence, the very land itself suffers and loses its productivity. The interrelation of ecological decay, destructive personal behavior, and the false mystique is set forth unforgettably:

> Hear the word of Yahweh, O people of Israel;
> for Yahweh as a controversy with the inhabitants of the land.
> There is no faithfulness or kindness,
> and no knowledge of God in the land;
> there is swearing, lying, killing, stealing, and committing adultery;
> they break all bounds and murder follows murder.
> Therefore the land mourns,
> and all who dwell in it languish,
> and also the beasts of the field,
> and the birds of the air;
> and even the fish of the sea are taken away.
> (Hos. 4:1-3.)

This sweeping condemnation must have amazed those engaged in zealous violence. It implied that, contrary to the popular mystique, no crusade or murder then being performed was a matter of covenant loyalty to God. It cut the very nerve of Zealous Nationalism, which assumed that God called men to exercise faithfulness by killing sinners. Moreover, it flatly insisted that the religious consensus contained no knowledge whatsoever of God. Deluded by zeal, religionists had a completely distorted perception of Yahweh's justice. The result of this radical perversion, much like the current consensus in America, was a boundless crime wave. Each crime Hosea mentioned is a breach in the respect for persons which covenant loyalty to Yahweh had enjoined. "Swearing," for instance, was "an imprecation or malediction invoking a divinely caused misfortune on another";[36] it was a matter of gaining precisely the vengeance in personal matters that Zealous Nationalism sought in public matters.

The connection between public zealotry and private violence should be obvious. If it is proper to kill without trial in zealous campaigns, why should it be wrong in cases of personal injustice? If one can lie in connection with the crusade against evil, why should it be objectionable when the individual is pitted against personal threats? If great figures become rich and gain power through their participation in public crusades, why should common citizens not be justified in taking what they need if their motives are pure? Once infected by the short circuit of zeal, in which the aims of the self are identified with the aims of God, one finds it natural to break across all restraints. Life becomes cheap. For if those massacred by a Jehu or a Calley had no intrinsic worth, surely no one will care if an old man is set afire for fun in a New York park, or beaten to death for the money in his pocket.

An obscene appetite for sadism is growing among us. One can document it in the changing taste in movies and reading materials. Formerly, horror stories were placed in a make-believe setting which was conducive to psychic release. Now there is a demand for realism in horror. When the movie *Straw Dogs* was shown in Chicago, the audience cheered and laughed through the horrible rape scene, as well as at the torture of the retarded boy and the pet cat. In reporting this, Bob Greene of the *Chicago Sun-Times* notes the acting out of such brutal impulses in incidents such as the basketball game in Minnesota in which the Ohio State players were badly injured after being kicked. The cheering crowd reacted to the injury of the players by pouring out of the stands to add their heels to the writhing bodies.[37]

The congruence between crimes of violence and publicly sponsored crusades has been visible in America for a long time, but it seems never to have been examined in detail. Our incidence of homicide and other crimes of violence is so many times higher than that of other nations in similar circumstances that cultural rather than natural factors must play the decisive role.[38] How else can one explain the astounding fact that our homicide rate is fifteen times that of Holland, eight and one half times that of England, four and one half times that of neighboring Canada?[39] I would submit that Hosea's oracle offers the most perceptive answer. And it can be confirmed by any number of comparisons between crusading and noncrusading cultures. An interesting confirmation comes by comparing the American frontier experience with that of Canada, a country that has always resisted the Puritan type of crusading. The Canadians have relied on normal processes of law rather than zealous campaigns to keep the peace. Seymour Martin Lipset[40] points out the striking fact that the Canadian Mounted Police force of only three hundred men, organized in 1974, succeeded within a short time in pacifying the vast region from Manitoba to the Rockies. By impartial justice they eliminated the whisky traffic to the Indians, livestock stealing, land seizures, and major Indian conflicts. Lipset cites Edgar W. McInnis' study, *The Unguarded Frontier*: "An imaginary line separated Canada from the United States for a distance of 800 miles. South of that line strategic points were garrisoned by thousands of United States soldiers; an almost continuous condition of Indian warfare prevailed, and the white population in large measure ran free of the restraints of established authority." Shaped by two hundred years of zealous ideology, the American reliance on violence to keep evil at bay seemed actually to encourage lawlessness. It allowed far too much space for violent solutions to conflicts, outside the purview of the courts or the democratic process. With violence widely popularized as a means of social redemption, respect for law and order was strikingly low and the tolerance of crimes of violence strikingly high. Can the same not be said concerning our own time, a century later? If violence is redemptive for the nation as a whole, surely it remains efficacious for the individuals therein.

The ecological results of violence are provocatively pictured in the Hosea oracle. That the land itself should "mourn" and the beasts "languish" may strike one at first glance as a curious fragment of ancient superstition. How could such "a loss of vitality by land and population, . . . a terrible diminution of life-forces which tends to a total absence of life"[41] be related to the violent mystique? A quick glance at what happened to the land of Palestine as a result of zealous crusading may provide a clue. Forests were ravaged for siege timbers and campfires; vineyards and orchards were destroyed by raiding troops and abandoned by depopulated villages; waterways and irrigation systems were damaged and fell into disuse; pastures and grainfields were trampled by battles and ruined by neglect when their owners were killed, subsequently to be eroded beyond usefulness. Streams were polluted and wells were poisoned. And between the violent campaigns the vital energies of survivors were directed to military preparedness rather than constructive agriculture and industry. The landscape of Palestine began to assume the appearance it has presented in modern times: barren, denuded of natural forests, lacking in vineyards and orchards, eroded by the winter rains, and parched by the summer heat. A land flowing with milk and honey was ruined by the mystique of violence.

Surely a similar "mourning" and "languishing" of the very earth itself is visible today as well. In the United States, how long has it taken for the ravaged South to recover its strength or productivity after the Civil War? Have the desert canyons of the Navahos ever regained their fertility after the the marvelous peach orchards and fields and livestock were destroyed by American soldiers more than one hundred years ago? How many generations will it take for the poisoned fields and blighted forests of Indochina to regain their verdure? If the still-ruined terrain of Verdun is any guide, it may never take place. The shattered, shell-torn earth, like the now-barren hills of the Palestinian wilderness, may be permanently ruined by the modern methods of *herem*.

There is an unspeakable ruthlessness in actions such as our attempts to set the great forests of Vietnam afire, to seed the clouds to cause destructive floods, or to destroy the dikes built up by generations of patient work. Like the Israel of Hosea's time, we have truly broken "all bounds" of divine law and human decency. And the judgment against such sin is the chain reaction of ecological disaster as well as the decline in the contstructive goals of man. When whole generations are taught the lust for wanton destruction, it becomes natural for their energies to be directed in violent exploitation and crime rather than in the slow, patient labor of peace. Can we not hear the "controversy" God has against such behavior? Can we not see the judgment against it in the exploited and ruined land, even in what used to be America the beautiful?

The violent mystique causes a *perversion of democratic ideals.* By encouraging brutality and crimes against others, it gradually drives a society into totalitarian practices. The institutions of law and order, whose aim is the preservation of life through the equal treatment of all persons, begin to condone violence against certain groups and types. The principle that a person is innocent until proven guilty is set aside in the case of certain enemies of the state. Suspects are tortured on the premise that they are guilty anyway and are incapable of responding to anything but brute force. One by one, the Constitutional protections of the rights of citizens drop away until the Government changes from an agency of justice to the very opposite.

The perversion caused by the spell of the violent mystique is described by Hosea in a sharply formulated oracle directed against the legal and religious authorities of his time. Though they were ostensibly Yahweh's ministers of impartial justice, they had been "making a quarry of others instead of being their protectors and benefactors."[42]

> Hear this, O priests!
>     Give heed, O house of Israel!
> Hearken, O house of the king!
>     For judgment pertains to you;
> for you have been a snare at Mizpah,
>     and a net spread upon Tabor.
>
> (Hos. 5:1)

The image of the wild game traps reveals the callousness in the treatment of fellow human beings. It is a suitable image for our modern forms of police brutality, our dehumanized court and prison systems, and the disinterest in impartial treatment on the part of law enforcement officers. If violence is truly redemptive, and if the source of evil is identifiable on the basis of popular stereotypes, then the Constitutional protections can be dispensed with. The presumably guilty parties are issued an immediate form of violent justice, whether their guilt has been proved before an impartial bar of justice or not. Police officers routinely search for suspects in ghetto neighborhoods, weapons drawn and often blazing. Prison authorities bear down with brutal force on "troublemakers," often managing to carry out the capital punishment which the courts had refused to order. The eyewitness accounts of the George Jackson slaying in San Quentin indicate precisely this kind of pattern.

Even Presidents get caught up in this perversion of due process of law. While scolding the press for its coverage of the Manson case in August 1970, President Nixon made a statement that presumed the guilt of the defendant, in gross violation of the legal and Constitutional provisions he had sworn to uphold: "Here is a man who was guilty, directly or indirectly, of eight murders without reason."[43] The *Boston Globe* editorial pointed out that this was "a shocking statement from a man who is himself a lawyer. . . . The observation that needs to be made is that the presumption of guilt before it is proven is all too prevalent these days."[44] The cause of this growing prevalence is revealed in an editorial in the *Arizona Republic* which defended the President's statement:

> We are not among those who think President Nixon did irretrievable damage to our judicial system. . . . We know of no law that says an individual cannot presume the defendants guilty. . . . What needs changing, and what President Nixon is trying to change, is the ploys used by criminals and their lawyers to defy the vast majority. . . . The important thing about the Nixon statement in Denver was that it again put the Administration clearly on the side of law and order. The President spoke for the vast majority of Americans when he criticized the defense lawyers for their contemptuous attacks on the judge. He told the absolute truth when he said a new respect for the legal system would have to be created, or the system would be destroyed.[45]

Here is the perverted form of "law and order" that Hosea had in mind. Eschewing legal restraints, it seeks to enact violent justice on those it presumes guilty. If the "vast majority" are convinced that such punishment should be carried out, no impertinent lawyers should hinder it. But, contrary to Nixon and the *Arizona Republic,* such zeal does not create "new respect for the legal system"; it is the most effective way to destroy it. For the victims of such partial justice, who turn out to be the minorities, the poor, and the nonconformists, as well as those who are actually guilty of some crime, lose their respect for the legal process and for the Government itself.

The capacity of the violent mystique to undermine respect for law and order is portrayed in telling fashion by one of Hosea's oracles. It cites the cynical remarks of his fellow countrymen who experienced the perverted forms of violent justice:

> For now they [the disillusioned citizens] will say:
> "We have no king,
> for we fear not Yahweh,
> and a king, what could he do for us?"
> They [the authorities] utter mere words;
> with empty oaths they make covenants;
> so judgment springs up like poisonous weeds
> in the furrows of the field.
>
> (Hos. 10:3f.)

If the king's justice is partial, based on stereotypes and executed in impatient violence, why should those who experience it continue to offer their respect? And if such perverted justice is really Yahweh's justice, as it claimed to be, let God be damned as well! The result is a growth of lawlessness, in which the social cement of respect for authority has dissolved. But the prophet sees much more clearly than our current majority the source of such "poisonous weeds." It is in the very defenders of the perverted law and order, who call violence justice and who discard the priceless treasure of equality before the law.

A final consequence of the violent mystique is the *militarization of foreign policy*. If the exercise of military power is thought to be redemptive, ridding the nation of threats to its existence, then the tedious and humble business of accomodating the nation to living with reality falls into disrepute. Diplomacy gives way to militarism. George F. Kennan noted such a process in connection with the development of the containment policy in the 1950's. American leaders thought of it in strictly "military terms." Kennan claims that our Government failed to take advantage of the opportunities for useful political discussion when, in later years, such opportunities began to open up, and exerted itself, in its military preoccupations, to seal and to perpetuate the very division of Europe which it should have been concerned to remove."[46] Donald McDonald explains: "Foreign policy becomes militarized when, at critical moments, it is the military who seem to offer the crisp, definite, tangible options—while those who argue for negotiation, diplomacy, and respect for the decent opinion of mankind seem to be offering the unattractive, endlessly prolonged, and inconclusive options."[47]

Our experience belies the easy promises of military solutions. The promises they seem constantly to set before us turn out to be tracks into the swamps of endless violence. The Vietnam debacle was an excellent example. Hosea has a succinct description of this paradox, i.e., that the clear-cut solution of militarism drives a nation into far worse dilemmas and dangers than it initially confronted. He likens the military option to the east wind of Palestine, the searing sirocco which destroys everything green in its path:[48]

> Ephraim [i.e., Israel] herds the wind,
> and pursues the east wind all day long;
> they multiply falsehood and violence;
> they make a bargain with Assyria,
> and oil is carried to Egypt.
>
> (Hos. 12:1.)

Like the militarized foreign policy, the wind from the eastern desert is clear-cut, tangible, and undeniably potent. But it seems to defy herding! A nation can devote itself to the task with all the care of the German general staff and all the resources of the Pentagon, but the sirocco inevitably runs amok. Rather than achieving what it promises, it redoubles the "falsehood and violence." All the shrewd arrangements of military diplomacy, like the vassal treaty with Assyria and the bribing of Egypt to help break it,[49] cannot provide salvation from the cycle of destruction.

This oracle renders a telling judgment on the self-defeating policies of postwar America. It also sheds a piercing light on Metternichian manipulations of power politics. How much have our military alliances and our military interventions added to our security? Has militarized diplomacy really been effective in Southeast Asia or in Latin America? Have we been any more successful than ancient Israel in taming the east wind?

If we are honest, we must admit the validity of this oracle. And we must be forthright enough to see that the mystique of violence has proved anything but redemptive in our own recent experience. Rather than holding violence at bay, or keeping evil within bounds, it has added to it ten and twenty fold. It has led us like the sirocco to destroy everything in our path. Young Americans have participated routinely in torture and execution of prisoners or suspects. A Vietnamese woman, Do Thi Thanh, characteristically reports concerning the routine operations in 1968: "I remember three years ago when the Americans came many times by sea and helicopters. They shot anything—any people they saw anywhere in the hamlet, on the beach, or outside the hamlet, in the fields. . . . One time, after the Americans had come by sea and then left, I went down to the sea, and saw 10 bodies floating in the water."[50] Even the bombing of hospitals became accepted. The French press agency correspondent's report of July 1927 provoked no outrage when it sketched the details of the bombing of the Bach Mai hospital about a mile from the center of Hanoi: "About 30 bombs fell right on the hospital shortly before 9 a.m. One, weighing approximately 1 ton, dug a crater of a circumference of 40 feet. Beds and wheelchairs were broken, operating rooms damaged, electronic control equipment in shambles, and everywhere glass splinters and heaps of plaster."[51] Following the logic of the east wind, there were scarcely any limitations in the level of destruction we were routinely working to inflict. The laws of war are helpless to harness the gale. Richard Wasserstrom's thoughtful study of this process sets forth the current consensus: "The laws of war permit and treat as legitimate almost any practice, provided only that there is an important military advantage to be secured."[52] The destructive logic of the east wind brooks no arbitrament of law, of reason, or humanity. If violence is redemptive, then one must be willing to follow it to the end.

The classic statement of this logic was offered by an American major during the Tet offensive early in 1968. The town of Ben Tre had been overrun by Viet Cong attackers, so American fighter bombers carrying bombs, rockets, and napalm were ordered in to level it. The number of casualties in the town of thirty-five thousand is unknown, but military observers estimated that at least five hundred civilians were killed. The officer explained that "it became necessary to destroy the town to save it."[53] For many critics of the war this statement was the epitome of absurdity. But it fit precisely into the structure of the violent mystique. To redeem a town from the grip of evil, the application of *herem* is sometimes necessary. If bombing saved the world in World War II, it could surely save a river town in the Mekong Delta! The logic of the east wind was never more clearly stated.

## 5

Is there anything that can reverse this awful process of destruction? Can anything set people free from the perverse sirocco of violence? Hosea was the first thinker in world history, I believe, to wrestle with this question in something like its modern form. James D. Smart describes his conclusion in the following terms:

> Hosea came to see most clearly the fearful dilemma of man's evil. Sin, by its disruption of the personal relation on which life depends, brings blindness, callousness, and despair, which lead to yet more violent sin. The human being, once started on this disastrous downhill course, is helpless to stop the tragic cumulative process. There must be an intervention from beyond. Someone, with love for the sinner in spite of the sin, must break in upon the deadly process and by sheer grace create for the prisoner of sin and death the possibility of a new beginning. This was Hosea's final word concerning God.[54]

This theme is developed in the following oracle, which pictures Yahweh in daring terms as the lover who will "allure" his people, taking them into the "wilderness" which was the site of their covenant relationship during the time of the exodus and the wandering. He would draw her away from the site of Canaanite civilization, with its manipulative attitude toward the world and its reliance on coercion. He would also reverse the dread legacy of *herem* which had so perverted the substance of the faith. The prophet describes Yahweh as calling to his people:

> Therefore, behold, I will allure her,
> and bring her into the wilderness,
> and speak tenderly to her.
> And there I will give her her vineyards,
> and make the Valley of Achor a door of hope.
> (Hos. 2:14f.)

Achor was the barren, rock-strewn site where Achan and his family were presumably stoned for violating the terms of *herem*. This horrible tradition will be reversed so that the Valley of Achor will no longer symbolize wrath and death. It will become the hopeful path into the verdant vineyards of the future. The chapter proceeds to describe the restoration of harmony between humankind and the natural world which would come in the wake of this reversal. "And I will make for you a covenant on that day with the beasts of the field, the birds of the air, and the creeping things of the ground; and I will abolish the bow, the sword, and war from the land; and I will make you lie down in safety." (Hos. 2:18.) The power of God's love would evoke a sense of repentance which would mark the end of the rule of the violent mystique over the human heart (Hos. 14:3). It would one day draw Israel away from the militarism which was destroying her and setting the very balance of nature awry.

This strategy of redemptive love was taken up by Jesus of Nazareth. What for Hosea had remained in eloquent words alone came into concrete human experience with Jesus. The passionate love of God came to earth, full of sensual, yearning, creative power. Love was expressed to persons obsessed by the mystique of violence as well as to those suffering under its brutal impact. It proved as redemptive as Hosea had promised. Small groups of restored persons began to emerge, reaching out to others in their violence-prone society, with a vigor and joy which only love can produce.

With violence relegated to the nonredemptive role of enforcing civil law and order so that men may survive together until they all have been set free from the poisonous residue of a perverted past, love came into its own. It accepted enemies just as they were, in the very midst of alienation, and offered them a chance to break free. Its form of conversion was the very opposite of *herem*. It offered antagonists a possibility of remaining true to themselves while accepting others as they felt accepted. Redeemed by the power of such acceptance, the races, the sexes, the generations, and the classes discovered that they could exist together. The joy of reconciliation and the new stimulations to creativity served to confirm the power of love and make its further communication a matter of pleasure. Thus a new form of mission emerged. Rather than thrusting itself upon neighbors in the zealous demand to lose identity and be absorbed into the superior community of the saints, it offered restored relations with neighbors precisely as they were. Unconditional acceptance replaced aggression, joy took the place of rage, and a zeal for love overcame the zeal to destroy.

Two paths thus lie open to those who would reform our society today, or take up America's calling to serve the world. There is the way of redemptive violence which may take the form of the great revolution or the great crusade. This path promises to shatter the injustice with a righteous fury, punishing the evildoers, emancipating those who have been exploited, and making the world safe for virtue. There is also the way of redemptive love. Its promise is less clear-cut, and it leads to much less predictable results. For when love is enacted, persons become free. New impulses awaken which no one can master ahead of time. So this is the way for the audacious and the large in spirit, who can live without idols and face an uncertain future unafraid. It is for those who dare to coexist with all sorts and conditions of humans. They who follow it will be thrust out into the no-man's land between the rigid fronts of zealous conflicts, out where the wounded are, the shell-shocked and the lost. Their impulses of creative love will draw them into the prisons and the ghettos, onto the streets and the way stations, even into the lands that have been ravaged by our crusades. Whatever their occupation or place of service, they will give way to the spontaneous impulse within them to overcome alienation with love and despair with joy. They will seek and save the victims as well as the violent ones, not by pious admonitions or zealous evangelism, but by the sort of unconditional acceptance they themselves have received. Many of them will perish in the times ahead, victims of hatred and suspicion. But their work will redeem, even as they forgive their executioners and pray for the lynching mobs. They stand in a great and noble company, not with Elisha and Jehu and John Brown, but with Hosea and Jesus and Saint Francis and Martin Luther King.

The present crisis is one in which these two paths, which have been hopelessly confused in the American mind, stand as sharply opposed alternatives, awaiting our choice. If our path be redemptive love, then the policies and the mystique of violence must be repudiated once and for all. And if it be the path of violent zeal, all pretensions of carrying out the goals of love should be dropped. The two paths are mutually exclusive. May the God of justice, whose wisdom far transcends our poor powers to comprehend or to convince, guide our nation onto the path which truly leads to peace.

# 9

# NEITHER HUMILIATION NOR DEFEAT

In his speech defending the invasion of Cambodia in May 1970, President Nixon gave voice to the theme of this chapter: "We will not be humiliated. We will not be defeated." He went on to declare his willingness to suffer political death, if necessary, in order to prevent such reversals. "I would rather be a one-term President than to be a two-term President at the cost of seeing America become a second-rate power and see this nation accept the first defeat in its proud 190-year history."[1]

What is there about defeat that evokes so fundamental a consideration as political suicide, as it does repeatedly in Presidential speeches and interviews? Have other nations not experienced defeat, and yet survived and even recovered with more strength and determination than before? Why should a reversal in so obscure and distant a battlefield as Indochina seem to threaten the very foundation of American pride?

The key to answering these questions was suggested by the historian D. W. Brogan. While discussing the mounting impatience about the seemingly unwinnable war in 1967, he noted that "the desire to be right as well as victorious is deeply embedded in the American psyche."[2] David E. Larson similarly suggested that our isolation from the realities of international power "is *primarily* due to the Puritan ethic. Or, that 'somehow, some way, right will prevail over might.'"[3] A necessary connection between being right and being victorious is in view here. And the obvious corollary of such a position is that to be defeated is to be wrong. Given this premise, to accept defeat is to acknowledge national guilt, perhaps even to give up the favored people concept. If the implications are really so drastic, a Zealous Nation might be willing to take the most desperate steps, even to the point of self-destruction, to avoid defeat.

To account for this phenomenon we must trace the impact of the Biblical models of the triumphant God and his victorious people as understood in the moral framework of right producing victory and wrong producing defeat. The zealous solutions to defeat need to be explored and the psychic impact of unresolved defeat examined. After noting the disastrous consequences of refusing defeat, we shall draw upon the resources of Prophetic Realism to suggest creative alternatives.

## 1

The Song of Miriam summons the faithful community to break forth in ecstatic song, for Yahweh "has triumphed gloriously" (Ex. 15:21). Yahweh is viewed especially as the powerful warrior (Ex. 15:3), invincible in battle. Psalm 24 calls forth the liturgical question, "Who is the king of glory?" The answer is prescribed: "Yahweh, strong and mighty, Yahweh, mighty in battle!" This tradition developed into the highly stylized promises of victory which were announced before the battle in every instance of zealous warfare. The promises were stated in the past tense, as if the victory were already complete before the battle had opened:[4]

> And Yahweh said to Joshua, "See, I have given Jericho into your hand." (Josh. 6:2.)

> "Do not fear or be dismayed.... I have given the king of Ai into your hand." (Josh. 8:1.)

The Israelites who heard and believed such promises went into battle with "the perfect certainty of victory."[5] It was as certain as an event that had already occurred, and to doubt this was to doubt the power of Yahweh himself. The exhortation not to fear the enemy but to believe in Yahweh, so frequently connected with promises of victory in the early accounts of zealous warfare, may actually have been the earliest form of the Israelite faith.[6] And there is little doubt that it was an effective force in evoking the courage to face enemies who were often better armed and trained than the Israelite peasant volunteers.

From a rather early time in Biblical history this faith had to confront the uncomfortable fact that the victories did not always come as expected. There were defeats by desert tribes at the time of the invasion of Canaan as well as by the Philistines, which culminated in the loss of the Ark of the Covenant at the battle of Aphek, nearly shattering the tribal confederacy (I Sam., ch. 4). In the later period came defeat by the great empires and the ultimate destruction of Israel and Judah. Any one of these defeats could have led to the dissolution of faith in Yahweh as a triumphant God. What kept this from occurring was the development of the "Deuteronomic Principle" which linked Israel's virtue with victories and her sin with defeats.

In its classic form the "Deuteronomic philosophy of history, with its rhythm of righteousness-prosperity and wickedness-ruin"[7] offered a simple but harsh explanation of defeats. They were due to the wrath of God which was evoked by Israel's disobedience. The book of Deuteronomy has Moses exhort his people as follows: "But if you will not obey the voice of the Lord your God or be careful to do all his commandments . . . Yahweh will cause you to be defeated before your enemies" (Deut. 28:15, 25). The explication of this scheme forms an important part of the book of Deuteronomy; the aspects of the curse are matched at every point with the blessings of prosperity and victory for obedience (Deut. 28:1 to 32:52). The great national disasters as late as the time of Deuteronomy were interpreted as the result of disobedience. Inferior military resources, unwise leadership, or lack of preparedness were completely overlooked in this simple explanation of defeat. A sharply stereotyped view of history thus emerged. It was projected backward in the Deuteronomic History, written in the early period of the Babylonian captivity, so that the complex pattern of success and failure in the preceding six hundred years was explained by a simple formula (cf., e.g., Judg. 2:11-20).

The moral of this Deuteronomic Principle was to be good so as to be again triumphant. All Israel had to do, according to this principle, was to obey God's commandments, and "rest" from its enemies would automatically be given. Israel would earn unbroken peace and prosperity, and even enjoy a position of international supremacy. Thus Deut. 28:1 naively asserts: "If you obey the voice of Yahweh your God, being careful to do all his commandments which I command you this day, Yahweh your God will set you high above all the nations of the earth."

## 2

This Deuteronomic Principle gave distinctive shape to the American experience. John Winthrop stated while aboard the *Arabella* on the way to America in 1630 that if the settlers obeyed the covenant, God would grant them domestic peace, prosperity, victory over their enemies, and a status superior to all other nations. "Wee shall finde that the God of Israell is among us, when tenn of us shall be able to resist a thousand of our enemies, when hee shall make us a prayse and glory, that men shall say of succeeding plantacions: the Lord make it like that of New England: for we must Consider that wee shall be as a Citty upon a Hill, the eies of all people are uppon us." But Winthrop warned in the words of Deut., ch. 30, that if they turned away they would "surely perishe."[8]

This scheme lies at the heart of political sermons throughout American history. Nicholas Street preached on the Deuteronomic theme of "The American States Acting Over the Part of the Children of Israel in the Wilderness and Thereby Impeding Their Entrance Into Canaan's Rest" in 1777. The calamities the colonists were experiencing were due to God's wrath provoked by their sins. Peace would not be restored until they repented. The following excerpt from Street exhibits the Deuteronomic flavor:

> God has a righteous controversy with us in this land; and our iniquities have arrived to that aggravated height, that they have called for these sore calamities that we feel! And the British nation are the rod of God's anger to scourge and chastise us for sins.... Therefore let us be humble, kiss the rod and accept the punishment of our sins... that God may be intreated for the land, spare his heritage, and not give it up to a reproach but restore to us our liberties as at the first, and our privileges as at the beginning.[9]

At the conclusion of the Revolution, Ezra Stiles preached before the Connecticut General Assembly on the theme of "The United States Elevated to Glory and Honour." His text from Deut. 26:19 led him to claim that "God's American Israel" was being lifted by God "high above all nations." He linked the victorious outcome of the war with American virture and divine pleasure.[10] Samuel Langdon, in his Election Day sermon before the General Court at Concord, New Hampshire, in 1788, stated the same Deuteronomic theme very clearly. He challenged his hearers to adhere to the principles of the God-given Constitution. "By this you will increase in numbers, wealth, and power, and obtain reputation and dignity among the nations; whereas, the contrary conduct will make you poor, distressed, and contemptible."[11] He exhorted the new American nation: "RISE! RISE to fame among all nations, as a wise and understanding people! political life and death are set before you; be a free, numerous, well ordered, and happy people! The way has been plainly set before you; if you pursue it, your prosperity is sure; but if not, distress and ruin will overtake you."[12]

These sentiments came to popular expression during the War of 1812 in a poem by Francis Scott Key which quickly became a national favorite. "The Star-spangled Banner" stated the deuteronomic Principle in its third stanza, which claims the inevitable victory for those who trust in God. "Then conquer we must, when our cause it is just, And this be our motto: 'In God is our Trust.'"

The conditions for victory were precisely those of the book of Deuteronomy: the justice of the cause and the faithfulness of the people. Adverse power factors played no role, and the tragic reverses of history were overlooked. Even after the Civil War, when such dimensions should have been clearly visible, these Deuteronomic sentiments, rather than the tragic vision of Lincoln, prevailed in the victorious North. The Civil War monument in Des Moines, Iowa, expressed the thought in its essential form: "Right is right, since God is God. And right the day has won." The conviction was that the North won the war not because it was more powerful but because it was on the side of divine rightness.

This mythic belief played a decisive role in the *laissez faire* economic system, which became the arena for victory in the post-Civil War period. The conviction was that prosperity marked the reward for virtue, that no person in America would be in poverty unless he or she had done wrong. The famous Brooklyn preacher, Henry Ward Beecher, stated this clearly: "There may be reasons of poverty which do not involve wrong; but looking comprehensively through city and town and village and country, the general truth will stand, that no man in this land suffers from poverty unless it be more than his fault—unless it be his sin."[13] He put it another way in one of his sermons: "Nowhere else does wealth so directly point towards virtue in morality, and spirituality in religion, as in America."[14] The widely quoted sermon by Bishop William Lawrence on "The Relation of Wealth to Morals" states the same Deuteronomic point: "In the long run, it is only to the man of morality that wealth comes. . . . Put ten thousand immoral men to live and work in one fertile valley and ten thousand moral men to live and work in the next valley, and the question is soon answered as to who wins the material wealth. Godliness is in league with riches."[15] The Horatio Alger tales and the popular stories about the giants of industry were based on precisely the same principle. Success in the competitive economic system became the sign of divine favor tended to drop aside, but the premise of success as a sign of virtue remained.

On the basis of these adaptations of the Deuteronomic Principle, the popular American belief in its own superiority stands forth in mythic clarity. That America is the most prosperous nation on earth is proudly boasted, not because wealth has served to overcome inequities or eliminate human need, but because it proves our virtue. The statistics concerning American military and industrial power are proudly displayed in debates concerning the validity of current policies and attitudes; statistical superiority is taken to prove moral superiority. That America has never started or lost a war was a boast which every school child learned. Its appeal obviously is more mythic than historical. It is not based on a balanced appraisal of the causes and the outcome of the War of 1812, the complicity of the nation in provoking the Mexican War and the Indian Wars, or the degree of American responsibility for the sinking of the *Maine*, the torpedoing of the *Lusitania*, the vulnerability of the fleet at Pearl Harbor, or the incident in the Gulf of Tonkin. The appeal of the myth is so fundamental that disclosures of complicity in these instances do little to alter popular consciousness. If we believe we have never started a war, this confirms in our minds our virtuous lack of aggressiveness. And if we have never lost, this is clear Deuteronomic proof that "our cause it is just."

These flattering implications of the popular myth that we are "the number one nation of the world" are deeply threatened, however, if the nation should happen to lose or fall behind. It is not that such eventualities actually threaten the physical survival of the nation; rebuffs to client regimes, the loss of competitive superiority in some aspect of production, or defeat in some United Nations vote or in the race for gold medals at the Olympics cannot rationally be viewed as mortal threats. But they are psychic threats. They are fiercely resisted and bitterly resented by Americans because they threaten the mythic base of moral superiority.

There can be little argument that avoidance of such defeat became a primary goal in the dreadful Vietnam War. Long before 1968, when the hopes for a clear-cut American victory had been shattered by the Tet offensive, Pentagon analysts frankly admitted in a confidential memo that 70 percent of our aim in Vietnam was to avoid an embarrassing defeat.[16] It was clearly the primary goal in Nixon's secret plan for disengagement. As he stated in the January 24, 1973, message announcing the peace agreement, "Throughout the years of negotiations, we have insisted on peace with honor."[17] The content of such "honor" as spelled out in his earlier addresses was to retrieve our prisoners without admitting defeat, to ensure the preservation of our "allies" in South Vietnam, and to save face during the transition period by some form of international controls. The package was restated in the peace agreement message. "Now that we have achieved an honorable agreement let us be proud that America did not settle for a peace that would have betrayed our allies, that would have abandoned our prisoners of war or that would have ended the war for us, but would have continued the war for the 50 million people of Indochina."[18] To avoid the possibility of defeat during the withdrawal process was the stated purpose of the Laos invasion. To force the other side to acquiesce in a face-saving solution to keep such honor intact was the reason for the bombing and mining in North Vietnam which gradually evoked the revulsion of the civilized world. And if the twenty thousand additional servicemen, not to speak of several hundred thousand Vietnamese, who were killed during Nixon's first term died for any cause, it was precisely this kind of "honor." Their deaths were the price of forestalling defeat and thereby salvaging the image of our virtue.

In a penetrating article on the moral consequences of the war, Francine du Plessix Gray notes this dominant concern to maintain the image of American innocence. The "cornerstone" of the Nixon-Kissinger strategy, she writes, "was the obscene rationale of the 'decent interval': the United States must choreograph its eventual departure from Vietnam—thousands of lives lost in the process—in such a way that it does not *appear* to abandon the Saigon regime, thus absolving us of guilt in the tragedy. This search for a false and abstract purity has been but a new modulation of our traditional obsession with American innocence. It is based on myths of moral perfection as theologically antiquated as they are symbolically false."[19]

It should be noted, however, that Kissinger was apparently much more willing to settle for the modest interval between American withdrawal and the inevitable South Vietnamese collapse than was Nixon himself. This became apparent in the fate of the first draft of the peace agreement which was not signed as scheduled in October 1972. It contained unequivocal references to the territorial integrity of Vietnam and to the complete cessation of American aid to the current South Vietnamese government. There were ambiquities in wording which allowed the impression that the interim "Council on National Reconciliation and Concord" would be a coalition government which would replace the current regime in the south. The President rejected this draft because, according to Richard Wilson, it would link him with defeat in the eyes of history.[20] Dana Adams Schmidt, of *The Christian Science Monitor*, expressed this reasoning: "In the President's larger view of affairs, the danger loomed that in five or ten years, people would be asking; 'Who lost South Vietnam?' much as they once asked 'Who lost China?' "[21] When the

North Vietnamese refused the subsequent new demands to recognize the sovereignty of the current South Vietnamese government, and upped their own conditions in return, the President retaliated with the Christmas bombing of the North Vietnamese cities. This brutal act of mass terror was so clearly linked with the petulant quest for "honor" that even previously pro-American newspapers such as *Die Welt* concluded that we could no longer claim to be fighting for freedom and democracy in Vietnam.

The final terms of the peace agreement, after the horrible pressure of the leveling of approximately 20 percent of Hanoi's residential areas, differed somewhat from the October draft.[22] It was in effect a cease-fire agreement, not a real peace treaty, as President Thieu quickly pointed out. With the massive infusion of arms between October and January, and the retention of American airpower, the President made it plain that defeat should continue to be forestalled. A bleak period of continued strife was in prospect, despite the rhetoric of "a lasting peace." As long as current attitudes prevail, it will be the determination to preserve our "honor" which will guarantee that the tragic conflict and others like it will continue.

The theological implications of this current version of the Deuteronomic Principle are thoroughly idolatrous. That victory for one side or the other may reveal the justice and the power of God is a matter which may be glimpsed at times, but only "in a glass darkly," with the eyes of faith. To claim that such justice is unequivocally visible in the victory of any nation is to lose the sense of the transcendent. And to claim it for one's own nation, with an aim of proving one's selflessness, is nothing short of idolatrous. It places the honor of self or nation in the position of ultimate significance. Whenever this occurs, a terrible distortion in perception follows. Having lost its due sense of finite worth, a nation embarks on campaigns to sustain its presumed infinite superiority, utilizing means that are the very antithesis of the virtues it seeks to defend. It refuses to admit such realities, because to do so would threaten the graven image of perfect virtue and good intentions. Since the idolatrous center of such a system is so fragile, it calls for a defense in every theater of competition. The sense of proportion disappears as the nation squanders its energies against specters on every hand. Every battlefield, no matter how dubious, is pronounced holy. And every victory, no matter how bloodily bought, is thought to confirm the rightness of the cause. This chain of illusions is particularly taut in a secular area in which a vital sense of transcendence has been lost and the perennial threat of *hubris* has been forgotten. In such an era the Deuteronomic Principle can transform the nation into a terrifying Moloch, the idol whose insatiable appetite is for the blood of its own and its enemies' children. It is then that the God of history, whose righteous purposes cannot be thwarted by human pride, calls forth the hammer of adversity to shatter the clay-footed idol.

## 3

When defeat threatens a zealous nation, it is rare that any element of divine justice is discerned. To admit the hammer blows are deserved is to give up the idolatrous view of one's own virtue, as long as the Deuteronomic Principle is intact. So one resorts to mythic solutions to adversity.

The first of these is the *betrayal theory*. If defeat has come to a righteous nation, it must be due to evil conspirators. Someone must have betrayed the cause, thus thwarting the natural rhythm in which goodness brings victory and sin brings defeat. All one has to do is find the traitors, eliminate the obstruction, and victory will once more be assured. The solution is deceptively simple.

This is the initial reaction pattern of any nation that believes in the conspiracy theory of evil. One of the most striking examples is the "stab in the back" idea which emerged in Germany in 1918. A Lutheran clergyman was supposedly the first to formulate the conviction that the German armies had been thwarted by traitors in the homeland. Hindenburg's testimony on the responsibility for the outbreak and length of the war in November 1919 placed the blame on civilian leaders who attempted to negotiate peace while the war was still on: "The German Army was stabbed in the back."[23] This line was used to masterful advantage in the Nazi propaganda which destroyed the Weimar Republic.

The betrayal theory emerged on the center stage of American politics the moment the frustration of the cold war was felt. D. W. Brogan cited this reaction in his 1952 article entitled "The Illusion of American Omnipotence." Since Americans felt that their virtue assured them of victory in any circumstances, frustration of that victory was taken as a sign that betrayal had occurred. The conviction was that "any situation which distresses or endangers the United States can only exist because some Americans have been fools or knaves."[24] The traitors in this case were thought to be Communists and their sympathizers within the government itself. Such men must have been responsible for the Yalta agreements, the Russian domination of Eastern Europe, and the chaotic decline of Nationalistic

China after 1945.

One of the first politicians to seize on this possibility was Richard Nixon. In the 1946 California Congressional campaign he charged the Democratic incumbent, Jerry Voorhis, with being a tool of the Communist labor movement. Nixon's slogans featured the line, "A vote for Nixon is a Vote Against the Communist-dominated PAC" [Political Action Committee of the C.I.O.].[25] The times were such that his opponent, who had long been an energetic foe of Communism, was shattered.[26] The same strategy was employed to defeat Congresswoman Helen Gahagan Douglas in the 1950 California Senatorial race. Although "she was actually a vigorous foe of the Communist Party," to use the words of Nixon's biographer Earl Mazo,[27] her political career was destroyed by the betrayal charge. Nixon suggested that her record in Congress "discloses the truth about her soft attitude toward Communism" and hinted that "if she had had her way, the Communist conspiracy in the United States would never have been exposed. . . . It just so happens that my opponent is a member of a small clique which joins the notorious Communist party-liner, Vito Marcantonio of New York, in voting time after time against measures that are for the security of this country."[28] Mrs. Douglas retorted that Nixon had voted with Marcantonio on such issues as aid to Korea. But Nixon's role in having exposed Alger Hiss rendered him invulnerable to such a charge.

The political adaptation of the betrayal theory has since been refined, with underlings increasingly carrying out the business of formulating accusations of betrayal. But the basic strategy remains the same. At times of national frustration and defeat, the desire of a zealous public to destroy scapegoats is shrewdly channeled into the political process. The technique is to combine traditional statements about American virtue and invincibility with the suggestion that the elimination of one's opponent will remove the only impediment to America's triumph. This tactic is much more appealing to a morally fastidious public than the old-fashioned form of elimination which a Phinehas, a John Brown, or a Lee Harvey Oswald could provide. Hatred and self-righteousness are channeled into the voting booth rather than into the rifle barrel. A "generation of peace" is offered on the sole condition that the opposition candidate, whose ideas would presumably betray the essential American dream, be destroyed at the polls. A discussion of the issues, one is solemnly assured, need not take place, for the single "overriding" issue is "peace with honor and never peace with surrender."[29] The difficulty is that the betrayal theory works much better in the polling booth than in the arena of international conflict. That the majority of the American voters can be induced to vote against an ostensible traitor to the national dream is no proof of the validity of this myth.

The second solution is the Deuteronomic form of *repentance*. Although this is less primitive than the scapegoat idea, it is as old as American nationalism itself. Its premise is visible from John Winthrop's admonitions down through the latest political sermons: that the sin of the chosen people is the cause of any dilemma it might presently face. As one looks at our political sermons, whether sacred or secular, the curiously reactionary stamp of the book of Deuteronomy makes itself felt. Repentance is seen as a turning backward to recover former values. And the call to return is accompanied by glowing promises of the elimination of defeat and humiliation. This form of repentance, in contrast to the radical kind of self-examination and sharpened moral responsibility demanded by the great prophets, lends itself very nicely to political rhetoric. The promise of restoration of victory and honor is flattering to the fragile sense of national superiority. And the recovery of spiritual values is placed on so abstract a level that the actual misdeeds of the nation do not have to be admitted. As in the book of Deuteronomy, one confesses cultic sins and spiritual faults in lieu of admitting actual historical transgressions.

This Deuteronomic form of repentance is implicit in the frequent references to "spiritual" factors in political rhetoric. It played a key role in Eisenhower's first inaugural address, which set forth the "laws of spiritual strength that generate and define our material strength."[30] In the face of the frustrations and perils that confronted the nation in 1953, he called for a renewal of faith in the principles of democratic decency as well as "a conscious renewal of faith in our country and in the watchfulness of a Divine Providence."[31] The Deuteronomic rationale of this kind of rhetoric was stated very concisely by Dulles: "The sum of the whole matter is this, that our civilization cannot survive materially unless it be redeemed spiritually."[32] The great material power of America was being frustrated, not because of an atomic stalemate and the rivalry of superpowers, but because America was not adhering to her spiritual principles. If she regained her hold on those principles, she would surely prevail against Communism.

The resurgence of religiosity in the '50s reflected this "spiritual" form of repentance. It was inspired by Eisenhower's "private prayer" which opened his inaugural address, by the White House prayer breakfast which he initiated, and by the close liaison he developed with leading clergymen such as Billy Graham and Norman Vincent Peale. The pledge of allegiance to the flag was changed in 1954 after the President heard a sermon by Rev. George M. Docherty on the nation "under God." Declarations of faith, both private and public, were viewed as the forms of repentance which would guarantee victory in the cold war. In thoroughly Deuteronomic fashion, frequent religious ceremony was the means whereby God's favor would be assured and the frustration of foreign threats removed. As Eisenhower stated in 1953: "The churches of America are citadels of our faith in individual freedom and human dignity. This faith is the living source of all our spiritual strength. And this strength is our matchless armor in our world-wide struggle against the forces of Godless tyranny and oppression."[33] Leading clergymen such as Edward L. R. Elson dedicated their books of sermons on "America's spiritual recovery" to the President, "who by personal example and public utterance is giving testimony to the reality of America's spiritual foundations."[34]

This "spiritual" form of repentance was what President Nixon called for in his first inaugural address, in a line that was framed in numerous pious living rooms and offices throughout America: "To a crisis of the spirit, we need an answer of the spirit."[35] The content of this answer is essentially that of Nixon's predecessors back to the book of Deuteronomy. The subsequent lines in the Inaugural spelled out the source: "And to find that answer, we need only to look within ourselves. When we listen to the 'better angels of our nature,' we find that they celebrate the simple things, the basic things—such as goodness, decency, love, kindness." The concrete application of this answer a few lines later was "to lower our voices . . . stop shouting at one another"—an obvious criticism of the vociferous protests that had so unsettled the country. The social evils that had provoked them were not to be confronted and overcome; instead, we were to return to the very ideals that had produced them, and the evils presumably would melt away. No change of the national motivations and policies was necessary. "I know America. I know the heart of America is good."

The application of this concept to the threatened defeat in Vietnam was spelled out in the November 3, 1969, speech to the "great silent majority" which retained the Deuteronomic ideals. Vietnamization was offered as a way to avert defeat and keep all the traditional ideals intact. The exhortation was to return to the great principles and hold to them with tenacity.

> Our greatness as a nation has been our capacity to do what had to be done when we knew our course was right. . . .
>
> I know it may not be fashionable to speak of patriotism or national destiny these days. But I feel it is appropriate to do so on this occasion. . . . The wheel of destiny has turned so that any hope the world has for the survival of peace and freedom will be determined by whether the American people have the moral stamina and the courage to meet the challenge of free world leadership.
>
> Let historians not record that when America was the most powerful nation in the world we passed on the other side of the road and allowed the last hopes for peace and freedom of millions of people to be suffocated by the forces of totalitarianism. . . .
>
> Let us be united for peace. Let us also be united against defeat. Because let us understand: North Vietnam cannot defeat or humiliate the United States. Only Americans can do that.[36]

Defeat is possible, in short, only if America lacks "the moral stamina and the courage" to hold to the zealous values. Those who protest should repent and become "united" with the silent majority. The solution is internal, a matter of holding the prescribed values and acting on them. External circumstances do not count. That is why the effectiveness of this peculiar form of repentance is pictured in such grandiose terms. The factors hindering "peace and freedom" throughout the world are thought to be entirely subject to the direct application of American resolve. Our strength is presumably such that only one question remains: whether the chosen nation will have enough stamina to apply it.

What this appeal overlooked was that the new weapons of Vietnamization would not suffice to transform a corrupt and dictatorial Saigon regime into a model of democratic justice, capable of attracting popular support. Something much more than American resolve was required, especially when that resolve was guided more by the desire to sustain our own virtue than to advance the cause of representative government. These fundamental considerations were set aside, however, as the public responded in overwhelming support of this mythic appeal. Richard Wilson concluded, "No more effective single speech ever was made by a President, certainly in this century." It disoriented and isolated the Moratorium movement, "muted" Congressional dissent, and "won more time for the Vietnamization of the war."[37]

While this Deuteronomic form of repentance has potent capacities for manipulating a zealous public, it should never be mistaken for true repentance. It is vastly different from the repentance to which the great prophets called their people. It turns a nation backward to the old idolatries, to the very beliefs and actions that defeat is demonstrating to be false. It confirms the overblown view of our virtue. And thus it impedes a realistic appraisal of the evils we have wrought, the actual possibilities of our situation, or the transcendent justice of God. True repentance is not turning backward in time, but turning back from one's bondage to time. It is a turning away from the destructive idols of yesterday's religion, and at the same time a turning toward the God of history whose justice stands always before us.

So long as these zealous solutions to defeat are relied upon, the reality of our situation remains disguised. But defeat cannot thereby be averted, no matter how attractive these inappropriate forms of power may seem. It is merely postponed a bit and rendered more corrosive in its coming.

## 4

The corrosion of defeat may be traced in the history of any zealous nation. It is most destructive when the defeat is not honestly and directly confronted. If leaders explain defeat away, laying the blame on scapegoats or demanding reactionary forms of repentance, it will gradually consume the ideal of a servant nation. It will hollow out even the most precious forms of civil religion. And if circumstances permit, it can provide the atmosphere in which reactionary and self-destructive revivals can occur.

This process is visible in archetypal form in Israel's experience after the Deuteronomic reform of 621 B.C. Soon after King Josiah had inaugurated a nationalistic revival, he was killed in battle. He was attempting to thwart the Egyptian expeditionary force moving through Israelite territory in order to intervene in a power struggle in the fertile crescent. The exemplary Yahwist king and his small but holy army anticipated triumph over the wicked Pharaoh and his invaders. Had not Deuteronomy given assurances in such a case? "When you go forth to war against your enemies, and see horses and chariots and an army larger than your own, you shall not be afraid of them; for Yahweh your God is with you . . . to give you the victory." (Deut. 20:1, 4) But Josiah was killed by a stray arrow, seemingly directed by destiny because the king was disguised and could not have been picked out by the archers. Martin Buber noted that this shattering defeat was "a most important incision in Israelite religious history. The question 'Why?' presses upon all hearts. Why has the king, who unlike his predecessors did Yahweh's will in everything, been snatched away in the prime of his life and in the midst of his plans for the realization of God's word, at the hour when he went forth undismayed, trusting in God's word (Deut. 20:1), to fight the superior force?" The theological implications were that the "ready teaching about reward and punishment in the life of the individual and community is shaken. This deity is no more to be formulated.... He has become an enigma."[38]

Nevertheless, Israelite leaders clung ever more fiercely to the zealous dogma. Past traitors and former sins were deemed responsible for the reversal.[39] A dozen years later Israel suffered shattering defeat at the hands of the Babylonians. Within yet another decade the Israelites opened a suicidal war against their overlords, and Jerusalem was leveled. A handful of fanatics later assassinated the Babylonian governor. When Yahweh failed to destroy the Babylonian relief columns, the Israelite remnant fled to Egypt. Jeremiah assured Israel of Babylonian amnesty (Jer. 42:7-22), but the leaders left the "promised land" and the dream of restoring its destiny. With the civil religion discredited by defeat, perceptive and skeptical minds had sought solace in nihilism and occultism, such as the worship of the "queen of heaven," a degenerate deity popularized during the dark ages of Assyrian domination (Jer., ch. 44). A fatal decline of moral integrity, public spirit, and common sense had ensued, diminishing Israel's capacity to survive. Only a structure thoroughly rotted from within could have crumbled like that.

The irony of our situation at the end of the Vietnam War was that the convulsive efforts to avoid defeat lest our morale be broken actually led to this same sort of inner corrosion. President Nixon often stated his fear of what defeat in Vietnam would do. "Our allies would lose confidence in America. Far more dangerous, we would lose confidence in ourselves. . . . Inevitable remorse and divisive recrimination would scar our spirit as a people."[40]

What the nation little suspected, perhaps, was that the very effort to achieve such goals produced the fatal corrosion. Our self-confidence is doomed as long as it is linked to the achievement of incredible results, such as producing a democratic society by taking the reactionary side in a local power struggle or by ensuring peace for the entire world by continuing the most destructive bombing raids in history. Even if we were to succeed in these unlikely enterprises, the faith thereby sustained would be an empty mockery of our religious heritage. Its boast of total unselfishness is as far as one can possibly depart from the spirit of true religion which admits realistically,

"No one is good except God alone" (Luke 18:19). Any nation that attempts to sustain such illusions about itself has already become demonic. Its actions will be so rash and destructive that the national virtue thereby affirmed is already a grotesque caricature of the good.

Since no nation can succeed in transcending its finite limitations, this illusory kind of confidence is bound to crumble. As it does, efforts to reconstruct the shattered self-idolatries become more and more frantic, and more and more violent. That such efforts could evoke the "confidence" of allies or encourage trust in democratic "self-determination" elsewhere in the world, is preposterous. Only a public that is prepared to face reality, about both its finite virtue and its limited capabilities, can elicit the respect of world opinion. And the finite variety of self-confidence is the only kind that can survive under the pressure of history.

When the national destiny and religious heritage are linked to such an effort to shore up weakened self-confidence, the collapse is all the more destructive when it comes. The idealistic aspects of the civil religion are the first to go down in the wreckage. To support this idolatrous effort, as Billy Graham, Norman Vincent Peale, and other clergymen have done,[41] is to prepare the way for the kind of religious and moral skepticism that generations of zealous warfare have produced in Christian Europe. It is to strengthen the forces that seek to replace the definition of national destiny as democratic servanthood with doctrines of pure national self-interest. When the degenerative process is complete, all that is likely to be left is "every man save himself." As our recent diplomacy illustrates, this is already the dominant line in our negotiations with Japan, Europe, and Latin America. The noble traditions of disinterested and fair-minded diplomacy, which received such approbation during the time of the Marshall Plan, is now passé, but a public deluded by idolatrous visions of being "totally unselfish" does not even mark its passing.

Above all, the sense of national or personal significance is jeopardized as it is linked with the doomed Deuteronomic dogma. If the life of the community and the individual have meaning only in victory, defeat thrusts it into the abyss of meaninglessness. This lies behind the oft-stated argument that if we were to lose the war, all those who died therein would have died in vain. Between an idolatrous significance predicated on victory and the complete lack of any significance whatsoever there is no middle ground, no basis for a healthy, finite, and resilient sense of meaning. The fact that meaning is always fragmentary, shot through with the tragic stuff of personal and national folly, yet somehow visible in the mysterious purposes of divine righteousness—the key thesis of Lincoln's Gettysburg Address and his second inaugural address—is frosted over by zealous dogma. A people nurtured on this dogma will allow the most atrocious acts to be committed in its name, so long as they promise to hold off defeat a while longer. The psychic conviction is that to submit to the blow is to give up the most precious of all possessions: the sense of meaning. But what significance remains when defeat finally is ineluctable? None whatever! National and personal nihilism are the results.

Yet no matter how frantically a nation twists and contorts to avoid the pain, the blow of defeat comes ever and again. No nation, including the most powerful on earth, can avoid it indefinitely. Although it may be particularly humiliating to experience the reversal at the hands of a small and primitive nation like North Vietnam, whose major resources are its wits and its stamina, the proper question is not how to avoid it, but how to respond to it creatively.

## 5

Perhaps the most promising approach would be to appropriate the tragic yet realistic heritage of our great prophets, writers, and artists. They who have explored the depths of the human situation, who have experienced the shattering of their dearest idols and the bitterness of defeat, offer us the resources we need. For unlike the situation of victory which leaves the self complacently anchored in its certainties, our present crisis calls us to radical transformation. We have to learn not only to live without our former idols but to take modest steps toward the construction of a healthier culture. No one can do this for us; the agony of death and rebirth must be suffered by each of us. But we cannot hope to undergo this alone, enacting the isolated destiny of lonely martyrs while the public remains unchanged. We must undertake the process as a culture.

The essential starting point is to get the message of defeat straight. This requires a break with the idolatrous and morally evasive forms of the Deuteronomic dogma. We see this in the incident in which Jesus was asked to comment on the implications of Pilate's recent massacre of suspected insurrectionists and on the construction accident at the tower of Siloam (Luke 13:1-5).[42] The Deuteronomic message regarding both of these incidents was that the victims must have sinned to deserve their fate and thus that one should continue to applaud the business of killing culprits who offend divine justice.

Such explanations would allow the self to retain its assumed innocence and cling to the vicious dogmas that were catapulting the nation into a catastrophic war with Rome. The larger message was that the Deuteronomic dogmas were being refuted by current history, and that to continue to follow them in the zealot uprisings against Rome would lead to national suicide. To follow Jesus' admonition—"Unless you repent you will all likewise perish" (Luke 13:5)—would be to turn away from the dogmas and their political enactment. It would be to turn toward the kingdom of God, which accepts enemies unconditionally and calls them into the tasks of reconciliation.

This is precisely the call we must hear today. For the current interpretations of our crisis, with the typical setting of blame and the naive resolve that we will "never make a mistake like Vietnam again," simply lock us into the very complacent dogmas which got us there in the first place. They confirm in us the conviction that we are the innocent in a world in which the guilty should be bombed. What is required of us, both as a nation and as individuals, is to repent of these fatuous beliefs. If we refuse to repent, we shall destroy ourselves by acting out the Deuteronomic scenario till the end. That is the clear message of the defeats of the Galilean insurrectionists and of the American crusaders in Vietnam. What is required is the sort of fundamental shift that Abraham Lincoln called for in his time: "The dogmas of the quiet past are inadequate to the stormy present. The occasion is piled high with difficulty, and we must rise with the occasion. As our case is new, so we must think anew and act anew. We must disenthrall ourselves, and then we shall save our country."[43]

To "disenthrall ourselves" from Deuteronomic dogmas brings us face to face with our finitude, both national and personal. It is to admit that we have not been innocent lambs in a wicked world, that our violent crusades have sometimes been misguided, and that we do not have sole accesss to the wisdom about what other nations should do. It offers us access to the pragmatic wisdom of the Bible, whose premise is: "Be not wise in your own eyes; fear Yahweh, and turn away from evil" (Prov. 3:7). To acknowledge this is to follow also the admonition of the Delphic oracle which underlies so much of Greek philosophy and drama: "Know thyself—that thou art but a mortal."

If we made this discovery for ourselves and our nation, the deepest meaning of the cross might also be accessible. One of the contributing factors in our culture's blindness to tragedy has been the superficial grasp of the theology of the cross by our dominant Protestant tradition. The Christ event is interpreted under the rubric of the resurrection as a sign of triumph and immortality. That the tragic death of Christ is virtually inexplicable may be seen by dropping into some half-empty Protestant sanctuary to hear the fumbling Good Friday meditations. Contrast that with the self-assured mood in the same sanctuary jammed with the Easter morning crowd. This too must change if we are to lead our people to confront defeat. What American ministers need today is Paul's theology of the cross, with its grasp of the tragedy of life, its forthright acceptance of human weakness, and its bulwarks against human pride. We need to hear the message of a man who lived with defeat throughout his ministry, and who confessed he had received this answer to his yearning to be released from the discomfiture of his "thorn in the flesh": "The Lord . . . said to me, 'My grace is sufficient for you, for my power is made perfect in weakness.' I will all the more gladly boast of my weaknesses, that the power of Christ may rest upon me. For the sake of Christ, then, I am content with weaknesses, insults, hardships, persecutions, and calamities; for when I am weak, then I am strong" (II Cor. 12:8-10).

Here is a faith that confronts defeat with courage. It provides a proper humility without the self-pity that marks the "humiliation" we are striving so desperately to avoid. It faces squarely the realities of our human situation and lives creatively out of the power of God. We need preachers today who will proclaim such a faith, messengers who will interpret the good news in such a way as to face our humiliation and defeat, rather than disguise it with platitudes. We need forthright men and women who will resolve today to "preach the gospel" as Paul did in Corinth, but "not with eloquent wisdom, lest the cross of Christ be emptied of its power" (I Cor. 1:17).

In the last analysis, to admit defeat should be to acknowledge the transcendent justice of God. To admit defeat should mean to have discovered that the justice which we have striven to accomplish in Vietnam since 1954 is not identical with divine justice, and indeed has been repudiated by it. For the healthy way to face a defeat of the Deuteronomic dogma is to discard the idolatry while retaining the sense of divine justice which works its mysterious way throughout history. If we fall prey to the logic of the dogma and continue to identify divine justice with our own, defeat will shatter our moral sense and thrust us into skepticism or nihilism. We must grasp the prophetic insight that adversity is the discipline of sonship, and that defeat is a sign not of divine rejection but of suffering love (Hos., ch.

11; Heb., ch. 12). Our sense of having been chosen as a nation must be refined and purified in the "furnace of affliction" (Isa. 48:10) before we can begin to take up our rightful task of being a light to the nations and a servant of justice.

These prophetic resources of tragic vision must be adapted into the popular idiom if our culture is to be transformed. From the comic books to the television programs, vivid images of realism and courage must be developed. The powerful vehicles of rock and country and western music need to be used to present the deeper dimensions of our human situation. Those who deal in mythic and symbolic forms of communication must take a particular responsibility at this point, Writers and educators whose task it is to communicate our cultural legacy have a similar calling, as do parents and youth workers.

Our communities and our organizations must begin to carry out this task, knowing full well that in a democratic society our destiny is shaped as much by our neighbor's outlook as by our own. Our local governments must take up the cultural task of preparing us for life amid defeat. The publicly supported theaters which present the great tragedies are now essential to our survival. The opera houses and recital halls which offer the possibility of creative but tragic catharsis are not luxuries we can allow to be reserved for the wealthy, but maturing institutions which our citizens need for weathering the crisis which will not disappear. No longer can we allow our children to be educated on the shallow assumption that there is no importance in the past, and that there are no languages and cultures besides our own which are worthy of mastery. For to master the language and artistic heritage of others is to gain a sense of solidarity with humankind: that tragedy-prone, irrational, but noble species to which we Americans must finally discover we belong.

We must, in short, begin to develop a tragic sense of life if we are to cope with tragedy. We must take up the sort if instruction Herman Melville yearned for in his prose supplement to *Battle-Pieces and Aspects of the War*, poems published after the Civil War. "Let us pray that the terrible historical tragedy of our time may not have been enacted without instructing our whole beloved country through pity and terror."[44] What this means in our current crisis is yet to be worked out, but no one can experience the pity and the terror for us. Following the path of those who have experienced humiliation and defeat before us, we must adapt their insights for ourselves. The task is clearly there to be accomplished, but who will take it up?

We need thinkers who will work out the current implications of

Hosea's vision that in the defeat of Israel lay both the wrath and the love of God. As Bernhard Anderson put it: "To us, the 'wrath' and the 'love' of God may seem contradictory, but to Hosea God's love surpasses human understanding. It has both the dark side of judgment and the promise of hope and renewal (see Hosea 11:10-11). Israel would learn, as did the poet Francis Thompson, that her gloom after all was but 'the shadow of His Hand outstretched caressingly.' "[45]

We need novelists and composers who will portray for us in secular terms what Isaiah meant when he sensed Yahweh's word about Israel after its catastrophic defeat. "Behold, I have refined you, but not like silver; I have tried you in the furnace of affliction." (Isa. 48:10.) That tragedy can refine, rather than destroy; that it can burn out the impurities of illusion and pride—such profound possibilities must be translated for us into images with which we can identify and into structures conducive to our transformation.

We need playwrights, actors, and actresses who will create for us dramas like Job, taking up that poet's courageous stand against the destructive dogmas of his day, and celebrating that moment of dialogue when the Eternal breaks through and speaks to persons caught on top of the dung heap. It is crucial for our cultural health to experience the creative, though completely secular, impulse that Archibald MacLeish caught in the climax of *J.B.*, as the wife places the chair back on its legs and begins the process of putting things back together again. To experience such a play, powerfully performed, is to discover that to be fully human is to undergo tragedy and move beyond it in faith.

The most powerful means of catharsis is not in the theater, however, nor on the psychiatrist's couch, but in the prophetic interpretation of current experience. Jeremiah was a pioneer in this regard. He saw the defeats of his time as divinely ordained means to bring the nation back to reality. He insisted upon the recognition of personal responsibility, not just by the leaders but by the entire public. For only as the tragedy touched the individual so as to transform the twisted heart could it produce rebirth rather than annihilation. No evasion of responsibility was possible with an oracle like this:

> Your ways and your doings
> have brought this upon you.
> This is your doom, and it is bitter;
> it has reached your very heart.
>
> (Jer. 4:18.)

We need interpreters who will take up this forthright style of commentary on our current events. We need reporters and historians who will take up the task of holding us to our responsibilities for the tragedy now unfolding, and who will do so in such a way that it reaches the center of motivation and action which for Jeremiah was the "heart." We need teachers and parents who will take up such a diagnosis for themselves, then adapt it for those in their charge.

Our current dilemma is a time of judgment, of opportunity, and of decision. The judgment has already fallen on our mistaken version of Deuteronomic justice. The opportunity to be transformed by defeat lies open before us. So the decision must fall as to which path we shall follow. The way into the pit is the path of Zealous Nationalism. Its end has already been determined if we remain enthralled by the dogmas of our past. The alternative is the hard, narrow path of realism. This is the path of which the prophets have spoken, the one which leads directly through the fields of adversity and the slough of despair.

# THE FUTURE

# 10
# THE HOPE OF REALISM

The realist expects the unexpected. He never believes that the application of past solutions will bring him security. He avoids illusions such as that the world can be made safe for his ideals or that winning one more war will guarantee a generation of peace. Unlike the myth-bound zealot, he is never certain ahead of time that the cause of disorder is demonic, that his adversaries are irredeemable or always corrupt enough to have their price, that violence in his own hands is always redemptive, or that the defeat of his own interests will necessarily be unjust or even disadvantageous in the long run. Thus his responses to crises cannot be charted on mythic maps. He experiences the creative freedom which derives from a fresh assessment of the evidence and is stimulated by a vision of transcendent justice. His aim is more modest than the zealot's: not to eliminate the crisis but to advance gradually through it toward the goal which he acknowledges he may never reach.

Whereas Zealous Nationalism is dominated by the past, Prophetic Realism is marked by the pull of the future. In Lincoln's political ethic, for example, the vision was the gradual approximation of the principle in the Declaration of Independence that "all men are created equal." In the debates with Douglas in 1858 Lincoln insisted that the Founding Fathers had been fully aware that equality was not yet a reality and could not quickly be achieved. "They meant to set up a standard maxim for free society, which should be familiar to all, and revered by all; constantly looked to, constantly labored for, and even though never perfectly attained, constantly approximated, and thereby constantly spreading and deepening its influence and augmenting the happiness and value of life to all men of all colors everywhere."[1] It was the recognition that this vision would never be fully achieved which kept Lincoln from becoming a fanatic. Yet it was the retention of the vision which kept him from being merely a political opportunist.

We must begin therefore by sketching out a vision toward which the nation might strive, weaving it out of the warp of traditional American ideals and the woof of Isaiah's dream of the role of government in ushering in the age of coexistence. It is not an alien vision, though it is vastly different from the one we have recently been following. It lies buried in one half of our nation's divided heart, obscured by its long fusion with an incompatible counterpart. And though it can be seen only dimly, it is submitted here in the hope that others may go on to grasp it more fully.

## 1

Isaiah composed his oracles concerning the ideal government at the time of the accession of King Hezekiah in 715 B.C.[2] Although Isa. 9:2-7 and ch. 11:1-9 were later interpreted as predictions of Christ, it is clear that their original purpose was to provide healthy goals for the new regime at a time when government had gone drastically off its track. The fact that the young king did not accept these goals, choosing instead a revival of militarism, which led to disaster, serves only to accentuate their power and wisdom. Spanning the centuries, their content is amazingly close to the healthy traditions of American nationalism:

> The people who walked in darkness
> have seen a great light;
> those who dwelt in a land of deep darkness,
> on them has light shined.
> Thou hast multiplied the nation,
> thou hast increased its joy;
> They rejoice before thee
> as with joy at the harvest,
> as men rejoice when they divide the spoil.
> For the yoke of his burden,
> and the staff for his shoulder,
> the rod of his oppressor,
> thou hast broken as on the day of Midian.
> (Isa. 9:2-4.)

Joyous anticipation is linked here to a government which takes up the task of liberation. To set people free from the "oppressor" implies the release not only from foreign exploitation but also from social subordination. It is the same vital purpose which is stated in the Declaration of Independence: the achievement of equality, life, liberty, and the pursuit of happiness. The motif has been characteristic of American nationalism and was clearly stated in the Four Freedoms declaration prior to World War II. But the striking thing is that this task is not to be accomplished by foreign crusades, as in the popular Israelite and American traditions. The prophet explicitly repudiates the militarization of government in the very next lines:

For every boot of the tramping warrior in battle tumult
and every garment rolled in blood
will be burned as fuel for the fire.
(Isa. 9:5.)

It is not just the enemy boots and tunics which are to be burned, but "every" relic of military glory! This strikes at the heart of the fallacy in our national ideology: that human liberation is achieved through death in selfless crusades.

The alternative method is stated in the companion oracle depicting the ideal ruler:

He shall not judge by what his eyes see,
or decide by what his ears hear,
but with righteousness he shall judge the poor,
and decide with equity for the meek of the earth;
and he shall smite the earth [or the "bully"][3]
with the rod of his mouth,
and with the breath of his lips he shall slay the wicked.
Righteousness shall be the girdle of his waist,
and faithfulness the girdle of his loins.
(Isa. 11:3-5.)

The "poor" and the "meek" are to be liberated by equity in the courts and by equal access to material advantages. The government has the unique task of providing justice for those who cannot fend entirely for themselves, and this means contending against exploitation not on the battlefield but in the enforcement of law. "Righteousness" in judgment and "equity" before the law are the means by which this must take place. They are the very antithesis of the qualities Zealous Nationalism engenders: stereotyping of the poor, illusions about the virtues of the rich, and scorn for due process of law. Impartiality in the sense of not judging by external appearances must be linked with compassion for the oppressed if true liberation is to occur. This method of approximating the goal of equality is worlds apart from government for the sake of wealthy interest groups, with its benign neglect of those who experience partial justice in every sphere because of their color, class background, or level of educational development. Ask them what they desire most "as with joy in the harvest" and the answer will be, "We demand the equal chance we have never had!"

## 2

The implications of Prophetic Realism are not just national in scope. The passion for justice includes the poor of other nations as well: the "meek" of the *earth,"* not just of Israel or America. The ruthless exploitation of lesser nations by the industrial powers of our time is a clear violation of this ideal. It creates smoldering resentment and disorder, which cost far more in the long run than would equity itself. The essence of impartiality in Isaiah's sense as well as in our own tradition that "*all* men are created equal" is its indivisibility. We are inhabitants of the one Spaceship Earth, to use Barbara Ward's expression, and our compassion must transcend national boundaries if we are to survive. To translate this into effective measures, however, requires impartial law with force behind it. Isaiah was much more realistic at this point than many modern idealists in his insistence that judgment of the ruler's "mouth" and "breath" must have the power to "smite" and even to "slay" oppressors. He recognized that law without enforcement loses its majesty and its capacity to coerce by consent. Our experience with the ineffective resolutions against aggression by the League of Nations confirms his wisdom. And it should not be forgotten that the power of government to coerce compliance with law is an essential component of our Constitutional system. What must be clarified is the distinction between the minimal violence controlled by law which acts in behalf of impartial justice and the crusading violence which shatters restraints in behalf of some biased vision. When Isaiah's ideal ruler has to "smite," it is by his lips in the courtroom and not by his hands on some foreign battlefield.

The results of such firm justice are depicted in the closing lines of Isaiah's magnificent vision:

> The wolf shall dwell with the lamb,
>   and the leopard shall lie down with the kid,
> and the calf and the lion and the fatling together,
>   and a little child shall lead them.
> The cow and the bear shall feed,
>   and their young shall lie down together;
>   and the lion shall eat straw like the ox.
> The sucking child shall play over the hold of the asp,
>   and the weaned child shall put his hand
>     on the adder's den.
>
> (Isa. 11:6-8.)

A mutually transforming coexistence between cultures and classes will be produced by equality under law. Those who lived by exploitation take up the higher pleasures of mutual enjoyment. For justice defuses conflict and allows each to maintain his integrity without aggression. Each is then free to take up the admirable traits of his former enemy. The prophet dares even to envision the lion, the aggressive symbol of his own Judah, adopting the peaceful attributes of the ox. And those who benefit most are the "sucking child" and the "weaned child" who find their playgrounds safe again. The references to the snakes imply the reversal of that destructive pride which led from the first mythic enmity between man and the serpent in Gen. 3:14-15 down to the nationalistic pretensions of Isaiah's time and ours. The appeal of this ideal is as visible in the songs of the counterculture as it is in the old tradition of the melting pot, which we are now discovering is a matter of retaining cultural identity while undergoing a transforming interaction.

It was late in Isaiah's ministry, after the terrible invasion of 701 B.C. had buried his country's preference for other ideals, that the prophet developed the international implications of his vision.[4] Here is the oracle whose final lines are chiseled in the United Nations Building in New York—the origin of a modern hope for world peace:

> All the nations shall flow to it,
>   and many peoples shall come, and say:
> "Come, let us go up to the mountain of Yahweh,
>   to the house of the God of Jacob;
> that he may teach us his ways
>   and that we may walk in his paths."
> For out of Zion shall go forth the law,
>   and the word of Yahweh from Jerusalem.
> He shall judge between the nations,
>   and shall decide for many peoples;
> and they shall beat their swords into plowshares,
>   and their spears into pruning hooks;
> nation shall not lift up sword against nation,
>   neither shall they learn war any more.
> (Isa. 2:3-4.)

The attraction of Zion's law and the prophetic "word of Yahweh," so powerful that the nations are envisioned as voluntarily bringing their disputes before it, lay in impartiality. The law when rightly administered was no respecter of persons. And the Yahwist prophets dared to pronounce judgment even against the behavior of their own nation.[5] These institutions correspond to the judicial and legislative roles in a modern constitutional system. Compliance depends in large measure on public respect, though requisite amounts of coercive power are available. There is a need for such prestigious institutions on the international scale, attracting the adherence of those they serve by the quality of justice they administer. Like the American Constitution, such institutions require no claim of divine origin to evoke such loyalty. It suffices that they are guided by impartiality and blessed in that task by suitable ceremonies of a global, civil religion. The organic growth of devotion is required to make such institutions stable, but with the communications system now available such a process may for the first time be feasible within the finite span which is available in our threatened circumstances.

## 3

The United States is uniquely suited by its Constitutional heritage to participate in bringing this vision of a peaceable kingdom to international fruition. We have experienced the gradual transfer of loyalty from township to state to nation. We have demonstrated the feasibility of allowing local agencies of government to administer affairs in certain areas while allowing for national jurisdiction in others. Sealed by the tragedy of the Civil War, our Union is such that it never even occurs now to the leaders of a state to settle their disputes with a neighboring state by unconstitutional means. This is an immense cultural achievement which demonstrates that when higher tribunals are revered, states no longer "lift up sword" against each other.

There are signs that the 1980s may witness a resurgence of this realistic tradition. The nuclear freeze resolutions that swept through hundreds of local elections were followed by the immense throng of three quarters of a million marchers on the occasion of the United Nations Conference on Disarmament on June 12, 1982. This amazing grass-roots movement, reflecting the resolve of thousands of neighborhood, professional and religious groups across the country, is concerned with more than purely national survival. It reflects the recognition that international cooperation and the support of international institutions of peace and order are more realistic means of conflict resolution than increasing weaponry. One of the persons I interviewed on the march was a secretary from New York. "It's one world to blow up and it's a one shot deal," she said. "This thing is larger than the Russians and it's larger than Reagan. There's only one moon, one atmosphere, one world. If we go up, we all go up together." A young man from Vermont spoke about "a major conceptual shift" away from nationalistic ideals toward "global unity." Looking around at the sea of faces and banners, he said, "The parochialism of the United States has been busted." Many people spoke of how good it felt to turn away from the cynicism and despair of the 60s and to take part in a movement that involved nations other than our own. In fact one of the unique features of this demonstration was that it was initiated in response to movements in Europe and Asia. For many participants, both in the convocation for religious leaders at the Cathedral of St. John the Divine on June 11 and the U.N. march on June 12, the high points were the speeches and actions of Japanese delegates. The presence of our former enemies, particularly those from Hiroshima, provided a sobering and exhilarating sense of world community. The possibility of "beating swords into plowshares" captured the imagination and began to replace the vision of a burned out planet.

The recovery of realistic imagination is the most pressing need in the atomic age. The effect of Jonathan Schell's work, *The Fate of the Earth*, was to allow thousands of people to grasp imaginatively what a full scale atomic war would do to destroy any hope of long-term survival of human life on the planet. It helps dispel the illusions in plans like that disclosed in Secretary of Defense Weinberger's defense guidance plan published in the summer of 1982, claiming that this country would not only survive but also prevail in an escalation of nuclear exchanges. Schell allows to grasp the logic of the system of mutual deterrence whose "basic dictate . . . is that if in the opinion of any nuclear power any other nuclear power seriously breaks the rules, then all powers are to be annihilated."[6]

Some critics dismissed Schell's book as an alarmist, apocalyptic fantasy. But when it was followed in the fall of 1983 by the studies of Carl Sagan and his colleagues of the climatic consequences of atomic exchanges, the element of realism has become undeniable. The scientific community of East as well as West is now in agreement that "even small nuclear wars can have devastating climatic effects." The cold, dark, radioactive world left after a nuclear war would destroy "global civilization" in both the Northern and the Southern hemispheres. To continue on the present path of nuclear deterrence entails "a real possibility of the extinction of the human species."[7]

One of the most controversial aspects of Jonathan Schell's analysis is that deterrence for its own sake is not the core of the problem facing the global community. "National sovereignty lies at the very core of the political issues that the peril of extinction forces upon us. Sovereign is the 'reality' that the 'realists' counsel us to accept as inevitable, referring to any alternative as 'unrealistic' or 'utopian.' "[8] The irony is that what passes for realism in the atomic age turns out to be the rashest form of self delusion. What we need now, it seems to me, is Prophetic Realism that sees beyond the limited resources of military logic or traditional idealism. While Schell refrains from discussing the political solution to the nuclear stalemate, and the nuclear freeze movement limits itself for the time being to the urgent necessity to turn the current escalation around, the task of Prophetic Realism is to rethink the Constitutional logic of our own American tradition.

To extend this Constitutional legacy into the international arena is the direction Isaiah's vision and our historic sense of mission beckon us. Even experienced analysts of international relations view such a vision as feasible. In his October 1972 article in *Foreign Affairs*, George F. Kennan suggested that we aim at the "restructuring of the international community and the development of the full potential of the United Nations." Such problems as the fragmentation of the world, the imbalance of the voting pattern in the UN, and the rigidities of national sovereignties "call out for the sort of study of the problem and leadership in attacking it which the United States is outstandingly equipped to give."[9] But before we can hope to succeed at such a mission, we must disentangle ourselves from the distortion of our heritage which adherence to zealous myths has produced. Unlike Isaiah, we cannot hope for the redemptive monarch who will suddenly do justice for the poor and usher in the golden age. No one will do it for us: neither a king, nor an all-powerful president, nor even a superhero who rides in from the plains. In the modern world, only an informed public can carry out such tasks. We must become the redeemer nation we are called to be, taking up the task of cooperating in world order without illusions and without self-righteousness: not because we are superior, or somehow have a right to lead, but because we are called to be a servant and a light to the world. This is the vision that should lighten the horizon which we shall never fully reach.

The American sense of mission, scorned by current cynics and disappointed idealists alike, needs to be transformed rather than abandoned. Its sense of how the world should be led to peace has simply been misguided by zealous myths. The absolutizing of our moral impulses, the delusions of the Grand Conspiracy, the distortions of popular stereotypes, the mystique of violence, and the idolatrous grasp of the Deuteronomic Principle have distorted our sense of mission and impelled us toward scenarios of annihilation. Our calling now is to separate ourselves from this legacy and to enter a long, twilight struggle against what is dark within ourselves. It is not our adversaries alone who must change. It is ourselves. But this cannot be accomplished alone. It calls for the transformation of the mythic forms which mark our culture and define the patterns of our politics. It calls for a creative rechanneling of Captain America's impulse to "fight for right." Only when America's realism qualifies its zeal can it be said in Melville's words that it bears "the ark of the liberties of the world."

# NOTES

## *Introduction*

1. Mark Mayfield, "Americans Support Grenada Invasion," *USA TODAY*, October 31, 1983, p. 7A.

2. "Transcript of Address by President on Lebanon and Grenada," New York *Times*, October 28, 1983, p. 5.

3. *Idem*.

4. Arthur Schlesinger, Jr., "The Two Faces of American Foreign Policy," Chicago *Sun-Times*, October 16, 1983, p. 4.

## *Chapter 1. Tracing the National Complex*

1. "Address by President on Lebanon and Grenada," *Op. Cit*.

2. Herman Melville, *White-Jacket*, cited from *The Works of Herman Melville*. Reproduced from the Standard Library Edition (16 vols., [1922-1924], Russell & Russell, Inc., Publishers, 1963), Vol. VI, p. 189. *White-Jacket* was first published in 1850.

3. Frederick Merk and L. B. Merk, *Manifest Destiny and Mission in American History: A Reinterpretation* (Alfred A. Knopf, Inc., 1963), p. 261.

4. *The Annals of America*, 18 vols. (Encyclopaedia Britannica, Inc., 1968), p. Vol. XII, p. 343.

5. Cited by Ernest Lee Tuveson, *Redeemer Nation: The Idea of America's Millennial Role* (The University of Chicago Press, 1968), p. 212.

6. Richard M. Nixon, *Six Crises* (Doubleday & Company, Inc., 1962), p. 68.

7. "Captain America," *Marvel Comics*, Vol. CXXXI, Nov., 1970.

8. Cited by Schlesinger, *Op. Cit*., p. 4.

9. New York *Times*, September 7, 1983.

10. Samuel Lubell, "Hidden Crisis in American Politics," *Los Angeles Times*, June 21, 1970, p. F-1.

## *Chapter 2. A Rod of Iron or a Light to the Nations*

1. In Scripture quotations in this book, the Revised Standard Version has been employed for the most part. I have also made my own translations as well as adaptations of established versions.

2. Frank Moore Cross, Jr., "The Divine Warrior in Israel's Early Cult," in Alexander Altmann (ed.), *Biblical Motifs: Origins and Transformations* (Harvard University Press, 1966), pp. 11-30.

3. Rudolf Smend, *Yahweh War and Tribal Confederation: Reflections Upon Israel's Earliest History*, tr. by Max Gray Rogers (Abingdon Press, 1970).

4. Cf. Gerhard von Rad, *Der heilige Krieg im alten Israel* (Göttingen: Vandenhoeck & Ruprecht, 1965[2]), pp. 26 ff.
5. Josephus, *The Jewish War*, VI. 5. 2-4.
6. Cf. Tuveson, *Redeemer Nation, pp. 1-51; David E. Smith, "Millenarian Scholarship in America," American Quarterly*, Vol. XVII (1965), p. 535-549.
7. Tuveson, *Redeemer Nation*, pp. 197-202.

## *Chapter 3. America's Zeal to Redeem the World*

1. Winthrop S. Hudson (ed.), *Nationalism and Religion in America: Concepts of American Identity and Mission* (Harper & Row, Publishers, Inc., 1970), p. 7.
2. John Fiske, *The Beginnings of New England; or, The Puritan Theocracy in Its Relations to Civil and Religious Liberty* (Houghton & Mifflin, 1889), p. 147.
3. Michael L. Walzer, *The Revolution of the Saints: A Study in the Origins of Radical Politics* (Harvard University Press, 1965), p. 291.
4. *Ibid.*, p. 294.
5. *Ibid.*, p. 295.
6. *Ibid.*, p. 296.
7. Perry Miller, "Preparation for Salvation in Seventeenth-Century New England," Paul Goodman (ed.), *Essays in American Colonial History* (Holt, Rinehart & Winston, Inc., 1967), p. 178.
8. Tuveson, *Redeemer Nation*, pp. 97 ff.
9. Jonathan Edwards, *History of the Work of Redemption*, cited by Tuveson, *ibid.*, p. 100.
10. J. F. Maclear, "The Republic and the Millennium," in Elwyn A. Smith (ed.), *The Religion of the Republic* (Fortress Press, 1971), p. 190.
11. Cited from Tuveson, *Redeemer Nation*, pp. 105 f.
12. Perry Miller, "From the Covenant to the Revival," *Nature's Nation* (Harvard University Press, Belknap, 1967), p. 95.
13. *Ibid.*, p. 97.
14. Bernard Bailyn, *The Ideological Origins of the American Revolution* (Harvard University Press, 1967), p. 54.
15. Cf. Ralph Barton Perry, *Puritanism and Democracy* (Vanguard Press, Inc., 1944), pp. 147-218.
16. Cf. Sidney E. Meade, "The Nation with the Soul of a Church," *Church History*, Vol. XXXVI, No. 3 (1967), p. 280.
17. William G. McLoughlin, "Pietism and the American Character," *The American Experience: Approaches to the Study of the United States*, ed. by H. Cohen (Houghton Mifflin Company, 1968), pp. 44 f.
18. Albert K. Weinberg, *Manifest Destiny: A Study of Nationalist Expansionism in American History* (Johns Hopkins Press, 1935), p. 127.
19. *Ibid.*, p. 128.
20. Melville, *White-Jacket*, p. 189.

21. Cited by Harry J. Carman and Harold C. Syrett, *A History of the American People* (Alfred A. Knopf, Inc., 1952), Vol. I, p. 550.

22. Cf. Hans Kohn, *American Nationalism: An Interpretive Essay* (The Macmillan Company, 1957), pp. 62 f.

23. Cited by Richard D. Mosier, *Making the American Mind: Social and Moral Ideas in the McGuffey Readers* (King's Crown Press, 1947), p. 21.

24. George Bancroft, *History of the United States of America* (1883-1885), Vol. IV, pp. 12-13.

25. Cf. Harry V. Jaffa, *Crisis of the House Divided: An Interpretation of the Issues in the Lincoln-Douglas Debates* (Doubleday & Company, Inc., 1959).

26. Cited by Timothy L. Smith, *Revivalism and Social Reform: In Mid-Nineteenth-Century America* (Abingdon Press, 1957), p. 183.

27. Aileen S. Kraditor, *Means and Ends in American Abolitionism: Garrison and His Critics on Strategy and Tactics, 1834-1850*, 2d ed. (Pantheon Books, Inc., 1969).

28. Tuveson, *Redeemer Nation*, p. 191.

29. *Ibid.*, pp. 192 ff.

30. *Ibid.*, pp. 197 ff.

31. Hudson, *Nationalism*, p. 74.

32. John Hope Franklin, *The Militant South: 1800-1861* (Beacon Press, 1964).

33. Cited in *Ibid.*, p. 230.

34. Cited by James W. Silver, *Confederate Morale and Church Propaganda*, 2d ed. (W. W. Norton & Company, Inc., 1967), p. 31.

35. *Ibid.*, p. 17.

36. Cited by Robert Penn Warren, *The Legacy of the Civil War: Meditations on the Centennial* (Random House, Inc., 1961), p. 104.

37. Don E. Fehrenbacher (ed.), *Abraham Lincoln: A Documentary Portrait Through His Speeches and Writings*, (Signet Classics, The New American Library of World Literature, Inc., 1964), p. 278.

38. *Ibid.*, p. 279.

39. Thomas Harry Williams, *et. al.*, *A History of the United States Since 1865*, 3d ed. (Alfred A. Knopf, Inc., 1969), p. 19.

40. Cited from Ralph Korngold's selection of Congressional testimony in *Thaddeus Stevens: A Being Darkly Wise and Rudely Great* (Harcourt, Brace & Co., Inc., 1955), p. 305.

41. W. R. Brock, "Radical Ideology and the Weaknesses of Radical Reconstruction," in *Reconstruction: A Tragic Era?* ed. by S. M. Scheiner (Holt, Rinehart & Winston, 1968), p. 94.

42. Cited by William A. Clebsch, *From Sacred to Profane America: The Role of Religion in American History* (Harper & Row, Publishers, Inc., 1968), pp. 195 f.

43. Cited by Tuveson, *Redeemer Nation*, pp. 203 f.

44. Warren, *Legacy*, pp. 59, 69.

45. Maclear, "Republic," p. 206.

46. Merk and Merk, *Manifest Destiny;* Walter LeFeber, *The New Empire: An Interpretation of American Expansion 1860-1898* (Cornell University Press, 1963).
47. Cited in Hudson, *Nationalism*, pp. 112-117.
48. Cited by Maclear, "Republic," p. 211.
49. Cited by Hudson, *Nationalism*, p. 111.
50. *Louisville Courier-Journal*, April 20, 1898. Cited in *Annals of America*, Vol. XII, p. 196.
51. Cited by Hudson, *Nationalism*, p. 121.
52. Walter Mills, *The Martial Spirit: A Study of Our War with Spain*, 2d ed. (The Viking Press, Inc., 1965), p. xiii.
53. Cited by Hudson, *Nationalism*, p. 119.
54. *Annals of America*, Vol. XII, pp. 336-345.
55. Williams *et al.*, *History*, p. 387.
56. *Annals of America*, Vol. XIV, pp. 65-69.
57. *Ibid.*, pp. 77-82.
58. *Ibid.*
59. Theodore Roosevelt, *The Foes of Our Own Household* (1917; Charles Scribner's Sons, 1926), p. 33.
60. Jess Yoder, "Preaching on Issues of War and Peace 1915-1965," in *Preaching in American History: Selected Issues in the American Pulpit, 1630-1967*, ed. by DeWitte T. Holland *et al.* (Abingdon Press, 1969), pp. 239-257.
61. Cited by Ray H. Abrams, *Preachers Present Arms: The Role of the American Churches and Clergy in World Wars I and II, with Some Observations on the War in Vietnam*, rev. ed. (Herald Press, 1969), p. 55.
62. George Parkin Atwater, "Peter Stood and Warmed Himself," *Atlantic Monthly*, Vol. CXXI (1918), p. 523.
63. Cited by Abrams, *Preachers Present Arms*, p. 117.
64. Kohn, *Nationalism*, p. 209.
65. Williams *et al.*, *History*, p. 569.
66. Harry Scherman, "The Last Best Hope on Earth," *Atlantic Monthly*, Vol. CLXVIII, Nov., 1941, p. 567.
67. *Annals of America*, Vol. XVI, pp. 89 f.
68. *Ibid.*, p. 91.
69. *Ibid.*, p. 104.
70. *Ibid.*, p. 107.
71. Cf. William Henry Chamberlin, *America's Second Crusade* (Henry Regnery Co., 1950), pp. 285-310.
72. *Reader's Digest*, Vol. XL, May, 1942, p. 49.
73. Cited by Chamberlin, *Crusade*, pp. 236-237.
74. Peter Marshall, "Quicken the Spirit Within You," *Reader's Digest*, Vol. LXVI, Jan., 1945, pp. 1 f.
75. Stanley High, "War Boom in Religion," *The American Magazine*, Vol. CXXXIV, Nov., 1942, p. 132.
76. Yoder, "Preaching," p. 249.

77. *Christian Advocate*, Vol. CXVII, Jan. 22, 1942, p. 29.
78. James Bryant Conant, *Our Fighting Faith: Five Addresses to College Students* (Harvard University Press, 1942), pp. 21 f.
79. Williams *et al., History*, p. 620.
80. Chamberlin, *Crusade*, p. 342.
81. James Truslow Adams, "Why Are We Americans Different?" *Reader's Digest*, Vol. XLIV, April, 1944, p. 4.

## *Chapter 4. The Frustration of Zealous Nationalism*

1. James P. Warburg, *The United States in a Changing World: An Historical Analysis of American Foreign Policy* (G. P. Putnam's Sons, 1954), p. 416.
2. Cited by Eric F. Goldman, *The Crucial Decade: America, 1945-1955* (Alfred A. Knopf Inc., 1956), p. 30.
3. George F. Kennan, *Realities of American Forign Policy*, 2d ed. (W. W. Norton & Company, Inc., 1966), pp. 16, 23.
4. Cited by *Look* magazine, Aug. 26, 1969, p. 26.
5. Kennan, *Realities*, p. 83.
6. *Ibid.*, p. 118.
7. Cited by Goldman, *Crucial Decade*, pp. 78-79.
8. *Ibid.*, pp. 112 f.
9. Nixon, *Six Crises*, pp. 71, 1.
10. *Annals of America*, Vol. XVI, p. 436.
11. *Ibid.*, p. 563.
12. *Ibid.*, p. 565.
13 .Arthur A. Ekirch, *Ideas, Ideals, and American Diplomacy: A History of Their Growth and Interaction* (Appleton-Century-Crofts, 1966), p. 186.
14. *The Pentagon Papers*, commentary by Neil Sheehan (Quadrangle Books, Inc., 1971), p. 9.
15. Cited by Williams *et al., History*, p. 690.
16. *Ibid.*, p. 694.
17. *Ibid.*, p. 693.
18. Goldman, *Crucial Decade*, pp. 205 f.
19. *Ibid.*, p. 206.
20. Douglas MacArthur, *A Soldier Speaks: Public Papers and Speeches*, ed. by Vorin E. Whan, Jr. (Frederick A. Praeger Inc., Publishers, 1965), pp. 263 f.
21. Goldman, *Crucial Decade*, p. 208.
22. Cited by Louis L. Gerson, *John Foster Dulles* (Cooper Square Publishers, Inc., 1967), pp. 87 f.
23. *Ibid.*, p. 16.
24. John Foster Dulles, "World Brotherhood Through the State," *Vital Speeches*, Vol. XII (1946), p. 744.
25. Cited by R. D. Challener and John Fenton, "Which Way America? Dulles Always Knew," *American Heritage*, Vol. XXII, June, 1971, p. 87.
26. Gerson, *Dulles*, p. 26.

27. John Foster Dulles, "Collaboration Must Be Practical," *Vital Speeches*, Vol. XI (1945), p. 248.

28. Cited by Deane and David Heller, *John Foster Dulles: Soldiers for Peace* (Holt, Rinehart & Winston, Inc., 1960), p. 120.

29. Cited by John R. Beal, *John Foster Dulles: A Biography* (Harper & Brothers, 1957), p. 310.

30. Cited by Gerson, *Dulles*, p. 303.

31. Denna Frank Fleming, *The Cold War and Its Origins, 1917-1960* (Doubleday & Company, Inc., 1961), Vol. II, p. 692.

32. Gerson, *Dulles*, p. 175.

33. *Ibid.*, p. 185.

34. Fleming, *Cold War*, Vol. II, p. 694.

35. *Des Moines Register*, July 9, 1971.

36. Cf. George McTurnan Kahin and John W. Lewis, *The United States in Vietnam*, 2d ed. (Delta Books, Dell Publishing Co., Inc., 1969); Nina S. Adams and Alfred W. McCoy (eds.), *Laos: War and Revolution* (Harper & Row, Publishers, Inc., 1970).

37. Frederick L. Schuman, *The Cold War: Retrospect and Prospect*, 2d ed. (Louisiana State University Press, 1967), pp. 88 f.

38. Gerson, *Dulles*, p. 236.

39. Cecil V. M. Crabb, Jr., "American Foreign Policy in the Nuclear Age," in *The Puritan Ethic in United States Foreign Policy*, ed. by David L. Larson (D. Van Nostrand Company, Inc., 1966), pp. 15 f.

40. Cf. Schuman, *Cold War*.

41. *Annals of America*, Vol. XVIII, pp. 5-7.

## *Chapter 5. Consumed by Zeal*

1. Norman H. Snaith, "Jealous, zealous," *A Theological Word Book of the Bible*, ed. by Alan Richardson (The Macmillan Company, 1950), p. 115.

2. Johannes Pedersen, *Israel: Its Life and Culture* (London: Oxford University Press, 1926), Vols. III-IV, p. 620.

3. *Ibid.*

4. Albrecht Stumpff, "*zelos*," etc., in Gerhard Kittel (ed.), *Theological Dictionary of the New Testament*, tr. and ed. by Geoffrey W. Bromiley, Vol. II (Wm. B. Eerdmans Publishing Company, 1964), pp. 877 ff.

5. Cf. *The Random House Dictionary of the English Language* (Random House, Inc., 1967).

6. "Cromwell, Oliver," *Encyclopaedia Britannica* (1963 edition), Vol. VI, p. 797.

7. Walzer, *Revolution*, p. 72.

8. William Styron, *The Confessions of Nat Turner* (Random House, Inc., 1967), pp. 306 f.

9. *Ibid.*, p. 392.

10. Warren, *Legacy*, p. 22.

11 .Comer Vann Woodward, *The Burden of Southern History* (Louisiana State University Press, 1960), p. 43.

12. Allan Nevins, *The Emergence of Lincoln*, Vol. II, *Prologue to Civil War, 1859-1861* (Charles Scribner's Sons, 1950), p. 9.
13. *Ibid.*, pp. 95 f.
14. Thomas J. Fleming, "The Trial of John Brown," *American Heritage*, Vol. XVIII, Aug., 1967, p. 100; italics in original.
15. Woodward, *Burden*, p. 55.
16. Ralph Waldo Emerson, *Miscellanies* (Boston, 1884), p. 268.
17. Henry David Thoreau, *Anti-Slavery and Reform Papers* (Montreal: Harvest House, 1963), p. 44.
18. *Ibid.*, p. 64.
19. *Ibid.*, p. 54.
20. Hudson, *Nationalism*, p. xi.
21. Arnold S. Rice, *The Ku Klux Klan in American Politics* (Public Affairs Press, 1963), p. 24.
22. "Captain America," *Marvel Comics*, Vol. CXXXI, Nov., 1970.
23. Gerard W. O'Connor, "Dirty Harry: 'The Law Is Crazy,'" *Civil Liberties*, Vol. CCLXXXV, March, 1972, p. 2.
24. lMick Jagger, "Street Fighting Man," *Beggar's Banquet* (London album).
25. Cited in "Time Essay," *Time*, Aug. 29, 1969, pp. 52-54.
26. *Newsweek*, Nov. 12, 1970, p. 49.
27. Max Rafferty, *Sioux City Journal*, March 1, 1972.
28. Melvin R. Laird, *A House Divided: America's Strategy Gap* (Henry Regnery Co., 1962), pp. 176 f.
29. *Newsweek*, Sept. 29, 1969, p. 42..
30. Cited by Kohn, *Nationalism*, p. 185.
31. *Annals of America*, Vol. XII, p. 196.
32. *Ibid.*, Vol. XIV, pp. 77-82.
33. Allen Drury, "Inside the White House," *Look*, Oct. 19, 1971, p. 52.
34. Dee Brown, *Bury My Heart at Wounded Knee: An Indian History of the American West* (Bantam Books, Inc., 1972), p. 31.
35. "King, of the Royal Mounted," *Dell Comics*, Vol. CCCX (1945).
36. Peter Homans, "Puritanism Revisited: An Analysis of the Contemporary Screen-Image Western," *Studies in Public Communication*, Vol. III (1961), pp. 73-84.
37. Eric Severeid, "American Militarism: What Is It Doing to Us?" *Look*, Aug. 12, 1969, p. 25.
38. *American Report*, May 28, 1971.
39. Herbert C. Kelman and Lee H. Lawrence, "Violent Man: American Response to the Trial of Lt. William L. Calley," *Psychology Today*, June, 1972, p. 41.
40. Herbert Marcuse, "Reflections on Calley," *American Report*, May 28, 1971.
41. *Ibid.*, p. 45.

42. Owen C. Whitehouse, "Jehu," *A Dictionary of the Bible*, ed. by James Hastings (Charles Scribner's Sons, 1905), Vol. II, p. 565; cf. John Bright, *A History of Israel* (The Westminster Press, 1959), p. 235.
43. *Des Moines Register*, June 14, 1971.
44. Stanley Karnow, *St. Paul Pioneer Press*, Nov. 27, 1970.
45. From the speech by Lyndon B. Johnson, Aug. 29, 1964, at the Johnson Ranch. Cited in *Pentagon Papers*, p. 311.
46. *Ibid.*, p. 310.
47. Stanley Karnow, *St. Paul Pioneer Press*, Nov. 27, 1970.
48. *Des Moines Register*, May 2, 1970.
49. *Des Moines Register*, Nov. 8, 1971.
50. *Des Moines Register*, Jan. 31, 1972.
51. *Newsweek*, May 1, 1972.
52. Nixon, *Six Crises*, p. 347.
53. Des Moines Register, July 17, 1971.
54. Cf. the March 3 and 17, 1972, issues of *National Review*, which are devoted to "Thoughts on Chairman Nixon's Visit" and "Did Nixon Surrender?"
55. *New York Times*, Aug. 1, 1971, p. E-11.
56. Nixon, *Six Crises*, pp. xv-xvi.
57. Warren, *Legacy*, p. 20.
58. *Ibid.*, pp. 22-23.
59. Fleming, *Cold War*, Vol. II, p. 656.
60. Arthur Goldberg, "Guest Privilege," *Life*, Oct. 17, 1969, p. 30D.
61. Warren, *Legacy*, p. 74.
62. Cf. Gerhard von Rad, *Old Testament Theology*, Vol. I, tr. by D. M. G. Stalker (Harper & Row, Publishers, Inc., 1962), pp. 203-219; Ernst Käsemann, *Jesus Means Freedom*, tr. by Frank Clarke (Fortress Press, 1970), pp. 31-41.
63. John Lawrence, "The Moral Attractiveness of Violence," *Journal of Social Philosophy*, Fall, 1970, p. 5.
64. Horace J. Bridges, "The Duty of Hatred," *Atlantic Monthly*, Vol. CXXII (1918), p. 464.
65. Rollo May, *Love and Will* (W. W. Norton & Company, Inc., 1969), pp. 28-33.
66. Cf. H. L. Strack and P. Billerbeck, *Kommentar zum Neuen Testament aus Talmud und Midrasch*, Vol. III, pp. 94 f.
67. Cf. Bo Ivar Reicke, *The New Testament Era: The New Testament Era from 500 B.C. to A.D. 100*, tr. by D. E. Green (Fortress Press, 1968), pp. 127-195; Hugh J. Schonfield, *The Passover Plot: New Light on the History of Jesus* (Bernard Geis Associates, 1966), pp. 21-32.

## Chapter 6. The Grand Conspiracy

1. Louis J. Halle, *The Cold War as History* (Harper & Row, Publishers, Inc., 1967), p. 414.

2. Paul S. Minear, *I Saw a New Earth: An Introduction to the Visions of the Apocalypse* (Corpus Books, 1968).

3. Bailyn, *American Revolution*, pp. 158 f.

4. Arthur M. Schlesinger, *Nothing Stands Still* (Harvard University Press, Belknap, 1969), p. 182-184.

5. David Brion Davis, *The Slave Power Conspiracy and the Paranoid Style* (Louisiana State University Press, 1971).

6. Eric Foner, *Free Soil, Free Labor, Free Men: The Ideology of the Republican Party Before the Civil War* (Oxford University Press, 1972).

7. William W. Freehling, "Paranoia and American History," *The New York Review of Books*, Sept. 23, 1971, p. 39.

8. Robert K. Murray, *Red Scare: A Study in National Hysteria, 1919-1920* (University of Minnesota Press, 1955).

9. . *Ibid.*, p. 265.

10. Goldman, *Crucial Decade*, p. 123.

11. *Ibid.*, p. 212.

12. *Ibid.*, pp. 212 f.

13. Richard Harris, "The Annals of Politics," *The New Yorker*, Nov. 22, 1969, p. 113.

14. *Ibid.*, p. 171.

15. Billy James Hargis, *Communism, The Total Lie* (Christian Crusade, 1963), p. 7.

16. *Christian Crusade*, Vol. XV, Aug., 1963, p. 15.

17. *Ibid.*, Vol. XVIII, March, 1966, p. 12.

18. *Weekly Crusader*, Vol. III, Jan. 18, 1963, p. 6.

19. Cited by Peter Schrag, "America's Other Radicals," *Harper's Magazine*, Aug., 1970, p. 38.

20. Cited from *The Crusade of Higher Education*, Oct. 5, 1970, p. 5.

21. Kahin and Lewis, *Vietnam*, pp. 18, 30.

22. *Ibid.*, p. 31.

23. Hans Morgenthau, "Reflections on the End of the Republic," *The New York Review of Books*, Sept. 24, 1970, p. 39.

24. Heller and Heller, *Dulles*, p. 120.

25. *Pentagon Papers*, p. 6.

26. *Ibid.*, p. 7.

27. *Ibid.*

28. Paul Hemphill, "Merle Haggard," *Atlantic*, Sept., 1971, p. 103.

29. Halle, *Cold War*, p. 317.

30. Lewis H. Lapham, "Military Theology," *Harper's Magazine*, Vol. CCXXIII, July, 1971, p. 73.

31. *Ibid.*, p. 84.

32. Cited in *Harper's Magazine*, June, 1969, p. 37.

33. Cf. Joachim Jeremias, *The Parables of Jesus, tr. by S. H. Hooke, rev. ed. (Charles Scribner's Sons, 1963), p. 224-227.*

## *Chapter 7. The Good Guys and the Bad Guys*

1. Cf. R. H. Charles, *A Critical and Exegetical Commentary on The Revelation of St. John* (Charles Scribner's Sons, 1920), Vol. II, pp. 216 ff.
2. Cited by Walzer, *Revolution*, p. 285.
3. Cited by Kohn, *Nationalism*, p. 13.
4. Cited by Carman and Syrett, *History*, Vol. I, p. 502.
5. *The American Magazine*, Aug., 1944, p. 1.
6. A. Dale Tussig, "Education, Foreign Policy and the Popeye Syndrome," *Change Magazine*, Oct., 1971, p. 19.
7. *Ibid.*
8. Cf. Francis G. Hutchins, "Moralists Against Managers," *Atlantic*, July, 1969, p. 54.
9. *Sioux City Journal*, Nov. 13, 1967.
10. Cited in *I. F. Stone's Weekly*, Mar. 24, 1969.
11. *Ibid.*
12. Halle, *Cold War*, p. 209.
13. Cited by Challener and Fenton, "Which Way America?" p. 91.
14. Citations from Presidential addresses printed in the *Des Moines Register* on April 22, 1970; May 2, 1970; April 28, 1972; and May 10, 1972.
15. Cf. *Pentagon Papers*, pp. 3, 53-66, 234-306.
16. Paul Scott, "Gag on Viet Military Discussion," *Sioux City Journal* (date unknown).
17. Joseph Kraft, *Des Moines Register*, Oct. 10, 1969.
18. "The Third Indochina War. An Interview with Fred Branfman," *Liberation*, April, 1972, p. 7.
19. Joe Nicholson, Jr., *American Report*, Jan. 28, 1972.
20. Stuart Symington, "Government Secrecy: Threat to Our Welfare and Security," *Los Angeles Times*, Aug. 9, 1970.
21. *Liberation*, April, 1972, p. 15.
22. McLoughlin, "Pietism," p. 52.
23. Joe McGinniss, *The Selling of the President 1968* (Pocket Book, Inc., 1970).
24. Richard J. Whalen, "The Nixon-Connally Arrangement," *Harper's Magazine*, Aug., 1971, p. 32.
25. Cited from *I. F. Stone's Weekly*, May 19, 1969.
26. *Sioux City Journal*, April 11, 1968.
27. *Newsweek*, Nov. 9, 1970, p. 21.
28. Cited in *ibid.*, p. 22.
29. Cf. Oscar Cullmann, *Jesus and the Revolutionaries*, tr. by Gareth Putnam (Harper & Row, Publishers, Inc., 1970), pp. 62 f., n. 11.
30. *Ibid.*, p. 63, n. 14.

## *Chapter 8. To Convert Them or Destroy Them*

1. Cf. Martin Noth, *Exodus: A Commentary*, tr. by J. S. Bowden (The Westminster Press, 1962), p. 121.

2. Harvey H. Guthrie, Jr., *Israel's Sacred Songs: A Study of Dominant Themes* (The Seabury Press, Inc., 1966), p. 130.

3. Pedersen, *Israel*, Vols. III-IV, pp. 21-31.

4. A. Kuschke, "Jericho," *Die Religion in Geschichte und Gegenwart*, 3d ed. (Tuübingen: J. C. B. Mohr [Paul Siebeck], 1957-1962), Vol. III, col. 591.

5. Edwin M. Good, "Peace in the OT," *The Interpreter's Dictionary of the Bible* (Abingdon Press, 1962), Vol. III, p. 704.

6. Cf. Pedersen, *Israel*, Vols. I-II, pp. 311-316; typical statements are Judg. 8:9; II Sam. 19:24, 30; I Kings 22:27 f.; I Chron. 22:18; Jer. 43:12; Micah 5:5; Zech. 9:10.

7. Walzer, *Revolution*, pp. 278 f.

8. *Annals of America*, Vol. XVIII, p. 208.

9. Hudson, *Nationalism*, pp. 96-98.

10. John Elliot, *The Christian Commonwealth: or, the Civil Policy and the Rising Kingdom of Jesus Christ* (London, 1659).

11. Cf. Tuveson, *Redeemer Nation*, p. 105.

12 R. Pierce Beaver, "Missionary Motivation Through Three Centuries," in *Reinterpretation in American Church History*, ed. by Jerald C. Brauer (The University of Chicago Press, 1968), p. 121.

13. Cited in *ibid.*, pp. 137 f.

14. Hudson, *Nationalism*, p. 115.

15. Kohn, *Nationalism*, p. 183.

16. Langdon B. Gilkey, *Shantung Compound: The Story of Men and Women Under Pressure* (Harper & Row, Publishers, Inc., 1966), pp. 181 f.

17. Cited by Roy Harvey Pearce, *The Savages of America: A Study of the Indian and the Idea of Civilization*, rev. id. (Johns Hopkins Press, 1965), p. 23.

18. Robert F. Berkhofer, *Salvation and the Savage: An Analysis of Protestant Missions and American Indian Response, 1787-1862* (University of Kentucky Press, 1965), p. 15.

19. Ray A. Billington and James B. Hedges, *Westward Expansion: A History of the American Frontier* (The Macmillan Company, 1949), p. 572.

20. Tuveson, *Redeemer Nation*, pp. 191, 196.

21. *Ibid.*, pp. 203 f.

22. Weinberg, *Manifest Destiny*, p. 285.

23. Millis, *Martial Spirit*, p. 38.

24. Cited by William Fulbright, "Violence in the American Character," *Annnals of America*, Vol. XVIII, p. 209.

25. Franklin Delano Roosevelt, "The Spirit of Man Has Awakened," *Think Magazine's Diary of the U.S. Participation in World War II*, ed. by E. F. Hacket (New York, 1946), p. 320.

26. Harry S. Truman, "I Call Upon All Americans," *ibid.*, p. 337.

27. Francis Vivian Drake, "Bomb Germany—and Save a Million American Lives," *Reader's Digest*, Vol. XLIII, July, 1943, pp. 89-92.

28. Halle, *Cold War*, p. 92.

29. Sidney J. Slomich, "The Myths and Mores of Nuclear Weaponry," *San Francisco Sunday Examiner and Chronicle*, July 28, 1968, p. 19.

30. John Lawrence, "Violence," *Social Theory and Practice*, Vol. I, Fall, 1970, p. 48.

31. Cf. James Luther Mays, *Hosea: A Commentary* (The Westminster Press, 1969), p. 147.

32. The slight change in style between verse 13a and verse 13b may indicate two separate oracles were joined here by later editors, but both appear to be genuine, and the substantial congruence in thought makes it feasible to consider them together. Cf. Mays, *Hosea*, p. 148.

33. *Ibid.*, pp. 90 f.

34. Cf. H. Wheeler Robinson, "Hosea," *The Abingdon Bible Commentary*, ed. by F. C. Eiselen *et al.* (Abingdon Press, 1929), p. 759.

35. Cf. Mays, *Hosea*, p. 28.

36. *Ibid.*, p. 64.

37. Bob Greene, "Audiences Cheer Violent Scenes," *Des Moines Register*, Feb. 12, 1972.

38. Gobind Behari Lal, "Our Culture of Guns: Basis for Violence," *San Francisco Examiner*, July 1, 1968.

39. Cf. "Table 24: Death and Death Rates by Cause and Sex: Latest Available Year" (from 1966), *Demographic Yearbook 1967* (New York: United Nations, 1968), pp. 455-495.

40. Seymour Martin Lipset, "Revolution and Counter-Revolution—The United States and Canada," in *The Revolutionary Theme in Contemporary America*, ed. by Thomas Robert Ford (University of Kentucky Press, 1965), pp. 21-64.

41. Mays, *Hosea*, p. 65.

42. *Ibid.*, p. 80.

43. *Los Angeles Times*, Aug. 9, 1970.

44. *Ibid.*

45. *Ibid.*

46. George F. Kennan, *Memoirs: 1925-1950* (Little, Brown & Company, 1967), p. 365.

47. Donald McDonald, "Militarism in America," *The Center Magazine*, Vol. III, No. 1 (1970), p. 29.

48. Cf. Mays, *Hosea*, p. 160.

49. *Ibid.*, p. 161.

50. *Sioux City Journal*, June 8, 1971.

51. Anthony Lewis, "Back to the Stone Age," *International Herald Tribune*, July 4, 1972.

52. Richard Wasserstrom, "The Laws of War," *The Monist*, Vol. LVI, Jan., 1972, p. 12.

53. *Des Moines Register*, Feb. 8, 1968.

54. James D. Smart, "Hosea," *The Interpreter's Dictionary of the Bible*, Vol. II, p. 652.

## *Chapter 9. Neither Humiliation nor Defeat*

1. *Des Moines Register*, May 2, 1970.
2. D. W. Brogan, "Americans: 'Short Distance' Crusaders," *Des Moines Register*, Oct. 29, 1967.
3. David L. Larson, "Objectivity, Propaganda, and the Puritan Ethic," in *The Puritan Ethic in United States Foreign Policy*, ed. by David L. Larson (D. Van Nostrand Company, Inc., 1966), p. 23; italics in original.
4. Cf. von Rad, *Der heilige Krieg*, pp. 7-9, for a complete list.
5. Pedersen, *Israel*, Vols. III-IV, p. 15.
6. Cf. von Rad, *Der Heilige Krieg*, p. 31.
7. Cf. Robert H. Pfeiffer, *Introduction to the Old Testament*, rev. ed. (Harper & Brothers, 1948), p. 186.
8. Cited in Conrad Cherry (ed.), *God's New Israel: Religious Interpretations of American Destiny* (Prentice-Hall, Inc., 1971), p. 43.
9. *Ibid.*, p. 81.
10. *Ibid.*, p. 83.
11. *Ibid.*, p. 98.
12. *Ibid.*, p. 100.
13. Cited by Henry F. May, *Protestant Churches and Industrial America* (Harper & Row, Publishers, Inc., 1967), p. 69.
14. Cherry, *God's New Israel*, p. 239.
15. *Ibid.*, p. 246.
16. *Pentagon Papers*. Noted by David Halberstam, *The Best and the Brightest* (Random House, 1972), p. 515.
17. *International Herald Tribune*, Jan. 25, 1973.
18. *Ibid.*
19. Francine du Plessix Gray, "The Moral Consequences: Slum Landlords in Eden," *Saturday Review of the Society*, Dec., 1972, p. 78.
20. Richard Wilson, *Des Moines Register*, Dec. 8, 1972.
21. Cited in the *Des Moines Register*, Dec. 5, 1972.
22. James Goldsborough, *International Herald Tribune*, Jan. 25, 1973.
23. Andreas Dorpalen, *Hindenburg and the Weimar Republic* (Princeton University Press, 1964), p. 51.
24. D. W. Brogan, "The Illusion of American Omnipotence," *Harper's Magazine*, Dec., 1952, pp. 21-28.
25. Cf. Earl Mazo, *Richard Nixon: A Political and Personal Portrait* (Harper & Brothers, 1959), p. 46.
26. *Ibid.*, p. 43.
27. *Ibid.*, pp. 74 f.
28. *Ibid.*, p. 79.
29. *Des Moines Register* account of Richard Nixon's final election appeal, issue of Nov. 7, 1972.
30. Dwight D. Eisenhower, *Peace with Justice: Selected Addresses* (Columbia University Press, 1961), p. 32.
31. *Ibid.*, p. 28.

32. Heller and Heller, *Dulles*, p. 239.
33. Edward L. R. Elson, *America's Spiritual Recovery* (Fleming H. Revell Company, 1954), p. 135.
34. *Ibid.*, Dedication.
35. Richard M. Nixon, *Setting the Course: The First Year: Major Policy Statements by President Richard Nixon*, with commentaries by Richard Wilson (Funk & Wagnalls Company, Inc., 1970), pp. 5-7.
36. *Ibid.*, pp. 28-30.
37. *Ibid.*, pp. 19 f.
38. Martin Buber, *The Prophetic Faith*, tr. by Carlyle Witton-Davies (The Macmillan Company, 1949), pp. 170 f.
39. Cf. II Chron. 35:1-19 for the account of the elaborate Passover Josiah staged just prior to his demise; for the official explanation for Josiah's defeat, cf. II Kings 23:26 f.
40. Nixon's speech of Nov. 3, 1969, in *Setting the Course*, p. 28.
41. Cf. Charles P. Henderson, Jr., *The Nixon Theology* (Harper & Row, Publishers, Inc., 1972), p. 28 ff.
42. S. Maclean Gilmour, "The Gospel of Luke," *The Interpreter's Bible* (Abingdon Press, 1951-1957), Vol. VIII, p. 239; William Barclay, *The Gospel of Luke*, 2d ed. (The Westminster Press, 1956), p. 177.
43. Second Annual Message to Congress, Dec. 1, 1862, cited from Abraham Lincoln, *Speeches and Writings*, ed. by R. P. Basler (World Publishing Co., 1946), p. 688.
44. Cited by Warren, *Legacy*, p. 107.
45. Bernhard W. Anderson, *Understanding the Old Testament* (Prentice-Hall Inc., 1957), p. 248.

## Chapter 10. The Hope of Realism

1. Speech at Springfield, Illinois, 1857, cited by Jaffa, *Crisis of the House Divided*, p. 316.
2. Cf. R. B. Y. Scott, "Isaiah," *The Interpreter's Bible*, Vol. V, p. 232.
3. *Ibid.*, p. 249.
4. *Ibid.*, p. 180.
5. Cf. Norman K. Gottwald, *All the Kingdoms of the Earth: Israelite Prophecy and International Relations in the Ancient Near East* (Harper & Row, Publishers, Inc., 1964), p. 202.
6. Jonathan Schell, *The Fate of the Earth* (Alfred A. Knopf, 1982), p. 214.
7. Carl Sagan, "The Nuclear Winter," *Parade Magazine*, October 30, 1983, p. 7.
8. Schell, *Op. Cit.*, p. 218.
9. George F. Kennan, "After the Cold War: American Foreign Policy in the 1970s," *Foreign Affairs*, Vol. LI, Oct., 1972, p. 227.